Emotions, Media and Politics

Contemporary Political Communication

Geoffrey Craig, *Performing Politics*
Stephen Cushion & Richard Thomas, *Reporting Elections*
Robert M. Entman, *Scandal and Silence*
Max McCombs, R. Lance Holbert, Spiro Kiousis & Wayne Wanta, *The News and Public Opinion*
Craig Allen Smith, *Presidential Campaign Communication* (2nd edition)
James Stanyer, *Intimate Politics*
Katrin Voltmer, *The Media in Transitional Democracies*
Karin Wahl-Jorgensen, *Emotions, Media and Politics*

Emotions, Media and Politics

Karin Wahl-Jorgensen

polity

First published in 2019 by Polity Press

Polity Press
65 Bridge Street
Cambridge CB2 1UR, UK

Polity Press
101 Station Landing
Suite 300
Medford, MA 02155, USA

ISBN-13: 978-0-7456-6104-9
ISBN-13: 978-0-7456-6105-6 (pb)

A catalogue record for this book is available from the British Library.

Library of Congress Cataloging-in-Publication Data

Names: Wahl-Jorgensen, Karin, author.
Title: Emotions, media and politics / Karin Wahl-Jorgensen.
Description: Cambridge, UK ; Medford, MA, USA : Polity Press, 2018. | Series: Contemporary political communication | Includes bibliographical references and index.
Identifiers: LCCN 2018025189 (print) | LCCN 2018042704 (ebook) | ISBN 9781509531431 (Epub) | ISBN 9780745661049 | ISBN 9780745661056 (pbk.)
Subjects: LCSH: Mass media--Political aspects. | Emotions--Political aspects. | Political psychology.
Classification: LCC P95.8 (ebook) | LCC P95.8 .W35 2018 (print) | DDC 302.2301/9--dc23
LC record available at https://lccn.loc.gov/2018025189

Typeset in 10.25 on 13 pt Scala by
Servis Filmsetting Ltd, Stockport, Cheshire
Printed and bound in the UK by CPI Group (UK) Ltd, Croydon

Contents

Acknowledgments   vi

Introduction: Understanding Emotions in
Mediated Public Life   1

1   Taking Emotion Seriously: A Brief History of
    Thought   20

2   Emotions are Everywhere: The Strategic Ritual
    of Emotionality in Journalism   37

3   Authenticity, Compassion and Personalized
    Storytelling   66

4   Towards a Typology of Mediated Anger   90

5   Shifting Emotional Regimes: Donald Trump's
    Angry Populism   110

6   The Politics of Love: Political Fandom and
    Social Change   129

7   The Emotional Architecture of Social Media   147

    Conclusion: Nine Propositions about
    Emotions, Media and Politics   166

    Notes   175
    References   178
    Index   205

Acknowledgments

It is only suitable that this book on emotions, media and politics is, more than anything, a labor of love; a love that has been sometimes breath-taking and thrilling, at other times fraught with difficulty and challenges. The work that forms the basis for this book has evolved and grown over a number of years and has benefited from the feedback of many colleagues, to whom I remain eternally grateful.

At Cardiff University, I have had the greatest possible institutional environment for such a project, drawing on the wisdom and kindness of stellar scholars including but not limited to Stuart Allan, Lucy Bennett, Mike Berry, Cindy Carter, Simon Cottle, Stephen Cushion, Lina Dencik, Bob Franklin, Inaki Garcia-Blanco, Ross Garner, Janet Harris, Arne Hintz, Jenny Kidd, Jenny Kitzinger, Justin Lewis, Kerry Moore, Caitriona Noonan, Joanna Redden, Richard Sambrook and Andy Williams.

Elsewhere, I have pestered esteemed colleagues with endless talk of this project over the years. Some of those who have had the most to say in return include Chris Anderson, Charlie Beckett, Jen Birks, Bolette Blaagaard, Tammy Boyce, Lilie Chouliaraki, Mark Deuze, Cherian George, Alfred Hermida, Michael Higgins, Risto Kunelius, Nikki Layzer, Mirca Madianou, Donald Matheson, Mervi Pantti, Zizi Papacharissi, Chris Peters, Patrick Lee Plaisance, Verica Rupar, Steen Steensen, Einar Thorsen, Herman Wasserman and Tamara Witschge.

When I started working in this area, I was one of a handful of scholars in the field who thought it might be worth taking emotion in media seriously. I am endlessly pleased to see a new generation of academics focusing their work on related questions, and have been honored to examine a series of excellent PhD projects in the area, including those of Lyn Barnes, Tom Doig, Stephen Jukes, Morgane Kimmich and Jennifer Martin.

I have also been lucky enough to be able to take my project on the road: aside from burdening my Cardiff colleagues with several seminars on various chapters in the book, audiences at Ben-Gurion University of the Negev, the University of Oxford, the University of East Anglia, the University of Leeds, the University of Leicester, the University of Newcastle and the University of Westminster, as well as numerous conferences, seminars and symposia around the world, have all provided useful feedback, friendly advice and general hospitality. Stints as a visiting scholar at Gothenburg University, Monash University, Stockholm University, the University of Copenhagen and Universidad del Norte, Barranquilla, have exposed me to new ideas and given me space to think.

I am grateful to the editorial team at Polity Press, including Andrea Drugan, who originally commissioned the book, Ellen MacDonald-Kramer and Mary Savigar, who saw it to completion, and Justin Dyer, who expertly copy-edited the manuscript.

My thoughts have taken shape through a series of publications in the form of articles, book chapters, blog posts and encyclopedia entries. I have been writing about the relationship between emotions, media and politics in some form or another for my entire career. Many of the publications have been referenced throughout the book where relevant; others have helped to shape or sharpen my thinking on the subject. Parts of Chapter 2 represent an updated version of a study first published in Wahl-Jorgensen (2013b). Chapter 4 is based on an updated version of Wahl-Jorgensen (2018c). Chapter 5 draws on work published in Wahl-Jorgensen (2017b, 2018b). Chapter 7 is a shortened, updated and modified version of Wahl-Jorgensen (2018a).

Along with friends in Cardiff and beyond, Jacob Wahl-Byde and Wouter Poortinga have carried the largest burden: that of maintaining my sanity throughout the epic endeavor of writing about emotionality. To them I owe the greatest thanks of all.

Introduction: Understanding Emotions in Mediated Public Life

This book is based on the premise that emotions are central to our social and political lives, and to the ways in which we make sense of ourselves and the collectivities and communities we inhabit – a process which increasingly takes place through the media. This means that we have to understand the institution-alized and systematic ways in which emotions are constructed and circulate through forms of mediated discourse as pivots of public life. They are part and parcel of production practices and routines, mediated texts and audience experience and participation. This should be reflected in the way we think about the relationship between media practices and political life. The book therefore sees emotional expression as a key building block of mediated politics. It develops a new research agenda on this basis, drawing on a series of original studies of how emotions are constructed and circulate through mediated public life. Each of these studies sheds light on different aspects of the relationship between emotions, media and politics, though they share a common set of conceptual preoccupations. By examining specific cases, ranging from the role of emotion in award-winning journalistic storytelling to the anger of Donald Trump and the introduction of Facebook emoji reactions, this book seeks to develop new conceptual and methodological tools that render visible emotions and their consequences for mediated public life.

[handwritten margin notes: emotion corner, possibly >>) as key component of social/political life (=Mute) _ "mediation"]

A changing emotional culture?

This book arrives at a historical moment which is unusually alert to the role of emotion in our shared conversations. Some observers suggest that contemporary culture is increasingly characterized by emotionality. Such observations draw on perceived changes in the political landscape and in the tenor of our shared conversations. First, with respect to political cultures, there is clear evidence to support claims of a rise in forms of populism that rely heavily on emotional appeals to disenchanted citizens. Beyond the election of Donald Trump in the United States, recent years have seen the Brexit vote in the United Kingdom, along with the rise of right-wing populist figures such as Rodrigo Duterte in the Philippines and Sebastian Kurz in Austria (e.g. Hewitt, 2017b; Peter, 2017). As political scientists Fred Inglehart and Pippa Norris observed in 2016, in relation to the rise of right-wing populism:

> [T]hese parties have gained votes and seats in many countries, and entered government coalitions in eleven Western democracies, including in Austria, Italy and Switzerland. Across Europe [...] their average share of the vote in national and European parliamentary elections has more than doubled since the 1960s, from around 5.1% to 13.2%, at the expense of center parties. During the same era, their share of seats has tripled, from 3.8% to 12.8%. Even in countries without many elected populist representatives, these parties can still exert tremendous "blackmail" pressure on mainstream parties, public discourse, and the policy agenda. (Inglehart and Norris, 2016, p. 2)

These new populist movements are not restricted to the right: on the left, there have been examples such as Syriza in Greece and Podemos in Spain, which have arisen in response to the inability of mainstream political parties to address public anger with austerity and economic hardship (e.g. Gerbaudo, 2018). Around the world, we have seen a collapse of trust in institutions. The post-colonial writer Pankaj Mishra

(2017) has suggested that we may be witnessing the rise of an "age of anger," fueled by global disenchantment with the inability of political institutions to effect social change.

This populist turn has been accompanied by a shift in the emotional climate of public discourse. As Chapter 5 explores in more detail, contemporary populisms draw on rhetoric which is often based on appeals to negative emotion, particularly anger (see also Berry and Sobieraj, 2014; Ott, 2017). *[emotion in political life]*

Alongside these developments in the political arena, we have seen the perceived rise of an emotional culture; one where emotion is granted a central place in contexts ranging from the workplace, to education and media. It is now widely considered essential not just to be in touch with and aware of our emotions, but also to be willing to discuss them openly *[in everyday life]* with others. For example, the rise of a confessional culture which addresses and validates emotions in public and privileges emotional expressiveness (e.g. Wright, 2008) has been extensively documented and, in some corners, bemoaned. As Frank Furedi argued in *Therapy culture*, his polemic against what he sees as a contemporary obsession with airing our dirty laundry in public, we "live in a culture that takes emotions very seriously" (2004, p. 1). Among other developments, we have witnessed a popular valorization of "emotional intelligence" – or the ability to identify and manage your own emotions and those of others (Goleman, 1996). Emotional intelligence is viewed as an indispensable life skill which is just as important as conventionally valued forms of intelligence (Goleman, 1996; Williams, 2001). Some observers link these transformations to social consequences of contemporary capitalism, resulting in the "commercialization of intimate life" (Hochschild, 2003) and the rise of "emotional capitalism" exemplified by practices including psychoanalysis and online dating (Illouz, 2007).

It is perhaps not surprising that some critics suspect that we have become *overexposed* to emotion in our everyday life to the extent that we suffer from "compassion fatigue" (Moeller

1999) or, even more drastically, that we have become over-whelmed with synthetic "quasi-emotions" to the point that we are no longer able to experience authentic feeling and there-fore, in fact, inhabit a "postemotional society" (Meštrović, 1996). Such arguments highlight the emerging centrality of emotion in society as a focus for debate and contestation.

Against these varied claims about shifts towards a more emotional culture, it is important to inject a note of caution: social interaction has *always* been suffused with emotionality, and societies have therefore always been intensely preoccu-pied with the management of emotions (e.g. Elias, 2000). It is therefore perhaps more accurate to say that particular eras are characterized by distinctive "emotional regimes" or normative emotions and ways of expressing them in public (Reddy, 2001, p. 129). Put simply, the ways in which emotions are managed in public has shifted over time. For example, in tracing shifts in the public management of manners and emo-tions since the late 1990s, Cas Wouters has detected a process of "informalization" which has involved "the code of man-ners coming to allow for an increasing variety of behavioral and emotional alternatives; manners becoming more lenient, more differentiated and varied for a wider and more differ-entiated public." (2007, p. 2). Wouters believes that although this process has enabled people to become more open in their expression and discussion of feelings through an "emancipa-tion of emotions," this has also led to increasing demands on self-regulation (2007, pp. 3–4).

Defining emotion

These debates not only signal the contested status of emotions in society, but more broadly raise fundamental questions about the meaning of the concept. I want to briefly specify how I understand emotions here.[1] The book is premised on taking seriously the study of emotions as they flow through news media, and I have appropriated ways of understanding the phenomenon which are most closely aligned with this aim. While the volume examines how groups and individuals, from journalists to audience members, experience emotions and react emotionally, much of it focuses on how emotions are *constructed* in mediated texts – ranging from Pulitzer Prize-winning articles, routine coverage of protest, and feminist Twitter hashtags to Reddit discussions of Donald Trump. What this means, I suggest, is that we need not only to understand what emotions *are*, but also to acknowledge that *their mediated construction* is distinctive from emotions as they *circulate through individual bodies.*

The word "emotion" was first recorded in use in the seventeenth and eighteenth centuries, but did not make it into scientific vocabularies until as late as the mid-1800s (Dixon, 2012). In 1884, the prominent pragmatist philosopher and psychologist William James wrote an essay, "What is an emotion?," which called for a new research agenda committed to understanding the psychological mechanisms underlying individual experiences of emotion. James lamented that the "aesthetic sphere of the mind, its longings, its pleasures and pains, and its emotions, have been so ignored" (James, 1884, p. 188).

Since James' initial call for research on emotion, the term has been hotly contested across fields of humanities and social sciences (Gendron, 2010; Lakoff, 2016). As early as 1934, Elizabeth Duffy cautioned, "[W]e should study these phenomena in their own right, and under precise labels that do not mean different things on different occasions and to different writers" (1934, p. 103). On the basis of this profound conceptual confusion, Duffy concluded that the idea of "emotion" should be abandoned altogether as a scientific construct. While this may be an extreme response, it highlights the difficulty of reaching a consensus on what, exactly, we mean by emotion, and alerts us to the resulting ways in which definitions have been associated with particular forms of conceptual baggage.

Scholars in psychology and sociology have paid extensive attention to emotion. Given the epistemological orientation of the former discipline, emotion has been largely understood as a feature of individual experience. For example, cognitive psychologists tend to understand emotions as an individual physical response. According to such accounts, "an emotion begins with an individual's assessment of the personal meaning of some antecedent event. This appraisal process may be either conscious or unconscious, and it triggers a cascade of response tendencies manifest across loosely coupled component systems, such as subjective experience, facial expression, cognitive processing, and physiological change" (Fredrickson, 2001, p. 218). In cognitive psychology, emotion is understood in terms of a "reaction triad" of physiological arousal, expressive behavior, and subjective feeling (Scherer, 1993). Dominant psychological definitions thus understand emotions as responses to a "personally meaningful circumstance" (Fredrickson, 2001). This approach has therefore added to our understanding of how emotions operate at an individual psychological and physiological level, while having less to tell us about the ways in which emotions and their expression are shaped by social interaction.

To advance an understanding more helpful to the preoccupations of this book, it is worthwhile revisiting debates around the distinction between affect and emotion. These debates have taken shape across several disciplines, particularly in psychology, philosophy and cultural studies. On the one hand, some scholars use the two terms interchangeably (Ross, 2015, p. 20). They argue that the distinction is unhelpful because it obscures the difficulties of separating such bodily felt – and possibly unconscious – intensity from conscious emotion (e.g. Williams, 2001, p. 54; see also Burkitt, 2014; Greco and Stenner, 2013). On the other hand, those who see the distinction between affect and emotion as salient have tended to view affect as a superordinate label which understands emotion as just one of multiple affective processes (e.g. Kleinginna and

Kleinginna, 1981). For example, Zizi Papacharissi (2015), the media scholar most closely associated with work in the area, has drawn on this approach to define affect as an umbrella term which encompasses emotion:

> Emotion is subsumed within affect, and perhaps the most intense part of affect. Yet affect itself extends beyond feeling as a general way of sense-making. It informs our general sensibility toward the world surrounding us. (Papacharissi, 2015, p. 15)

One of the most important articulations of the distinction between affect and emotion can be found in the work of Brian Massumi (2002). He proposed that affect is best understood as a bodily sensation in an individual, a reaction to stimuli characterized by intensity and energy, but without a conscious orientation and interpretation. By contrast, an emotion is

> a subjective content, the sociolinguistic fixing of the quality of an experience which is from that point onward defined as personal. Emotion is qualified intensity, the conventional, consensual point of insertion of intensity into semantically and semiotically formed progressions, into narrativizable action–reaction circuits, into function and meaning. It is intensity owned and recognized. (Massumi, 2002, p. 28)

Though Massumi described emotional reactions as *personal* and individual first and foremost, his distinction has also become an important resource for sociologists and political scientists interested in *collective* behavior, insofar as it is premised on emotion as both interpretation and narrativization of affect, or its placement in the nexus of social relations. This offers us a way out of a narrowly individualist understanding of emotion in foregrounding the "fundamental principle that an emotion cannot be seen purely as an internal, individual, and private phenomenon" (Boehner et al., 2007, p. 280). It enables us to understand emotion as a potentially politicized or politicizing interpretation of bodily affect in the context of public discourse.

I therefore find it helpful to maintain the distinction between affect and emotion, and to define emotion as *the relational interpretation of affect experienced in individual bodies* (see also Davidson and Milligan, 2004) – one that may become public and collective through naming, articulation and circulation. Such a definition of emotion has several implications. First, it is closely aligned with a sociological approach which sees emotions as *fundamentally relational, evolving out of the interactions of individuals with culture and underlying social structures* (Burkitt, 2014; Clay-Warner, 2014; Holmes, 2004; Stets and Turner, 2008). This also means that emotions evolve through ever-ongoing, dynamic and interactive processes (Boiger and Mesquita, 2012). This is not to say that emotions are purely "social, cultural and political constructs" (Flam, 2005, p. 19) and therefore do not exist outside of their discursive construction. Rather, the approach taken in this book suggests that it is both relevant and interesting to consider *which* emotions do gain purchase in the public sphere, *why*, and *with what consequences.*

The book also makes a distinction between emotions as circulating in individual bodies and emotions as discursively constructed through media texts – or what I refer to as "mediated emotion." Mediated emotional expression is carefully staged, for a particular purpose, and is a fundamental driver of social and political action (Wettergren, 2005). Whenever individuals display their emotions in public, these displays should be understood as "strategic performances in front of an audience of selected others" (Svensson, 2014, p. 21; see also Barrett, 2014; Turner and Stets, 2005).

Historian William Reddy proposed that emotional expression can be understood as a kind of speech act – when we speak of our emotions, we make them come alive. To Reddy, the expression of emotion, or "emotives," constitutes "a type of speech act [...] which both describes [...] and changes [...] the world, because emotional expression has an exploratory and a self-altering effect on the activated thought material of emotion" (2001, p. 128). Understanding the expression of emotion as a *speech act* with concrete consequences in the world and the lives of the people inhabiting it is central to the project of this book. Emotions circulate in public discourse in patterned ways that have profound social and ideological ramifications. The approach of this book is that how we speak about emotions in public matters hugely precisely *because* such speech is performative: It reflects the prevalence of particular emotional regimes (Reddy, 2001) and associated feeling rules (Hochschild, 1983).

News media are particularly interesting as an object of study because of the significance and distinctiveness of the articulation of emotion, which contributes to both establishing and challenging emotional regimes. First of all, if emotions are relational, and people "acting in concert develop shared repertoires of emotion" (Ross, 2015, p. 1), media are crucial to the ways in which these shared repertoires of emotion emerge. As Andrew Ross observed, "[E]motionally significant social interactions are increasingly involving dispersed participants connected through communications technologies such as radio, television, cell phones, electronic mail, social networking – and often many of these together" (2015, p. 5).

Compared to other kinds of talk between people, news media content is, in fact, explicit in both articulating and eliciting emotion (Wettergren, 2015, pp. 118–22). Journalists will often ask sources how they *feel*, as a way of generating drama and compassion, bringing the audience closer to the story (Back, 2017). That is to say, despite its historical allegiance to an objective style of reporting, news is dependent – for the drama and appeal of its narratives – on explaining the emotions of actors and characters, and engaging the emotions of audiences. In doing so, it tells us important things about our society, our ideologies – whether shared or contested – and our relationships to other nations and groups.

If journalism is one of the key vehicles used for both establishing and perpetuating particular emotional regimes, it also facilitates the particular legitimate ways of sharing our feelings. The ways in which we talk about our feelings in the media, in turn, set out the conditions of possibility for shared action. Michel Foucault's (e.g. 1978, 1980) understanding of discourse as a site where common sense and rationality are refracted through dynamic power relations has much to offer this project. This, in turn, entails an appreciation of news media as "a set of institutionalized practices embedded within a web of sometimes overlapping, sometimes conflicting discourses that generates social meanings" (Carlson, 2016, p. 353). Looked at this way, discursively constructed emotions play a key role in shaping these social meanings and are, in turn, profoundly shaped by power relations.

Thinking of emotions in these terms helps to highlight the *performative, social, collective and potentially political consequences of their mediated construction.* It involves "performances of status and power in that feelings and expressions of emotion serve to reflect and reinforce existing hierarchies" (Clay-Warner, 2014, p. 316). Precisely because emotions are in part socially constituted and profoundly shaped by power relations, their public articulation – particularly in mediated contexts – tells us about more than merely how individuals feel: it tells us about how we collectively and socially narrate emotions for larger purposes. It provides an emotional compass that we – as audience members and citizens – can use to orient ourselves in a confusing world. It directs us in particular ways to make sense of events unfolding around us, ranging from economic crises to natural disasters and elections.

Towards a nuanced analysis of emotions

Among scholars who have taken seriously the role of emotion in political life, we can discern a spectrum of responses which acknowledge that emotions can be both disruptive and constructive, and that the same emotions may do different kinds of work depending on who articulates them and in what context. The insight that emotionality, rather than existing in binary opposition to rationality, actually operates in complex and differentiated ways is foundational to this book. It underpins the remaining chapters, which focus on discerning the multiple and variegated ways in which emotion moves through mediated politics. Here, I will briefly outline some of the key fault lines of these arguments, which form a vital backdrop for the book.

The relationship between the valence – or the positive and negative orientation – of emotions and their roles in mediated politics is not a straightforward one. Some emotions – ranging from anger and grief to love and happiness – are readily articulated in public, while others may be "dark" (Jalan, 2015) or "ugly" (Ngai, 2005) – such as envy, irritation, anxiety, paranoia and disgust. These are widely viewed as socially undesirable and are therefore rarely shared with others, let alone in public.

Further complicating matters, evidence suggests that individuals are motivated to act politically on the basis of what are often *negative* emotions, including anger, fear, hatred and disgust towards groups or ideas that are discursively marked out as different or "Other." Indeed, in mediated narratives, as in everyday talk, we tend to see a preponderance of negative emotions – such as fear, anger and worry – over more positive ones – such as hope and love (Martin and Rose, 2003; Wahl-Jorgensen, 2013a, 2013b).

Such concerns have gained increasing urgency in the era of social networking, where platform affordances facilitate the rise of "toxic technocultures" (Massanari, 2017) through the uninhibited circulation of hate speech (Ben-David and Matamoros-Fernandez, 2016). Social media enable hate groups to spread and legitimate their ideas through a "borrowed network of associations" that facilitates the sharing of verbal and visual images as well as "links, downloads, news threats, conspiracy theories, politics and even pop culture"

(Klein, 2012, p. 428). The public expression of negative and divisive emotion may therefore undermine broader forms of public debate, even as it strengthens bonds within particular communities that are premised on exclusionary identities. For Sara Ahmed, the expression of disgust "generates a community of those who are bound together through the shared condemnation of a disgusting object or event" (2004, p. 94), even as it "others" those who are deemed disgusting. Another negative emotion which plays a similar role is that of fear: many political projects – ranging from the campaign for the British referendum on European Union membership (Wahl-Jorgensen, 2016) to former Australian Prime Minister John Howard's attempts at garnering support for military action in Iraq (De Castella et al., 2009) – rely on mobilizing particular populations by appealing to it (Enroth, 2017; Robin, 2004). Corey Robin's book *Fear: The history of a political idea* explores the evolution of what he refers to as "political fear" or "a people's felt apprehension of some harm to their collective well-being – the fear of terrorism, panic over crime, anxiety about moral decay – or the intimidation wielded over men and women by governments or groups" (2004, p. 2). Although fear may be seen to generate unity and energy, Robin believes it is more helpful to view it as "a symptom of pervasive conflict and political unhappiness" (2004, p. 3). An emphasis on fear, he ultimately proposes, creates divisions among groups in diverse societies and forecloses the possibility of a political culture that emphasizes freedom and rationality. As a result, it can never be a meaningful foundation for a constructive politics.

At the same time, ostensibly negative emotions can serve an empowering role. This book pays particularly close attention to the role of anger as an essential political emotion, which can be seen as a double-edged sword. On the one hand, anger is seen as a dangerous emotion which threatens social order (Lyman, 2004) and can never be normatively justifiable (Nussbaum, 2016). But, on the other hand, as social movements scholars have long established, anger is also vital to energizing and shaping the activities of activists representing groups that might otherwise be marginalized or disempowered (e.g. Flam, 2015; Gould 2010, 2012, 2015). As Chapters 4 and 5 explore in more detail, because anger in mediated politics is fundamentally *performative*, its consequences depend on who articulates it, to what end, and in what context (see also Berry and Sobieraj, 2014; Cramer, 2016; Hochschild, 2016).

Mediated politics & performative

What is very clear is that a discursive climate dominated by negative emotion, articulated with deliberate exclusionary intent, has serious consequences for views of political participation: in the context of a political culture characterized by a cynical attitude towards political engagements (e.g. Eliasoph, 1998; Stoker and Hay, 2016), those who venture forth to engage in political discussion are often dismissed as so extreme or even insane in their positions that their contributions can be ignored. As Gonen Dori-Hacohen and Nimrod Shavit noted in their study of Israeli online comments, it is a widespread practice of commenters to dismiss the contributions of their ideological opponents. For example, leftist commenters frequently portrayed rightists as fascists, violent and murderous, and psychos, whereas leftists, in turn, were described as peaceful and naïve delusionals by their rightist opponents (Dori-Hacohen and Shavit, 2013, p. 370). On this basis, they argued that participants "consistently condemn their counterparts as insane" (Dori-Hacohen and Shavit 2013, p. 369). As a result, "no consensus can ever be reached and the communal function of the communication is to maintain an apparent social schism between the participants from each camp" (Dori-Hacohen and Shavit, 2013, p. 372).

In fact, the emotional pain and uncertainty that comes with attempts at communicating across barriers of difference (Peters, 1999, p. 265) keeps many people from engaging in conversation with those from other backgrounds in the first place. With a proliferation of platforms ushered in by the digital age, it seems that the consequence has been a further fragmentation of public debate, leading to a multiplicity of discussions among like-minded participants, rather than ones which seek to face or overcome difference (Papacharissi, 2010). This is reflected in concerns over the "filter bubble" (Pariser, 2011) created by an environment in which our information universes are increasingly personally tailored by algorithms, and facilitated through the self-selective behavior we engage in through social media (Bakshy et al., 2015). As a result, we are less likely than ever to encounter disagreeable content. Though recent empirical research has failed to find support for the filter bubble thesis (e.g. Fletcher and Nielsen, 2017), the resonance of the concept speaks to the salience of concerns about the invisible curation of our information universe, including its emotional tenor.

On the other hand, there is a long-standing and significant body of work suggesting that emotionally engaged mediated politics may have an important role to play because it fosters the conditions for compassion with others who may be very distant and different from us (e.g. Chouliaraki, 2006, see also Zillmann 1991, 2013). This positive role of emotion in political life is explored in Chapters 2 and 3 in this book, which examine the ways in which forms of emotional and personalized storytelling might foster compassion by narrating concrete and embodied lived experience, and in Chapter 5, which looks at political fandom to understand how positive emotional attachments to political leaders can help to foster new forms of engagement, as well as new ways of talking about our shared problems.

Paying attention to emotion in mediated politics therefore entails seeing the nuance of how different emotions circulate across different contexts. In keeping with this preoccupation, the book illustrates how particular emotions – such as anger and love, discussed in Chapters 4, 5 and 6 – do not work uniformly, but rather operate in diverse ways, informed by interpretive contexts and power relations and shaped by media practices.

Overview of the book

The book navigates this complex landscape through a series of closely connected original studies which reflect specific engagement with the interplay of these key concepts: emotions, media and politics. While a brief book such as this one can only begin to scratch the surface of this interplay, it is aimed at investigating what I view as the most important and provocative contemporary sites and debates where it unfolds, while leaving many for others to discover. The book emphasizes the analysis of concrete empirical examples, which are invariably selective and context-dependent, but also gritty, textured and rich. It is premised on, and structured towards, building up a series of interconnected propositions about emotions, media and politics. These are intended to advance knowledge and open up for new debates and research agendas.

Chapter 1, "Taking emotion seriously: A brief history of thought," provides a conceptual introduction for the book, which lays out the foundations for the project. It does so, first of all, by examining why it is worthwhile paying attention to emotion, and how it has been investigated in social sciences and humanities disciplines. The chapter argues that even if emotion has historically been neglected, an "affective turn" has taken place in recent decades, which has spilled over into work on media and politics. Although attention to emotion in journalism studies has been slower to arrive, there is now an emerging body of work that examines the role of emotion in shaping journalistic practice, texts and audience responses.

Chapter 2, "Emotions are everywhere: The strategic ritual of emotionality in journalism," begins the journey towards centering emotion in political life in the context of media production, arguing that we need to understand emotionality as a central – and systematically overlooked – element of journalistic storytelling practice. Conventional scholarly wisdom has it that journalistic practices and genres are heavily influenced by what Gaye Tuchman (1972) referred to as the "strategic ritual of objectivity." Here, I find that a strategic ritual of emotionality is just as embedded in, and central to, journalistic practice. However, it does not call on the emotional expression of journalists in any straightforward way. Rather, such emotional expression is heavily policed and disciplined. Nevertheless, even if journalists are restricted in their *own* emotional expression, journalistic genres remain infused by emotion. This is because journalists *outsource* emotional labor to non-journalists – namely their sources, and particularly members of the public, who are authorized to express emotions in public. Drawing on an analysis of Pulitzer Prize winners – supposedly the exemplars of journalistic practice – across a range of categories, including breaking news reporting, international reporting, commentary, criticism, feature writing and investigative reporting, the chapter highlights how emotionality, far from being a burden bestowed on the public sphere by irrational citizens, is a fundamental force which underpins, structures and produces mediated public life.

Chapter 3, "Authenticity, compassion and personalized storytelling," builds on this argument, taking a step back by examining *why* particular forms of emotionality are valued by journalists and audiences alike. The chapter argues that personalized storytelling is viewed as more authentic, and has a powerful role to play in cultivating compassion and creating community. Drawing on a series of cases representing varied forms of personalized storytelling – including letters to the editor, user-generated content and hybrid formats like Humans of New York Refugee Stories – the chapter shows that to understand the experiences of others and make large and often abstract political happenings come alive, it is necessary to tell people's stories, although such storytelling can take many different forms.

Having focused on the ways in which emotionality and personal storytelling can enhance bonds of solidarity, the book then moves on to exploring the work done by *particular* emotions, with two chapters devoted to anger as a central political emotion. Chapter 4, "Towards a typology of mediated anger," defines mediated anger as a distinctive concept, suggesting it is performative, discursively constructed, collective and political. It then applies this typology to routine coverage of anger in protest coverage. The analysis demonstrates that anger serves as a cause of engagement and a barometer of the intensity of public feeling, ultimately forming an injunction to care. It sets out a spectrum of discursive constructions of mediated anger. On the basis of this spectrum, it argues that protesters can be simultaneously angry *and* rational, peaceful and legitimate. Mediated anger, the chapter argues, is always-already political and has the potential to change the world, for better or worse.

Chapter 5, "Shifting emotional regimes: Donald Trump's angry populism," examines one particularly distinctive formation of mediated anger by looking at the rise of Donald Trump as reflective of a shift in the prevailing "emotional regime" (Reddy, 2001) towards an "angry populism." The chapter focuses on how anger is discussed in coverage of Trump – from his election and up to the end of his first 100 days in office. It shows that angry populism – embodied by Trump – is based on a rhetoric which seeks broad appeal through the deliberate expression of anger. Indeed, as the analysis highlights, the mediated anger of Trump mattered because it became a political force in its own right. Through his astute reading of the Zeitgeist, Trump became an emotional performer, acting as the advocate of the people and the impersonator of their anger. The analysis implies that the anger of Trump, his supporters and his opponents is both salient and relevant to political life.

Having reclaimed the importance of anger as a political emotion, the book moves towards a more nuanced understanding of the place of emotion in shaping political engagement by looking at the role of *positive* affective bonds through an engagement with political fandom. Chapter 6, "The politics of love: Political fandom and social change," focuses on a very particular kind of love which is closely tied to forms of political discourse and action: it compares two recent cases of political fandom – those surrounding former British Labour leader Ed Miliband on Twitter and President Trump on Reddit. The chapter argues that these fandoms articulate in diverse ways, underpinned by the affordances of the media platforms on which they circulate, and the broader communities to which participants belong. Ultimately, the chapter shows that the position of the political fan creates a distinctive subjectivity that both facilitates and legitimates political engagement.

Chapter 7, "The emotional architecture of social media," looks in more detail at the relationship between affordances and emotion first raised in Chapter 6. It focuses on how forms of emotional expression are structurally encouraged in social media on the basis of design decisions. As with the architecture of other public spaces, these design decisions are sometimes *intended* to structure the forms of expression that are sanctioned in these social media, whereas in other cases, these consequences are coincidental and unexpected by-products. Increasingly, a great deal of thought goes into tailoring the emotional architecture towards far more positive forms of expression – in part as a result of the greater potential to monetize positivity and commodify users' emotional labor. The chapter takes an in-depth look at debates over the Facebook emoji reactions which have particular consequences for the horizons of mediated public participation enabled by the social networking site. If Facebook is now the world's most important news medium, the architecture of the platform matters hugely to the public sphere. The centrality of emotion in shaping the architecture of Facebook shows a paradigm shift in thinking about public debate as it takes place through social media. Whereas emotion has long been vilified as an enemy of rationality in the public sphere, it is now at the forefront of the concerns of the architects designing the social media platforms through which so many of us now get our news. The chapter demonstrates that there is a close link between emotional architecture, enforced positivity and the commodification of emotional labor in social media.

The conclusion, "Nine propositions about emotions, media and politics," summarizes the contributions of the book. It demonstrates that the book's reading of the practices of mediated politics through the lens of emotion highlights the need for a radical reconceptualization of theories of politics and media, grounded in lived experience which is often far messier and more emotional than dominant normative ideals might imply.

CHAPTER ONE

Taking Emotion Seriously:
A Brief History of Thought

In this chapter, I discuss why scholarship on news media and political life has been so slow in taking account of the place of emotion. The chapter begins by highlighting the suspicion of emotion embedded within the fabric of Western liberal democracy. This has meant that emotion has been viewed as the enemy of good citizenship – a view which informed the attention granted to emotion in the study of news media, as well as in other related disciplines. Nonetheless, there has been a turn to questions of emotion in recent years across the humanities and social sciences. For political communication scholars, important insights have been gained from research focused on the increasingly close relationship between politics and popular culture. In the study of news media, however, there has been a particular emphasis on journalistic objectivity, which has led to a strong aversion to emotion, often embodied in a fear of "sensationalism." This, alongside the fact that journalism studies has developed only relatively recently as a discipline, explains the late emergence of research on journalism and emotion. The chapter takes a closer look at how this research has taken shape, examining work on journalistic practices, texts and audiences which has informed this book.

The historical neglect of emotion in political life: celebrating rationality

Why has government been instituted at all? Because the passions of men will not conform to the dictates of reason and justice without constraint.

(*Alexander Hamilton*)

The way we have viewed the relationship between emotions, media and politics has been shaped by the framework of liberal democratic theory – the dominant mode of political organization in Western democracies. Built into the liberal ideal is an idealization of the rational, dispassionate and informed citizen, coupled with a clear understanding that emotional citizens make for bad subjects. Theorists have argued that political decision-making must be untainted by the passions, partialities and particularities which we all possess. Emotions are treated as "among the least reliable and most extendable human capabilities – merely private states with no proper place in intellectual deliberation over politics" (Ross, 2013, p. vii). Liberal democracy has been characterized by an "irrational passion for dispassionate rationality" (Rieff, 1979, cited in Williams, 2009, p. 140; see also Cepernich, 2016). As George Marcus and his coauthors put it:

> [The] Western tradition tends to derogate the role of affect in the public sphere. Being emotional about politics is generally associated with psychological distraction, distortion, extremity, and unreasonableness. Thus, the conventional view is that our capacity for and willingness to engage in reasoned consideration is too often overwhelmed by emotion to the detriment of sound political judgment. As a result, theories of democratic practice proclaim the importance of protesting against the dangers of human passion and political faction by building up institutions, rules, and procedures – all intended to protect us from our emotional selves. (Marcus et al., 2002, p. 2)

It is no coincidence that emotional engagement has been viewed with suspicion, while rationality has been widely celebrated as the panacea for good citizenship. The origins of this conception can be traced back to the birth of liberal democracy. As a political philosophy, it evolved in reaction to the long-standing dominance of the church and absolutist sovereigns (Holmes, 1995). These forms of governance were premised on the service of docile subjects, who were largely devoid of political agency and rights and considered incapable of rational political decision-making. This, in turn, necessitated the valorization of rationality, usually in opposition to emotion. As Zizi Papacharissi argued: "In the process of breaking the monopoly on knowledge held by the church and monarchies, frequently by affective means employed to control the masses, it became essential for scholars to prioritize reason and rationalization as a means of intellectual empowerment and greater enlightenment" (2015, p. 11).

The philosophical belief in the rationality of individuals and their ability and right to participate in politics followed on from the Renaissance. As an intellectual revolution, it heralded a renewal of interest in the ideas of Ancient Greece and Rome, and alongside it, a rediscovery of ideas of science and human rationality. Renaissance scholars embraced a humanist approach, emphasizing human dignity and the capacity for reason. The emergence of ideas of individual rationality gradually chipped away at the supremacy of sovereigns and the church and paved the way for the legitimation of individual rights, including liberty and equality. This resulted in transformations in political thought, which gradually came to reflect a belief in the possibility of democratic societies premised on the participation of rational dispassionate citizens (see also Held, 2006).

As a result of this historical trajectory, democratic thought struggled with the relationship between rationality and passion in political life. Passions were widely viewed as an inevitable part of human nature, but one which ought to be controlled and channeled. Recent rereadings have suggested that liberal political thought is, in fact, suffused with concern about emotions (Illouz, 2007). As philosopher Susan James noted:

> This wider concern with the importance of directing the passions is reflected in works aimed not specifically at rulers, but at a broader and predominantly male élite who occupy, or will occupy, positions of power. Taking over an ancient tradition, these treatises tend to identify the acquisition of self-knowledge with the ability to master and manipulate passion, and to associate both with a process of cure. (1999, p. 4)

In other words, if passions are undeniably part of our essential beings, we must become masters of human nature to tame these passions. As liberal thought developed over time and grew to encompass ideas of democratic governance and citizen rights and participation, the preoccupation with the question of how to control the emotions of the citizenry became ever more salient. On the one hand, a successful democratic society relies on involving citizens as rational and constructive participants in politics. But, on the other hand, such participation dictates the need to manage their passions – as individuals and collectives.

In response to this conundrum, Enlightenment thought became heavily invested in the celebration of rationality. For example, Immanuel Kant (1724–1804), one of the figures most closely associated with the movement, defended a normative hierarchy of knowledge based on the primacy of reason over the crudeness of the "senses." For Kant, all "our knowledge begins with the senses, proceeds then to the understanding, and ends with reason. There is nothing higher than reason" (Kant, 1998, Part 1.2.2.i). Emotional subjects are seen as "bad" subjects because emotion precludes the rationality required for political decision-making (Marcus, 2010, p. 6).

The elevation of reason over sensation reflects a broader preoccupation with the management of emotion in Western societies. As Norbert Elias argued in *The civilizing process*, Western civilization has always relied on affect control structures – systematic mechanisms which regulate individual behavior to ensure the smooth functioning of society. The control of aggression has been one of the key engines of modernity. Elias stipulated that when "the power of a central authority grows, if over a larger or smaller area the people are forced to live in peace with each other, the moulding of affects and the standards of the drive-economy are very gradually changed" (2000, p. 169). To Elias, no "society can survive without a channeling of individual drives and affects, without a very specific control of individual behavior" (2000, p. 443). His account highlights the centrality of emotion in everyday life – and the importance of governing its expression.

Emotion in scholarship on politics and news media
The concern with the control of emotion, and the preference for disembodied rationality over embodied emotionality, has spilled over into the understanding of how emotions circulate through news media and shape public life. Much of the work on the relationship between media and democracy takes as its vantage point Jürgen Habermas' (1989) influential notion of the public sphere, which shares key premises with liberal democracy. The public sphere is the site between the state and civil society where citizens deliberate on matters of common concern – facilitated through both face-to-face interaction and media. Habermas developed his ideas through a historical reconstruction of bourgeois publics in England, France and Germany in the seventeenth, eighteenth and nineteenth centuries. In writing about the rise and fall of the bourgeois public sphere as a historical, empirical case study, Habermas also articulated a normative ideal for how citizens ought to participate in public life; a vision of how democracies ought to function. Central to this normative ideal is the belief that citizens ought to hold government accountable through public discussion. The discussion should be rational, open

to all those with an interest in the issue, and participants in the discussion should be judged on the merits of their arguments, rather than on their social status. In his articulation of the public sphere ideal, Habermas implied that emotional expression, appeals and argument should be barred from the deliberative process to ensure its rationality.

Habermas has been particularly influential among scholars interested in mediated politics because his account demonstrates the centrality of news media to democratic societies (see Dahlgren, 1995, pp. 7–8). As such, the notion of the public sphere is a widely used shorthand for the institutions – including media – through which citizens deliberate about the common good and hold government accountable, or the "realm of social life where the exchange of information and views on questions of common concern can take place so that public opinion can be formed" (Dahlgren, 1995, p. 7). Because of its conceptual importance, the notion of the public sphere is widely used in literature on media and participation.

However, the insistence on the primacy of rationality and the undesirability of emotion and subjectivity reifies the liberal binary between rationality and emotion. In doing so, it obscures the messiness and conflict that inevitably characterize political discussion in "actually-existing democracies" (Fraser, 1992; Mouffe, 2005). As this book explores in more detail, such a position is not only at odds with lived realities, but also fails to reflect the ways in which we actually come to understand and appreciate the experiences of other people (Benhabib, 1992). More than anything, the commitment to rationality and consensus underpinning the notion of the public sphere precludes a recognition of the role of emotion and conflict in the shaping of communicative interactions (e.g. Crossley, 1998, pp. 17–18). This point is well made by proponents of radical democratic theory, who assume that politics is fundamentally shaped by conflict, tension and disagreement between groups and is therefore antagonistic in nature (e.g. Mouffe and Holdengräber, 1989). For radical democrats, the liberal desire to excise emotions – negative and positive – from political life to secure a one-sided consensus is a dangerous move that is based on an oversimplified view of the political (Mouffe, 2005). We should, instead, take seriously the role of "the passions" because these "affective forces [...] are at the origin of collective forms of identification" and constitute "one of the main moving forces in the field of politics (Mouffe, 2005, p. 24). A radical democratic understanding therefore also entails the recognition that political life *depends* on the mobilization of emotion (see also Ost, 2004, p. 239). Media are one of the main sites through which such emotions are mobilized and collective identities formed as a result (e.g. Dahlberg and Siapera, 2007). As we shall see throughout this book, they form the basis for affectively charged battles over the common good.

The affective turn

This book accepts the insights of radical democrats, and operates from the assumption that we need to take emotion seriously as a force in mediated public life – for better and for worse. In doing so, it aligns with what has been referred to as an "affective turn" (Clough and Halley, 2007) in cultural studies and humanities disciplines, which has spilled over into the social sciences.

Over the past few decades, political scientists, philosophers, sociologists, psychologists, historians and literary theorists have turned their attention to emotion. The aim of such work has been both to question the binary opposition between rationality and emotion, and to reclaim the centrality of emotion in social and political life. To mention just a few prominent examples, in political science George Marcus' work (e.g. 2010) has given rise to the idea of "affective intelligence" as a counter to the dominant rational choice theories of voter behavior. A group of historians are now charting the history of emotions, beginning from the vantage point of

William Reddy's (2001) ground-breaking work on changing emotional regimes. Central to such approaches has been the attempt at reclaiming the emotional dimension of history – including what people felt at particular historical junctures, how they thought they ought to lead their emotional lives, and which feelings were encouraged and discouraged (Lewis and Stearns, 1998, pp. 1–2; see also Hewitt, 2017a). In philosophy, Susan James (1999) has reread key political philosophers to understand the place of the passions in their work. To social movement scholars, the question of how movements mobilize emotional engagement has, in fact, long been a central preoccupation (e.g. Goodwin et al., 2001; Staiger et al., 2010) – a tradition of work which is central to this book and discussed in more detail throughout.

Paying attention to emotions allows us to see the world in a new way: it opens up a broad array of new research questions, and to reveal things that were previously invisible. This book's examination of how emotions circulate through various news media practices, forms, genres and platforms paves the way for new research agendas that render visible what has for so long been unseen by scholars of journalism and political communication.

Studying emotions in mediated politics

Informed by the insights of the affective turn, some scholars of politics now acknowledge the need to challenge the binary distinction between rationality and emotion (e.g. Williams, 2009, p. 150). This body of work is based on the premise that the *"political brain is an emotional brain*. It is not a dispassionate calculating machine, objectively searching for the right facts, figures, and policies to make a reasoned decision" (Westen, 2007, p. xv). Voters, though often well informed and politically aware, think "with their guts" (Westen, 2007, p. xv). Stephen Coleman echoes this view: his major study of "how voters feel" was carried out on the basis that "the performance of political democracy cannot be evaluated in purely instrumental terms; that what democracy *does* and how democracy *feels* are not separable considerations" (2013, p. 191).

Such approaches highlight the need for a more careful analysis of emotions in political life which recognizes their central role and shows that, "like rationality, emotion is neither good nor bad in itself. It harbors liabilities as well as benefits. [...] Emotion, like rationality, does not ensure desirable or good outcomes; emotion assists the democratic citizen in self-governance and can facilitate manipulation and error" (Brader, 2006, pp. 194–5). Rational decision-making, in other words, is both inseparable from and inextricably linked to emotion.

Looked at this way, it becomes important to recognize that citizens who participate are fueled by both rationality *and* emotions, ranging from love to hatred, and encompassing disgust, fear and care (Dahlgren, 2009, p. 8; see also Ahmed, 2004). Emotional engagement in politics may be both unavoidable and desirable: people participate because they *care* or feel passionately about an issue, and, conversely, the choice of *inaction* also comes about as a result of affective responses (cf. Berlant, 2007; Dahlgren, 2009; Gould, 2010, p. 32). In recognition of the increased awareness of the relationship between emotion, rationality and political life, scholars thus reflect on the rise of "passionate politics" (Goodwin et al., 2001), the "emotional public sphere" (Lunt and Pantti, 2007; Lunt and Stenner, 2005) and "affective publics" (Papacharissi, 2015), to mention just a few labels associated with emerging lines of investigation in the area.

Along those lines, scholars in political communication have, over the past decade, begun to take note of the increasingly close relationship between politics and popular culture (e.g. Jones, 2005, 2010; Stanyer, 2013; van Zoonen, 2005), proposing that rather than a "dumbing down" of public debate, this realignment opens up new forums and opportunities for emotional expression in public which might engage otherwise apathetic audiences (Lunt and Stenner, 2005). This work has demonstrated that politicians draw on the genres, languages and performative styles of popular culture, while figures from popular culture are becoming more and more involved in politics (Coleman, 2017; Ekström and Firmstone, 2017; Langer, 2010; Stanyer, 2013; Street, 2001; van Zoonen, 2005; Wheeler, 2013). This is, in part, illustrated by the success of celebrities in politics, particularly in the United States. Examples range from the presidency of Ronald Reagan in the 1980s, to Arnold Schwarzenegger's two-term career as governor of California from 2003 to 2011 and reality star Donald Trump's presidential election victory in 2016.

This development signals the importance of understanding the emotive roots of our political commitments, as well as our emotional responses to policies and politicians (see also Chapter 6). It necessitates the recognition that questions of rational policy-making may be dramatized in an emotional fashion through the theatre of public life (Richards, 2004, p. 339). The mediatization of political life, in turn, enables and underwrites such emotional dramatization: as Nigel Thrift has contended, "[P]olitical presentation increasingly conforms to media norms of presentation which emphasize the performance of emotion as being an index of credibility. Increasingly, political legitimation arises from this kind of performance" (2008, p. 184).

Such changes result, in large part, from the increasing scrutiny of the few and the powerful by the many, or the "transformation of visibility" (Thompson, 1995, 2005), facilitated by media that emphasize visual imagery, particularly television and online platforms, as well as genres such as television talk shows and Reality TV (Livingstone and Lunt, 1994; see also Chapter 3). As a result, coverage of politics has come to focus on the personalities and personal lives of political leaders (Langer, 2010). Political leaders, in their attempts to communicate with the public, are drawing on strategies of personalized and emotionalized storytelling, cultivating an "intimate politics" (Stanyer, 2013). For politicians, the ability to show themselves as "human" and "authentic" through emotional expression is now seen as a central quality for leadership (see also Chapter 3). The personalized and emotionalized performance is part of the ritual character test of the election campaign, as candidates now routinely subject themselves to the scrutiny of YouTubers, television talk shows and Twitter chats. This, in turn, signals the "informalization" of politics discussed in the previous chapter (Manning et al., 2017; Wouters 2007), through which political leaders have to increasingly communicate in a more casual fashion with voters to cultivate affective bonds.

Emotion and journalism

Scholarship on emotion and journalism has been somewhat slower to arrive, for several reasons. First, the relatively recent development of journalism studies as a discipline means that scholarship is still coming to terms with broader issues (e.g. Wahl-Jorgensen and Hanitzsch, 2009). Second, a strong commitment among professional journalists to ideals of objectivity (e.g. Schudson, 1978) has also shaped scholarly inquiry. Journalism, coming of age around the turn of the twentieth century alongside the rise of beliefs in positivist science and a commitment to the rationality of the modernist project, has been normatively invested in objectivity, understood in terms of the exclusion of values from the journalistic narrative (see also Maras, 2013). Objectivity has tended to be understood as the polar opposite of emotion. For example, Everette Dennis and John Merrill suggested that objectivity in journalism is tied to the aim of presenting "an emotionally detached view of the news" (1984, p. 111), while Michael Schudson argued that it "guides journalists to separate facts from values and report only the facts" using a "cool, rather than emotional" tone (2001, p. 150). Objectivity is characterized by a depersonalized narrative style, which erases the subjectivity of the journalist (Maras, 2013, p. 8). As Edward Epstein (1973) memorably put it, the norm of objectivity generates detached "news from nowhere" – a form of narrative which conceals the authorial voice of the journalist.

Objective journalism is normatively aligned with a view of journalism as a key institution in the public sphere. It is understood as the site for impartial, rational-critical discussion of matters of common concern. Subjectivity – and thus emotional expression and personal histories – is viewed as irrelevant and outside the scope of acceptable topics. Emotion has tended to be understood in terms of its deviance from ideals of the public sphere. As Mervi Pantti argued, "[E]motionality typically represents a decline in the standards of journalism and a deviance from journalism's proper social role; while 'quality' journalism informs and educates citizens by appealing to reason, other kinds of journalism focus on pleasing their audiences by appealing to the emotions" (2010, p. 169). These types of arguments are evidenced, among other things, in the concern over the sensationalist excesses of tabloid journalism. What gives rise to the moral panic associated with tabloid journalism is the very idea that it appeals to our *sensations*, and thus represents a preoccupation with the bodily and the emotional (Sparks, 2000), as opposed to our *reason*.

In recent years, however, as inquiry in the discipline has matured, journalism scholars have begun to take an interest in emotion, informed by the affective turn. Broadly, scholarship on journalism and emotion has been animated by interests in (a) understanding how journalistic practices are shaped by emotion and emotional labor, (b) studying emotion in journalistic texts, and (c) studying audience emotional engagement with news. Below, I discuss key studies in each of these areas to highlight the contributions of this work.

Scholarship on the role of *emotion and emotional labor in shaping journalistic practice* has demonstrated that journalistic practices have always taken emotion into consideration, but also shown that some of these practices may be evolving in response to technological, political and social change. Pantti (2010) was one of the first scholars to examine the role of emotion in journalistic practices, through her research on Finnish broadcast journalists' views on its appropriate use in reporting. While she identified highly critical views of "emotional news" amongst the journalists she interviewed, she also showed that journalists widely recognized the importance of emotional expression given its key role in facilitating audience understanding:

> On the one hand, presenting and interpreting "relevant" individual and collective emotions were seen as a part of journalism's aim to reveal reality, as "facts", without which the whole truth is not told; on the other hand, the main objective of emotional storytelling was to enhance the political and social knowledge of the audience, to facilitate the understanding of news. (Pantti, 2010, p. 179)

The notion that journalists recognize the value of emotional storytelling because of its ability to engage audiences has been a major theme of work on journalistic practices (see also Beasley, 1998), informing the approach taken in this book. Along those lines, Chris Peters has argued that the binary opposition between objectivity and emotion has obscured the fact that journalism has, in fact, always been emotional, given the central goal of "crafting an experience of involvement" (2011, p. 297). Journalists' awareness of the value of such storytelling also shapes their work in strategic ways. For example, Zeynep Gürsel's ethnographic work on photojournalism at an American news magazine demonstrated that to journalists, the anticipation of audience emotional reactions to stories informs deliberations over everything from photo selection to layout. She argued that the purpose of "wielding emotions" is to "bring the story closer" and educate the reader (Gürsel, 2010, pp. 40–1).

Scholarship on the intersection between emotion and journalistic practice has, in recent years, turned to examining the "emotional labor" – or management of feelings – amongst journalists (Hochschild, 1983). Such work has demonstrated that journalism's commitment to objectivity has meant that journalists are seen as detached and distant observers (Barnes,

2016; Hopper and Huxford, 2015, 2017; Jukes, 2017; Richards and Rees, 2011). This has made it difficult to recognize the emotional impact of journalistic work – whether it involves "death knock" interviews, (Duncan, 2012; Duncan and Newton, 2010) covering traffic accidents (Barnes, 2016), or reporting on wars and disasters (Jukes, 2017; Pantti et al., 2012). For example, Johana Kotišová's (2017b) work on Belgian journalists' experiences of covering a local terror attack highlighted how proximate disasters have a significant emotional impact on journalists, blurring boundaries between personal and professional lives and challenging conceptions of journalistic objectivity. In a separate study of Czech journalists' coverage of the 2015 refugee crisis and the Paris terrorist attacks, Kotišová (2017a) demonstrated the emergence of an "emotional culture" of cynicism which enabled journalists to maintain their sanity and distance against the backdrop of reporting on such traumatic events. Similarly, Stephen Jukes' (2017) research on journalists' reflections on the coverage of crises showed that professionals developed a "cool-detached" approach to shield themselves from the emotional impact of these events, through a set of practices consistent with the commitment to objectivity.

While these studies have contributed to a significant reappraisal of journalistic practices as they are informed by emotional responses – their own, as well as those of the imagined audience – there is also growing attention to the ways in which technological changes are transforming journalistic practices, carving out a space for emotional storytelling. Charlie Beckett and Mark Deuze (2016) have detected a trend "toward a more mobile, personalized, and emotionally driven news media" in the era of "networked news." Ros Coward (2013) investigated first-person writing in journalism, suggesting that while the rise of a more subjective and confessional form of journalism may have accelerated in response to the digital era and the emergence of social media, it has a long and complex history that can be traced back to the conventions of "New Journalism" in the 1960s and 1970s, as well as the influence of social movements such as feminism (see also van Zoonen, 1998).

Work on citizen journalism has made a particular contribution to understanding the drivers behind transformations in journalistic texts. Bolette Blaagaard's work on the affective practices of citizen journalists suggests that their narratives challenge the journalistic ideal of objectivity, introducing "situated, embodied, and political" registers (e.g. Blaagaard, 2013b). Such narratives are seen to have the potential to cultivate empathy and hence generate a new and enlarged moral imagination (Chouliaraki, 2010; see also Blaagaard, 2013a, 2013b). As Lilie Chouliaraki has demonstrated, the "ordinary witnessing" of citizens decenters journalists, replacing them with the citizen "as a guarantee of the authenticity of witnessing" (2010, p. 307).

Research on how emotionality is constructed and embedded in journalistic *texts* has contributed methodological tools and conceptual insights. Work in this area has developed ways of detecting the presence of emotions in journalistic texts, as exemplified in Maija Stenvall's discourse analytical work focusing on news agency copy (e.g. Stenvall, 2008, 2014; see also Wahl-Jorgensen, 2013a, 2013b and Chapter 2 in this book). A significant body of research has emerged on emotion in journalists' coverage of disasters as moments of heightened drama. Here, studies have acknowledged the particular significance of anger as a political emotion (e.g. Pantti and Wahl-Jorgensen, 2011; Pantti et al., 2012). This work shows that expressions of anger can facilitate calls for accountability and therefore often contribute to politicizing coverage of disasters. At the same time, work on how journalism represents suffering in disasters raises questions around conditions for the cultivation of compassion and cosmopolitan solidarity (Chouliaraki, 2006). The attention devoted to a spectrum of emotions and emotional responses in studies of disasters shows the complexity of emotional expression in journalistic texts and highlights the need for nuanced and systematic analysis.

Finally, an emerging body of research on *news audiences* demonstrates that audience conceptions of what constitutes valuable news may be at odds with the understandings of the profession (e.g. Costera Meijer, 2013; Schrøder, 2015; Swart et al., 2017). For example, consumers of news media frequently question the detached and disembodied stance of conventional journalism and seek out more emotionally engaging content (Costera Meijer, 2013). This work resonates with longer-standing research agendas in mass communication research, which have demonstrated the centrality of audience emotional engagement (e.g. Levy, 1979; Levy and Windahl, 1984) and that audience enjoyment is, in part, premised on narrative structure in ways that may challenge conventional journalistic genres. For example, Sylvia Knobloch and her colleagues found that higher "reading enjoyment for discourse structures typical for entertainment content implies that the classic inverted-pyramid news format does not maximize pleasure for print news users." On that basis, they called for "the importance of understanding affective appeals of reporting" (Knobloch et al., 2004, p. 282).

Together, these approaches to understanding the role of emotion in news media pave the way for a new set of research questions, premised on the understanding that emotion plays a role in shaping how journalists do their work, and how journalistic texts are crafted and received by their audiences. These processes are imbued with profound political significance, insofar as the research demonstrates how attention to emotion in the construction of journalistic narratives shapes audience reception and hence contributes to creating the conditions for political action and social change.

Conclusion

This chapter has demonstrated the central place of emotion in mediated politics. While the dominant liberal framework and the associated emphasis on the ideal of objectivity in journalism have contributed to rendering invisible the role of emotion, an "affective turn" across humanities and social sciences disciplines has shaped inquiry on politics and news media over the past few decades. Here, work on the increasingly close relationship between politics and popular culture has contributed to understanding the "informalization" of political life, and the growing role of personal and emotional narratives. At the same time, with the maturing of journalism studies as a field, we have seen emerging investigations into the role of emotions in shaping the practices of journalists, the forms of news texts and their reception amongst audience members. Such work alerts us to the need to take seriously questions of emotion and their circulation through media. We need to understand the complex interplay of the range of distinctive positive and negative emotions, and how they structure mediated politics. So, on the one hand, we should acknowledge the mobilizing potential of political emotion, and the power of the energy unleashed by it. On the other hand, we need to carefully analyze how particular emotions operate in mediated public life. Emotion should be understood as integral to the expressive forms of contemporary politics, and the ways in which citizens engage with it.

As the chapter has suggested, we must begin to engage with the concrete ways in which particular emotions encourage particular forms of public participation and expression while discouraging others. Such an interest is central to this book. To this end, the remaining chapters investigate the concrete ways in which emotions circulate through mediated politics. We start this journey by taking a closer look at the place of emotion in journalistic storytelling. It follows on from this chapter by drawing on a study of award-winning journalism which shows that despite the persistence of the ideal of objectivity, emotional storytelling is, in fact, central to the world-making powers of journalism.

CHAPTER TWO

Emotions are Everywhere: The Strategic Ritual of Emotionality in Journalism

This chapter takes a closer look at the place of emotion in Pulitzer Prize-winning journalism so as to begin charting the movement of emotion through news media, and its consequences for political life. It makes the case that despite the long reign of the ideal of objective journalism, the expression and elicitation of emotion are in fact central to audience engagement, and that emotional labor is central to journalistic professional practices. As a result, emotion is an elephant in the room that is journalism: it is a massive presence that has for so long been invisible and therefore unrecognized, even if understanding its role is key to unlocking the significance of the stories we tell ourselves as a society, and the forms of change rendered possible as a result.

As this chapter shows, Pulitzer Prize-winning stories consistently use techniques associated with outstanding storytelling – including the use of emotion and personal stories – to uncover and call public attention to what are often large, abstract and intangible events, entities and contexts. In doing so, they represent an instantiation of the relationship between emotions, media and politics, and dramatize the ways in which a rational understanding of the matters that concern us all can be best attained by engaging audiences emotionally.

As we discussed in the previous chapter, journalism's ideals – born out of its role as a key mediating institution of liberal democracy – have tended to value dispassionate and disembodied impartiality and derogate emotion (e.g. Jukes, 2017). Nonetheless, this chapter shows that in the day-to-day practice of journalistic labor, knowledge of how to incorporate emotion into storytelling is a crucial professional skill, and the correct display of this skill is valued and celebrated as exemplary.

The strategic ritual of objectivity

Ever since Gaye Tuchman first wrote about the strategic ritual of objectivity in journalism, it has been a well-established dictum that journalists mobilize a key set of professional practices to protect themselves from the risks of their trade. Tuchman argued that journalists "assume that, if every reporter gathers and structures 'facts' in a detached, unbiased, impersonal manner, deadlines will be met and libel suits avoided" (1972, p. 660). To Tuchman, the strategic ritual of objectivity could be seen as a survival mechanism; a response to the "risks imposed by deadlines, libel suits and superiors' demands." In drawing on the idea of ritual, she referred to "a routine procedure which has relatively little or only tangential relevance to the end sought. Adherence to the procedure is frequently compulsive. That such a procedure may be the best known means of attaining the sought end does not detract from its characterization as a ritual" (1972, p. 661).

This chapter picks up on Tuchman's sensitizing concept to suggest that there is also what might be referred to as a strategic ritual of emotionality, which operates alongside that of objectivity. The chapter finds that there is an institutionalized and systematic practice of journalists narrating and infusing their reporting with emotion, which means that journalistic storytelling, despite its allegiance to the ideal of objectivity, is also profoundly emotional.

This strategic ritual sometimes draws on practices of objectivity and, at other times, operates in tension with them. However, the strategic ritual of emotionality is as essential to journalistic practice as is the strategic ritual of objectivity, though it is rarely explicitly acknowledged because it is at odds with journalistic self-understandings. Unlike the ideal of objectivity, which is central to journalistic lore, the strategic ritual of emotionality constitutes a form of tacit knowledge, implicit in journalistic socialization processes and everyday work.

The chapter argues that the strategic ritual of emotionality does not call on journalists to express their *own* emotions. Rather, emotional expression is carefully managed to avoid journalists showing what they feel. Journalistic work in fact requires extensive emotional labor, but this labor remains unseen, hidden below the surface level of texts. Even if journalists are restricted in their own emotional expression, journalistic genres remain infused by emotion because of a neat trick: in telling stories, journalists rely on the *outsourcing* of emotional labor to non-journalists – the story protagonists and other sources (a) who are authorized to express emotions in public, and (b) whose emotions journalists can authoritatively describe without implicating themselves. This is consistent with the practices of the strategic ritual of objectivity as outlined by Tuchman, who argued that the "insistence on supporting 'facts' is pervasive, running throughout the editors' criticisms of reporters as well as the reporters' criticisms of editors" (1972, p. 667). On the basis of the availability of "facts" obtained through reporting, journalists are, in turn, authorized to describe the emotions of other individuals. In part, facts are verified through reliance on quotes from sources. Tuchman proposed that "[t]he newsmen view quotations of other people's opinions as a form of supporting evidence. By interjecting someone else's opinion, they believe they are removing themselves from participation in the story, and they are letting the 'facts' speak" (1972, p. 668). As we shall see, today's valorized journalistic forms operate on a somewhat more complicated set of epistemological assumptions, yet the premise of outsourcing emotional labor persists.

Based on an analysis of Pulitzer Prize winners – supposedly the exemplars of journalistic practice – across a range of news genres, including explanatory, international, national, investigative, feature and public service categories, the chapter uncovers the dynamics of the strategic ritual of emotionality. The chapter is premised on the idea that the regimented use of emotionality could be seen as a strategic ritual insofar as its correct display garners cultural capital in the field of journalism. It explores how emotion operates in these respective news genres so as to begin charting the complicated and bumpy terrain of emotional expression that journalists deftly negotiate on a daily basis and, more broadly, the movement of emotion and dispersal of emotional labor through the landscape of mediated politics.

Understanding the place of emotion in journalism

As we have seen, the ideal of objectivity as a central feature of journalistic self-understanding and practice enjoys a long and distinguished, if contested (e.g. Hartsock, 2000; Mindich, 1998), history in the field of journalism sociology (e.g. Schudson, 1978, 2001). Even if the ideal of objectivity had its heyday during a bounded and specific historical period (Schudson 1978), the central *practices* that it represents remain in force. Here, I argue that far from dispensing with the concept of objectivity, we can helpfully understand emotionality as a *complement* which draws on its practices and, through them, comes to be profoundly constitutive of journalistic narratives.

Proposing that emotionality is central to journalistic storytelling could be seen as both a contrarian and, in some ways, counterintuitive move. Mirroring its treatment in the history of liberal democracy as discussed in Chapter 1, in journalism emotion has often been denounced as a "bad object" by scholars and practitioners (Pantti, 2010). It has been seen as "a marker of unprincipled and flawed journalism" (Peters, 2011, p. 298) and has therefore rarely been taken seriously despite evidence of its prominence. For example, the sensationalized journalism of tabloid media is often denigrated in public and scholarly discourses precisely because the sensational is perceived to involve emotion in such a way as to preclude rationality and hence serious quality journalism (Sparks, 2000). While quality journalism is traditionally seen as objective and rational, tabloid discourse is considered to be anti-rationalist or sensationalist, in part due to its personalized storytelling and its intention to evoke emotional responses (Connell, 1998). In this vein, Bob Franklin argues that the purpose of tabloid journalism is "less to inform than to elicit sympathy – a collective 'Oh how dreadful' – from the readership" (1997, p. 8). This argument creates a binary opposition between "informing" and "eliciting sympathy," whereby emotion appears as the antithesis of the dominant vision of journalism as a "fact-centered" and rational discursive practice designed first and foremost to provide information (Chalaby, 1998). Other observers, however, have suggested that the creation of empathy is an indispensable prerequisite of political action (Boltanski, 1999). The work of the award-winning journalists examined here relies on precisely such an emotional response: it operates through storytelling which calls attention to larger social problems by eliciting emotional reactions in the audience and thereby securing their involvement. As the next chapter explores in more detail, this is, in fact, a common role of personalized storytelling in mediated discourse, but it takes a distinctive form in award-winning journalism.

Journalism's adversarial role, which is so central to the liberal democratic imagination, often implicates emotionality as a tool. Righteous indignation, mobilized on the part of a neglected majority, is a defining discursive strategy of populist politics (Higgins, 2008). Similarly, the indignation of celebrated interviewers like Britain's Jeremy Paxman is central to their success in acting as an advocate for the public, insofar as the aggressive journalist comes to represent the imagined emotional response of the audience (Higgins, 2008;

Higgins and Smith, 2016). As James Ettema and Ted Glasser (1998) pointed out, investigative journalists act as "custodians of conscience" through a consistent chain of reasoning which involves both the demonstration of systemic wrongdoing and the mobilization of moral outrage regarding this activity. Outrage is mobilized by getting a credible individual affected by the wrongdoing to denounce it in public, usually by sharing their own personal (and emotional) experience. Political scandal reporting – a related genre which is key to journalism's claims of holding the powerful to account – relies centrally on the elicitation of moral outrage at alleged transgressions through public denunciation (see also Thompson, 2000). Such coverage is seen to resonate emotionally with the public and is a necessary ingredient in the moral reasoning required to understand the complexities of claims for justice. As William Gamson (e.g. 1992) demonstrated, in studying how people talk about politics on the basis of news stories, citizens cultivate a sense of injustice precisely through the generation of moral indignation at an emotional level.

The idea that emotional expression has a role to play in some journalistic forms is not a new one. For example, Carolyn Kitch (e.g. 2000, 2003) has demonstrated that emotional storytelling is central to rituals of public mourning. Veteran British journalist David Loyn (2003) sought to recast the debate around objectivity by proposing that "[an objective] approach is not dispassionate. It can be hugely passionate, requiring emotional engagement and human imagination. But it is not about my passion, how I feel. The viewer or listener does not want to know how I feel, but how people feel on the ground."

The concern for the engagement of the reading public expressed by Loyn is echoed in the work of Liz Bird and Robert Dardenne, who go even further in making the case that compelling journalistic storytelling sits uneasily with practices of objectivity and thus fundamentally challenges core professional ideals: "[Journalists] face a paradox; the more 'objective' they are, the more unreadable they become; while the better storytellers they are, the more readers will respond, and the more they fear they are betraying their ideals" (1988, p. 78).

More recently, observers have suggested that social and technological change will increasingly place emotion at the forefront of journalistic practices, challenging conventional conceptions of professional roles (Beckett and Deuze, 2016; Jukes, 2017; Wahl-Jorgensen, 2014).

Nonetheless, an objective approach and compelling story-telling are not necessarily mutually exclusive. Verica Rupar and Marcel Broersma (2010), in their study of narrative practices in award-winning journalism, found that "objective reporting practices, in the form of allegiance to principles of accuracy, fairness, balance and impartiality, are understood both as minimal requirements and as attributes of excellence." That is to say, they are rarely used as explicit criteria for awarding prizes; instead, citations often focus on the excellence of journalistic storytelling. Techniques taken from New Journalism – including a delayed lead, human interest detail, realistic dialogue, scene-by-scene reconstruction, interior monologue and several narrators within the text – were privileged in awards decisions (Rupar and Broersma, 2010).

The evidence of the coexistence of objective reporting practices with emotional narratives is also backed up by research on journalists' professional reflections. As discussed in Chapter 1, Mervi Pantti (2010) concluded that while television journalists in both commercial and public service news organizations were critical towards "emotional news," they nevertheless believed that emotion did not pose a fundamental challenge to the rationales of factuality and objectivity. On the one hand, presenting and interpreting "relevant" individual and collective emotions were seen as a part of journalism's aim of representing reality, as "facts" without which the whole truth is not told; on the other hand, the main objective of emotional storytelling was to enhance the political and social knowledge of the audience and hence facilitate the understanding of news (Pantti, 2010; see also Richards and Rees, 2011).

Studying the strategic ritual of emotionality

This chapter takes an interest in delineating the strategic ritual of emotionality by answering the following questions: How is emotion built into journalistic stories? Who expresses emotion? How is it expressed? What role does emotional expression play in the narrative? To better understand the mechanics of the strategic ritual of emotionality, the chapter examines the extent and nature of emotional expression in the most highly valued examples of journalistic writing: award-winning stories. The decision to analyze award-winning journalism is based on insights from Pierre Bourdieu's field theory. To Bourdieu, "[A] field is a field of forces within which the agents occupy positions that statistically determine the positions they take with respect to the field, these position-takings being aimed either at conserving or transforming the structure of relations of forces that is constitutive of the field" (2005, p. 30). Bourdieu suggested that individuals advance their position within particular fields (including the professional field of journalism) through the accumulation of cultural capital. In the journalistic field, the specific cultural capital "is evident in those forms of journalistic excellence recognized by the US Pulitzer Prizes and other prestigious professional or academic forums" (Benson, 2006, pp. 189–90). As such, although Pulitzer Prize-winning articles may not necessarily give us a sense of what is *typical* of routine news reporting practices, and these stories may not accurately reflect the broad diversity of journalism practices in a global context, examining them identifies practices that are viewed as *exemplary* and as *models* to emulate (English, 2002).

The idea of looking at award-winning journalism as a marker of quality and excellence is not a new one. For some time, scholars have examined such stories and the journalists who write them to understand what counts as quality journalism, and which types of journalistic narratives are privileged and valorized within the profession as a result (e.g. Ettema and Glasser, 1998; Harbers and Broersma, 2014; Martin, 2017; Rupar and Broersma, 2010; Schultz, 2006).

The chapter focuses on how emotional storytelling operates in conventional news genres. To that end, I conducted a basic content analysis of a sample of Pulitzer Prize winners across the categories of news reporting conventionally assumed to be informed by ideals of objectivity,[1] including explanatory, international, national, investigative, feature and public service reporting. Each category is a distinctive genre, shaped by its own conventions and dynamic trajectories. But they also share some narrative features, including the use of emotional language and storytelling. These categories have been selected because they are the ones for which awards have been granted since 1995 – the first year for which the Pulitzer Prize online archive includes the texts of the winning stories – and up to 2017.[2]

As examples of the award-winning stories will demonstrate, there is little doubt that these journalistic narratives are profoundly infused with emotion. But because emotional intention, expression and reactions are both socially constructed and profoundly embedded in language, it is challenging to identify exactly how emotion operates in narrative, and scholars have grappled with this empirical problem for decades (see, e.g., Edwards, 1999; Lutz, 1988). Any attempt to come to terms with institutionalized discursive phenomena such as these requires both macro-level considerations about the nature of the narrative and micro-level analysis of particular word choices which shape the discourse. Emotions operate at several levels of journalistic discourse (e.g. Edwards, 1999). Most straightforwardly, they are at work in the use of emotive language – from the deployment of individual emotion words, such as "afraid," "happy," "elated" or "worried," to the use of detailed descriptions, judgments and appraisals of environments, objects and individuals. Emotions may also be *built into* the narrative: even in stories that do not use emotional language, dramatic tension is created through a variety of narrative strategies, including detailed description, juxtaposition and personalized storytelling, as the chapter will explore in more detail later. As Jacob Johanssen and Diana Garrisi (2017) suggested in their study of the coverage of acid attacks, stories based on "affective experiences" – or what I here call emotional storytelling – "are always already within *and* without, interior and exterior to discourse." This renders them complicated to analyze. The creation of dramatic tension draws on presuppositions, or claims based on shared normative assumptions that are taken for granted and implicit, "embedded within the explicit meaning of a text or utterance" (Richardson, 2007, p. 63), such as the idea that stealing and killing are morally wrong, that death is a tragic event, and that caring and loving are morally right. Indeed, Pulitzer Prize-winning stories, though dealing with a broad range of topics, are frequently premised on such presuppositions, and often deal with matters of life and death (Shapiro, 2006). Finally, at the extra-textual level, journalistic narratives are grounded in the anticipation of particular emotional responses in the audience (Gürsel, 2010).

Work in narrative journalism has taken an interest in the role of personalized storytelling (e.g. Bird and Dardenne, 2009) and the use, among other strategies, of the anecdotal lead (e.g. Rupar and Broersma, 2010). In analyzing the texts at the macro level, I used these two features – the use of an anecdotal lead and personalized storytelling – as markers of a strategic ritual of emotionality which have often been associated with a "softer" and more emotionalized form of journalistic storytelling (Macdonald, 2000). The anecdotal lead is an opening paragraph which does not use the conventional "inverted-pyramid" structure, characterized by "a style that conveys the most important information in the first paragraphs of a story, and one mentioned by textbooks and critics as part of 'objective' news writing" (Mindich, 1998, p. 13). Instead it tells a brief story, usually but not always personalized in nature, to draw in the reader (Itule and Anderson, 2003, p. 60). Personalized storytelling is defined as a narrative form which draws on the experience of a particular individual caught up in a story to dramatize a broader social issue. Anecdotal leads and personalized storytelling are thus closely related but one does not require the other: there are stories which have anecdotal leads but no personalized storytelling and, more rarely, stories which have other types of leads but feature the stories of individuals.

The chapter also draws on my previous research about the linguistic features of the texts in a smaller sample (Wahl-Jorgensen, 2013a, 2013b). This research used appraisal theory, an approach from the broader field of discourse analysis which focuses on how evaluations are made in commonly occurring genres of discourse (see Martin and Rose, 2003). The study examined how feeling is expressed in discourse through the use of affect - or emotion words (such as "happy," "elated," "optimistic," "hopeful"; "angry," "hurt," "worried," "ashamed"). In journalism, expressions of emotion are generally rather complex: they are often made on behalf of others, as when a journalist describes the feeling of a source ("Judge Robert Hilder felt *uneasy*") or a source describes the feelings of another individual or group ("'They were very *angry*,' added his wife"). It also considers judgments of individuals (e.g. 'elders are far more lenient') as a related form of appraisal which contributes to the building of dramatic tension.[3]

The chapter does not go into detail in analyzing the linguistic features of the texts, but instead describes systematic patterns in particular news genres and differences between them, making the general point that award-winning journalism is, across categories, pervaded by appraisal in general and emotion in particular, while the construction of emotion takes place in concrete and systematic ways.

Charting the strategic ritual of emotionality

If journalism has been conventionally understood as a fact-centered discursive practice (Chalaby, 1998), and the classic "objective" way of framing the facts in question has been the inverted-pyramid lead, characterized by a dispassionate, distanced narrative style (Itule and Anderson, 2003), the Pulitzer Prize-winning stories examined here give the lie to this received understanding. Instead, what prevailed, across all news genres, was a narrative form more closely resembling that of literary journalism (Hartsock, 2000), which draws on key storytelling tropes borrowed from fiction, and is characterized by anecdotal leads, personalized storytelling and widespread invocation of emotion. As Stephanie Shapiro (2006) put it in a tongue-in-cheek criticism of what she characterized as the "sob sister" style of award-winning journalism:

> Such human interest stories, molded by the techniques of fiction, put a face on the bewildering universe of medical ethics, risky procedures and end-of-life choices. Like the harrowing tales that yellow journalism's Nellie Bly and her sob sister descendants became known for, they also are calculated to snag readers by the emotions and not let them go until they burst, on cue, into tears.

Shapiro here tellingly described award-winning journalism as "calculated" and "molded by the techniques of fiction." This implies that the journalists who craft these stories deviate from the ideal of objectivity, as their storytelling practices are "less about providing information and more about manipulating emotions." For scholars who have studied storytelling in journalism, it is usually viewed as synonymous with a commitment to "telling stories with a plot and utilizing the medium's dramaturgical potential" to engage the audience (Ekström, 2000, p. 473). Such storytelling "is different from a simple chronological account, because it seeks coherence and meaning; a story has a point, and it exists within a cultural lexicon of understandable themes" (Bird and Dardenne, 2009, p. 207).

Along those lines, the exemplary American journalism of the two past decades could be more accurately described as carefully crafted and plotted storytelling with a moral purpose, which mobilized emotions – directly and indirectly – to engage audiences. Across all categories, anecdotal leads were the most prevalent, present in 66.2% of stories, compared to the conventional inverted-pyramid lead, which opened 17.6% of stories, while other types of leads (see Itule and Anderson, 2003, p. 60) accounted for 16.2%. There was, however, significant variation among genres, where anecdotal leads accounted for anywhere between 95.2% (in the case of feature reporting) and 34.8% (in the case of investigative reporting) whereas the percentage of inverted-pyramid leads ranged from none in the feature category to 29.2% in national reporting. This indicates variations which are also apparent in other respects and signals that specific practices may differ according to genre.

The role of the anecdotal lead was usually to draw the reader into a story with wider socio-political implications through the illustration of how it affected a particular individual or group. For example, the 2017 Feature Writing Pulitzer, won by C. J. Chivers for the *New York Times Magazine*, shows the horrors of war – and the difficulties of veterans in adjusting to life after its end – by telling the story of one marine's descent into violence following his service in Afghanistan:

> Sam Siatta was deep in a tequila haze, so staggeringly drunk that he would later say he retained no memory of the crime he was beginning to commit.
>
> It was a few minutes after 2 a.m. on April 13, 2014. Siatta had just forced his way into a single-story home in Normal, Ill., a college town on the prairie about 130 miles southwest of Chicago. A Marine Corps veteran of the war in Afghanistan, he was a 24-year-old freshman studying on the GI Bill at the university nearby, Illinois State. He had a record of valor in infantry combat and no criminal past.[4]

This lead, through the personalized tale of the desperate veteran, put a face on the complex social issue of the plight of veterans suffering from post-traumatic stress. Such personalized storytelling featured in 66.2% of stories, and there was a high degree of association between personalized storytelling and the presence of anecdotal leads: 90% of stories with anecdotal leads had personalized storytelling as opposed to only 4.2% of stories that opened with an inverted-pyramid lead.[5] While the frequency of anecdotal leads and personalized storytelling has remained remarkably stable over the time period included in the study, and there is therefore little evidence to suggest a change in the use of these practices, recent years have seen significant transformations due to the increasing use of multimedia formats. For example, the 2016 winner in investigative reporting, which was a collaboration between the *Tampa Bay Times* and the *Sarasota Herald Tribune*, explored violence in Florida's mental hospitals by combining personalized storytelling with photography and video. Similarly, the 2018 winner in explanatory reporting, by the *Arizona Republic* and the *USA Today Network*, used text, video, podcasts and virtual reality to explore the construction of the wall along the US border with Mexico. This indicates that award-winning journalistic practices are dynamic and adapt to the opportunities granted by the affordances of emerging technologies to enhance storytelling. However, the fundamental narrative building blocks – the use of anecdotal leads and personalized storytelling – remain intact.

As my previous research has shown (Wahl-Jorgensen, 2013a, 2013b), the expression of emotion was also widespread: in a smaller sample of Pulitzer Prize winners between 1995 and 2011, 86.1% of all stories contained expressions of affect by journalists, and 82.2% by sources.[6] When emotions were voiced, they were frequently negative: this was the case for 77% of journalists' expressions of affect and 65% of sources', involving terms such as "fear," "agony" and "threatened." On occasions when these expressions were positive, they often served as the basis for creating dramatic tension in the story by setting up a situation of "normalcy" that is then interrupted by a "remarkable event" or a "problem"; a common narrative structure in journalism and elsewhere (Martin and Rose, 2003, p. 130). For example, the story which won the Pulitzer Prize for feature reporting in 1997 for the *Baltimore Sun* dealt with the topic of a sick child: the son of a famous local umpire, John Hirschbeck. It opened with the description, through some expression of affect or emotion words, but also involving the extensive use of judgment of character of a "normal" little boy whose mundane but happy reality is then interrupted by a "problem," in the form of a deadly disease:

> Little John *could do anything*. He was *smart* and *adventurous* and *happy* and *healthy*. And then, mysteriously, silently, *he wasn't*. The trouble started at school. In first grade, John had *problems paying attention*. His writing looked shaky, and he'd lose his place in his work. (Emphasis added)

Here, the reversal in the tone of expressions of affect and judgments of Little John's character (from being *smart, adventurous, happy* and *healthy* to someone who *wasn't* and had problems *paying attention*) signals the dramatic tension which underwrites the story as a whole. The rich positive language thus serves a larger narrative purpose of investing the audience emotionally in the character.

Further complicating this picture was the fact that the most frequently mentioned positive emotion by sources was "hope" under what were usually discouraging circumstances. Richard A. Clarke, a White House counterterrorism official under George W. Bush, was interviewed for the *New York Times* series that won the 2002 explanatory reporting award. Clarke said about the possibility of capturing Osama Bin Laden that his "arrest, which we dearly hope for, is only one step along the road of the many things we need to do to eliminate the network of organizations." The prominence of hope in the discursive register means that most emotional expression calls attention to social and political problems that require solution, and that the positive emotions expressed tend to revolve around possible positive futures, rather than the present (see also Neiger, 2007). The overwhelming negative orientation of emotional expression is consistent with long-standing scholarly observations regarding the salience of news values of negativity and conflict (e.g. Galtung and Ruge, 1965), but also highlights journalists' construction of saddened subjects negotiating a dangerous and frightening world. On the other hand, this may reflect broader patterns in emotional expression: research demonstrates that negative emotion words are far more common in spoken language than positive ones (Bucy, 2003).

In the case of the Pulitzer Prize-winning stories, storytelling which is intensely emotional is clearly privileged. However, it is not emotional in the sense of journalists narrating their own emotions as storytellers. In fact, in *none* of the stories studied here did journalists discuss their own emotions. Instead, they described the feelings of groups and collectives in 43% of cases, story protagonists in 22%, and other individuals in 24%.

As such, there is clear evidence to suggest that journalistic storytelling outsources emotional labor – the responsibility for the expression of emotion contained within the news stories, and the elicitation of emotions on the part of the audience. In this, the emotional storytelling of journalism is validated by the evidence provided by sources. As Stephen Jukes has argued, this "well-rehearsed technique is a cornerstone of objective journalism practice since the reader or viewer is *not* being overtly confronted with the emotions of the reporter" (2017, p. 15).

Further complicating matters, as demonstrated above, stories which do not directly, or only sparsely, express affect can be intensely emotional through other means. The anecdotal lead cited below opened a series of Associated Press stories by Mark Fritz which won the 1995 International Reporting Pulitzer through illustrating the devastating consequences of the 1994 Rwandan civil war. The lead used the story of a geno-cide perpetrator to draw the reader into the broader account of the conflict:

> MUSHA, Rwanda (AP) – Juliana Mukankwaya is the mother of six children and the murderer of two, the son and daugh-ter of people she knew since she herself was a child.
>
> Last week, Mukankwaya said, she and other women rounded up the children of fellow villagers they perceived as enemies. With gruesome resolve, she said, they bludgeoned the stunned youngsters to death with large sticks.
>
> "They didn't cry because they knew us," said the woman. "They just made big eyes. We killed too many to count."
>
> [...]
>
> Virtually all of the prisoners recounted their horrific deeds in dull, emotionless voices, their faces a collection of impas-sive masks.

This story is a useful example of the complexities in chart-ing emotional expression, and a more detailed examination of its mechanics is illustrative. It makes very limited use of explicit emotion words ("*stunned* youngsters") even if it is rich in appraisals which set the scene to elicit audience emotional response ("*gruesome* resolve," "*horrific* deeds," "*emotionless* voices," "*impassive* masks") and, in fact, explicitly remarks on the absence of emotion in the accounts of the imprisoned alleged genocide perpetrators. The protagonist, Juliana Mukankwaya, likewise describes the absence of dra-matic emotional reaction amongst the victims ("*They didn't cry because they knew us. [...] They just made big eyes*"). But the emotional impact of the story, underlined by the appraisals, comes from the dramatic juxtaposition of the situation of nor-malcy ("*Juliana Mukankwaya is the mother of six children*") with the unexpected event (Martin and Rose, 2003: 130) ("*and the murderer of two, the son and daughter of people she knew since she herself was a child*"), a common narrative structure which here paints a resonant picture of the horror of the alleged crime without any use of emotion words.

Along those lines, the following story about famine in Afghanistan was relatively unusual insofar as the entire story contained no expression of source affect and only limited instances of appraisal. Yet the storytelling embodies profound emotion in its graphic description of the funeral of a young child:

> Abdullah looked like a child's doll in his perfect stillness. He was brought across the road and laid gently on a piece of yellow plastic. The father slowly tore off the boy's clothes – the parka, a green shirt, a good luck charm worn around the neck. Another man washed the baby with shampoo, rinsing the suds with water poured from a black kettle. Dabs of perfume were applied from a little bottle. Abdullah was then wrapped, first in the shroud, then in a tan blanket.
>
> [...]
>
> When it was time to lay Abdullah in his grave, it was already after 10 and the morning had turned bright. Wrapped in the shroud, and with the day pulsing with sunlight, the baby was finally warm when he was placed forever in the earth.

What both of these stories share is the presupposition (Richardson, 2007) that the death of a child is a tragic event. The horror of the very idea of children dying needlessly – in one case from the murderous actions of the mother of six children, and, in the other from starvation – serves as the consensual basis for the emotional resonance of the stories. In fact, as mentioned above, a significant number of Pulitzer Prize-winning stories told of dead or sick children as a way of illustrating broader themes, ranging from breakthroughs in DNA sequences to systemic failures in the care system (Shapiro, 2006). By contrast, one of the stories that most extensively used emotion words won the Pulitzer for feature reporting in 2008 for the *Washington Post*. It drew on the explicit invocation of emotion to engage the audience in a story about a violin virtuoso's unsuccessful attempt at busking in the Washington metro – one which appeared to require more explicit invocation of emotion to engender a connection with the audience:

> The violin is an instrument that is said to be much like the human voice, and in this musician's masterly hands, it sobbed and laughed and sang – ecstatic, sorrowful, importuning, adoring, flirtatious, castigating, playful, romancing, merry, triumphal, sumptuous.

Whether elicited through the explicit use of emotion words, or by deploying presuppositions and narrative conventions to generate an emotional reaction in the audience, Pulitzer Prize-winning stories use emotion as a journalistic tool in an institutionalized and ritualized fashion. Further, an ability to do so successfully is explicitly recognized as a criterion in the selection of winning stories. Several citations thus mentioned the emotional resonance of the journalistic storytelling.[7] For example, the citation for the 2016 international reporting award, given to Alissa J. Rubin of the *New York Times*, justified it as based on "thoroughly reported and movingly written accounts giving voice to Afghan women who were forced to endure unspeakable cruelties." Similarly, the 2009 feature reporting award was granted "to Lane DeGregory of the *St. Petersburg Times* for her moving, richly detailed story of a neglected little girl, found in a roach-infested room, unable to talk or feed herself, who was adopted by a new family committed to her nurturing."

Journalism, emotional intelligence and emotional labor

It seems, then, that the successful display of the strategic ritual of emotionality is a valued form of cultural capital in the journalistic field. Nonetheless, journalism, as an institution, has generally given scant recognition of the emotional labor of its professionals, though it would appear to be central to their work (Barnes, 2016; Hopper and Huxford, 2015, 2017).

As K. Megan Hopper and John E. Huxford noted in their study of how journalism textbooks address issues around emotional labor in journalism and its consequences, while "there are directives for journalists to manipulate their own emotions in order to be successful in their trade, there is little if any clear instruction on how this may be done" (2017, p. 90). More broadly, the emotional labor of media workers has received only very limited attention in scholarship (but see Hesmondhalgh and Baker, 2008, 2011; Richards and Rees, 2011). David Hesmondhalgh and Sarah Baker have pointed to the emotional labor of workers in the television industry, on the basis of an ethnography of the young television professionals working on a UK television show, demonstrating that "additional pressures are borne by these workers because of the requirements to undertake emotional labor, involving the handling of strong emotions on the part of talent show contributors, and to maintain good working relations in short-term project work, requirements generated by the need to ensure future employment" (2008, p. 107). In Barry Richards and Gavin Rees' work on journalists' emotional labor in traumatic situations, they found "a broad and fundamental ambivalence in the professional discourse of journalism between objectivity and emotional engagement, and a striking inattention to questions about the emotional impact of journalists' work upon audiences" (2011, p. 851). Similarly, after interviewing 25 journalists involved in covering traumatic events, Stephen Jukes concluded that "what emerges is a complex picture of journalists grappling with competing tensions – on the one hand a virtually hard-wired notion of what it is to be a professional journalist and, on the other hand, a visceral, empathic often instinctive affective dimension of practice" (2017, p. 4).

Clearly, however, journalistic work requires not merely the professional skills of information-gathering and writing which form part of the formal training and socialization, but also a set of skills now popularly referred to as emotional intelligence (Goleman, 1996), as discussed in the Introduction. In his popular book on the subject, Daniel Goleman defined emotional intelligence in terms of "self-awareness and impulse control, persistence, zeal, and the ability to motivate oneself, empathy and social deftness" (1996, back matter) – all central to journalistic work. He described emotional intelligence as an affect control structure (see also Elias, 2000); or a regime for facilitating the management of feeling (see also Reddy, 2001). Our emotions, "when well exercised, have wisdom; they guide our thinking, our values, our survival. But they can easily go awry, and do so all too often. As Aristotle saw, the problem is not with emotionality, but with the appropriateness of emotion and its expression" (Goleman, 1996, p. xiv).

The central role of emotional intelligence in journalism has been explored by a small group of scholars focusing on how coverage of traumatic events, such as disasters and conflict, impacts the emotional state of journalists (e.g. Barnes, 2016; Dworznick, 2008; Fröhlich, 2005; Jukes, 2017; Richards and Rees, 2011). This research opens up an important set of questions and allows us to begin exploring how *all* forms of journalistic work, by their very nature, require emotional labor and hence emotional intelligence. Having traced the manifest evidence of emotion in award-winning journalistic texts, it is also important to ask broader questions about the unacknowledged emotional labor which goes on "behind the scenes" and "below the surface" in the process of *producing* these journalistic texts. Journalism – like all other public-facing professions – requires extensive emotional labor. It does so in at least two specific ways: first of all, in enacting the requirement for professional objectivity; and, secondly, in managing interactions with sources.

The maintenance of objectivity could be considered a specific emotional regime in its own right (Reddy, 2001, p. 129). Across the board, professionals experience tensions between "the unrealizability of empathetic, personal concern and rational universal detachment" (Olesen and Bone, 1998, p. 127). As Arlie Hochschild has pointed out, one way of resolving these tensions is through attempting to "correct" for our feelings: "The word *objective*, according to the *Random House Dictionary*, means 'free from personal feelings.' Yet ironically, we need feeling in order to reflect on the external or 'objective' world. Taking feelings into account as clues and then correcting for them may be our best shot at objectivity" (1983, p. 31).

In journalism – as in other professional realms – correcting for emotions is in itself a kind of emotional labor. Journalists do so through the practices of the strategic ritual of objectivity. Though ensuring the absence of emotion is not the *sole* function of objectivity in journalistic storytelling, it is central to the underlying epistemological premise of liberal democratic journalism. Further, mastery of the strategic ritual of emotionality requires a great degree of emotional sensitivity with respect to "emotion rules" (Reddy, 2001) governing the correct public display of emotions. These include implicit rules about *who* should discuss their emotions (sources, not journalists), *how* they do so (on the basis of their own personal experience), and *which emotions* are appropriate in particular circumstances (grief is an appropriate response to bereavement; and joy to news of a victory), but also rules about how to anticipate audience emotional reactions by telling the story in a way that mobilizes the public display of emotion to generate an "injunction to care" about important issues.

Further, the ways in which the emotion rules surrounding the journalistic ideal of objectivity in journalism express themselves are distinctive given the fact that journalistic narratives are both public and highly scripted and regulated speech acts. In this respect, the emotional labor that journalists engage in through their writing has consequences for more than their own well-being – it impacts more broadly on the regulation of emotion in public discourse.

If the complex interaction between objectivity and emotionality in journalistic storytelling represents the public face of journalists' emotional labor, there is also a second and less visible sense in which journalists manage feelings: in their interactions with sources, they are required to carefully manage their own emotions and those of their sources. This calls for a set of complex skills, distinctive from the forms of emotional labor characterizing other public-facing professions, such as the airline hostesses studied by Hochschild, who had to put their "private capacities for empathy and warmth [...] to corporate uses" (1983, p. 89). Persuading a reluctant government source to go on the record, speaking to parents who have lost a child in an accident, or to victims of theft, disaster or wrongful dismissal, or getting homeless people or the neglected elderly to tell their stories are all part and parcel of the emotional labor involved in journalism (see also Barnes, 2016). The emotional labor of journalism is all the more demanding because the practices of journalistic news-gathering depend on violating a key expectation of interpersonal communication: that of reciprocal disclosure (e.g. Berger and Calabrese, 1975). The transaction between source and journalist requires that the journalist gets detailed and, in some cases, highly personal and emotional information from the source, without providing any such information in exchange. Through interviews, journalists bring new information into being which would not otherwise exist – a key premise of contemporary journalism, and one which has profound consequences for notions of journalistic responsibility.

Journalism is certainly not alone among the professions in performing this kind of emotional labor – it is central to the job description of social workers, psychiatrists and police officers, among many others. In fact, emotional labor is essential and emotional intelligence is increasingly seen as an indispensable skill across fields of capitalist production (Illouz, 2007). Journalism *is*, however, unique in one important respect: the knowledge that journalists generate through their emotional labor is subsequently made public, generating further risks – emotional and otherwise – for sources and, as discussed above, involving further emotional labor on the part of journalists in telling the story objectively. Further, as Richards and Rees argue, journalists' self-understanding does not sit easily with requirements for emotional intelligence or what they refer to as "emotional literacy" (2011, p. 865). As a result, there has long been a culture of silence around issues of trauma in the newsroom. As Lyn Barnes (2016) observed, rarely "are journalists taught how to deal with the range of emotions they are likely to encounter. [...] Because of a traditionally stoic culture and the socialization process within newsrooms, novice journalists feel the pressure to remain objective and suppress any emotions." While other professions that are frequently required to deal with traumatic incidents – including the police, the fire brigade and ambulance crews – have long been trained and counselled in dealing with trauma, journalism is only slowly coming around to the insight that such intervention might be necessary (Jukes, 2017, p. 22).

In doing the emotional labor of working with sources, journalists are aided by the widespread social acceptance of the professional privilege of journalists. But the power differential between journalists and sources, and the artificial social situation that it sets up, could nonetheless be seen as problematic. Along those lines, codes of ethics frequently recognize – implicitly or explicitly – the need for reporters to perform emotional labor by being "sensitive" to their sources. For example, the code of the US trade association the Society of Professional Journalists describes the principle of minimizing harm as follows:

> Ethical journalists treat sources, subjects and colleagues as human beings deserving of respect. Journalists should:
> – Show compassion for those who may be affected adversely by news coverage. Use special sensitivity when dealing with children and inexperienced sources or subjects.
> – Be sensitive when seeking or using interviews or photographs of those affected by tragedy or grief.
> – Recognize that gathering and reporting information may

cause harm or discomfort. Pursuit of the news is not a license for arrogance. (Society of Professional Journalists, 2014)

This statement is typical in highlighting the forms of emotional labor required in journalism. Most fundamentally, it emphasizes the significance of compassion – understood as emotional sensitivity and respect – while warning against arrogance, in the form of a failure to acknowledge the potential negative emotional consequences of discomfort and harm which may result from the journalist–source interaction. Along those lines, recognition of emotional labor as an important requirement tends to be largely implicit, rather than explicit, in trade discussions (Hopper and Huxford, 2015, 2017). For example, a blog for aspiring journalists and freelancers offered "10 tips for interviewing sources for articles," out of which the first three were centrally focused on the emotional labor involved in the interview process:

> 1. Know your own emotional issues. Certain topics are taboo (money, politics, religion, sex), which can make you feel awkward when asking sources certain questions. But, most sources are usually experienced and comfortable about talking about the issues at hand – else you wouldn't be interviewing them! When you're interviewing a source for an article, make sure your own issues aren't preventing you from asking direct, relevant questions.
> 2. Open up a *little* to establish rapport. Making a connection with your source via a common piece of history (e.g. the same alma mater), similar like or dislike, or even a person you both know can be a valuable way to establish rapport. Don't spend a lot of time sharing about yourself, though.
> 3. Listen to Rumi, and let there be "spaces in your togetherness." This tip for interviewing sources means "stop talking." Even a five second pause can feel endless – but those pools of silence will eventually reveal gems of information. Give your experts time to think, to reflect, and to figure out how to say what they want. Get comfortable with silence; it's a great way to discovering fascinating tidbits. (Pawlik-Kienlen, no date)

These tips hint at the complex dance that journalists perform in managing the emotional relationship with sources, including the concealment of their own "issues" and "discomfort," the appropriate extent of self-disclosure and the strategic use of silence as a marker of the intimacy of "togetherness." An article in the *American Journalism Review* went further in exploring the intimacy of the relationship, reflecting on the complications that arise from romantic liaisons between reporters and their sources:

> [T]he reporter–source relationship is an intimate one to begin with. Reporters want to be warm and friendly. They need trust, respect, rapport. A source may be giving them information that could cost the source his job. It's no surprise that, at times, these interactions turn to affection, whether it's a romance or a friendship. (Robertson, 2002)

The article goes on to consider the difficult lines reporters must negotiate in maintaining what several interviewees refer to as a "friendly, but not too friendly" relationship with sources. Ultimately, it advocates the importance of disclosing the ways in which the emotional impact of reporter–source relationships might affect journalists' ability to enact core professional values:

> But ethicists say the larger issue of what prejudices or feelings reporters bring to any story should also be discussed. "I believe a reporter, as well as photojournalists and line editors ... copy editors, producers should have continuing, substantive conversations with their supervising editors about what feelings they bring to a story whenever those feelings may impact on accuracy or fairness or any of the other values that govern our work," says the Poynter Institute's Bob Steele. (Robertson, 2002)

Different types of journalistic work require different types of emotional labor – witness the difference between a political reporter negotiating with a spin doctor over the interpretation of a policy proposal, as opposed to the feature reporter talking to a drug addict about their life history, and the local reporter interviewing school children about their sports day. These differences in types of emotional labor are informed by gender and power, as well as cultural capital in the journalistic field (e.g. Hochschild, 1983). However, as in other professions, the amount and nature of emotional labor in journalism do not necessarily map neatly onto power hierarchies: for example, the Pulitzer Prize-winning articles discussed here may well require considerably more investment of emotional labor (as well as other kinds of labor) than everyday routine news coverage. The much-celebrated and high-prestige genre of investigative journalism might require the most complex forms of emotional labor, as reporters wrangle reactions and the attainment of sensitive information from sources, and negotiate access and forms of attribution, as well as carefully calibrate the generation of moral outrage and, through that, solidarity with the sufferers of wrongdoing (e.g. Ettema and Glasser, 1998).

The fact that these complex forms of emotional labor are predicated upon organizational practices and vary across media institutions, genres and professional specializations reveals that journalism, just like other professions, relies on the commodification of private emotion in functionally differentiated ways (Hochschild, 1983). However, the profession's attachment to the ideal of objectivity and associated values of impartiality and independence has rendered the emotional labor of journalism largely invisible, and hence far more difficult to recognize and come to terms with (Barnes, 2016; Jukes, 2017). This chapter has sought to bring at least some of the manifestations of emotional labor to the surface, to offer a starting point for a discussion of the place of emotion in the production of the journalistic texts which shape our public discourse.

Conclusion

This chapter has revealed that in the case of award-winning journalism, emotion is everywhere: Pulitzer Prize-winning stories rely heavily on emotional storytelling, deploying what has been referred to as the strategic ritual of emotionality. The strategic ritual of emotionality is constituted by tacit rules of practice – ones that are rarely discussed or made explicit. But more than that, it emotion has been rendered invisible through the overriding emphasis on objectivity in discourses about the profession. Tom Rosenstiel and Bill Kovach (2005), in outlining journalistic "emotion display rules" in the context of disaster coverage, argue that "emotion ought to come at those moments when any other reaction would seem forced or out of place." The evidence presented here indicates that in fact emotional storytelling is a driving force behind award-winning journalism, with the aim of drawing the audience's attention to complex topics of social and political import and ultimately bringing about change. At the same time, long-standing practices of objectivity create particular parameters for the expression of emotion. Emotional expression is carefully policed, but extensive, systematic and routinized. Emotional labor is outsourced in such a way that journalists do not express their own emotions, but rather serve as ventriloquists for the feelings of their sources. Through this trick, journalistic storytelling elicits compassion for the subjects of their stories, or outrage directed at those responsible for injustice (see also Martin, 2017). This ultimately means that emotional storytelling enables journalists to act as watchdogs over the powerful.

But this emotional watchdog role comes at a cost: it entails significant emotional labor on the part of journalists. The chapter has shown that the strategic ritual of emotionality requires emotional intelligence which involves an understanding of how to craft stories that use emotional expression appropriately yet also consistently elicit an emotional reaction in the audience. Further, extensive "behind-the-scenes" emotional labor (Hochschild, 1983) is required to gain the rich – and emotionally resonant – stuff of which award-winning stories are made. As emerging scholarship in the area has demonstrated, journalistic work – particularly in covering traumatic or dangerous events – takes an emotional toll on journalists which has, up to now, gone largely unrecognized (e.g. Barnes, 2016; Jukes, 2017).

This chapter has indicated that emotional storytelling is central to making visible key social and political issues because it elicits compassion in audiences. The next chapter looks more closely at the question of why this is so – and what the consequences are of the emphasis on personalized storytelling. Specifically, the chapter develops the argument that the telling of personal and emotional stories in the public sphere is seen as a guarantor of authenticity, and therefore as a means of cultivating compassion.

CHAPTER THREE

Authenticity, Compassion and Personalized Storytelling

We've now established that emotion is a central ingredient in award-winning journalistic stories, enabling readers to make sense of the vast social, political and economic issues that are usually at the heart of them. Chapter 2 showed that the best of journalism uses personalized storytelling to anchor complex and abstract events of social and political importance in the lived experience of people on the ground. This, in turn, suggests that such storytelling may facilitate the audience's emotional engagement and understanding. The present chapter looks more closely at the reasons why this is the case. It does this by drawing on a series of examples, ranging from letters to the editor and vox pops, to user-generated content, social media hashtag campaigns and new forms of online hybrid storytelling represented by Humans of New York.

The chapter suggests that sharing emotions through the telling of personal stories in public is seen as a guarantor of authenticity, and, relatedly, as a means of cultivating compassion. The performative construction of mediated authenticity and of compassion are closely related and inseparable phenomena, and together generate a complex discursive dynamic: because of the powerful emotional resonance of stories that are constructed as authentic and capable of generating bonds based on compassion, such stories are widely valued by both news professionals and audiences, and strategically used by activists and non-governmental organizations. They have the capacity to foster new forms of community based on an understanding of concrete, lived experience. And these communities, in turn, have the potential to effect social change (Berlant, 2011).

The chapter investigates the cultivation of mediated authenticity and compassion by looking at a broad variety of instances where personalized storytelling is brought into the public sphere. Rather than being the preserve of award-winning journalism, the chapter proposes, such storytelling is, in fact, part and parcel of all the most important conversations that constitute mediated politics. The chapter demonstrates that to understand the experiences of others and make large and often abstract political happenings come alive, it is necessary to tell their stories, but that such storytelling can take many different forms.

Although personalized storytelling is frequently mobilized by journalists seeking to reach and engage mainstream media audiences, it also takes place via the increasingly variegated forums through which ordinary people are given voice, including social media, online platforms and user-generated content. Successive waves of technological change have had profound consequences in terms of broadening access as well as diversifying forms, platforms and genres through which such storytelling has taken shape, with these changes also spilling over into the mainstream media (see also Wahl-Jorgensen, 2014). However, despite claims that the recent proliferation of opportunities for individuals to share their stories in their own voice represents a "demotic turn" (Coleman and Ross, 2010; Turner, 2010) and a rise of the "personal voice" (Coward, 2013), the chapter will show that including the voices of "ordinary people" has long been a priority of news organizations.

The chapter will chart some of the consequences of these changes, while distinguishing between different forms of personalized storytelling and the ways in which they might facilitate compassion and the building of community.

Authenticity in personalized storytelling

Journalists, audiences and scholars all agree that personalized storytelling, in whichever form it may take, serves as a guarantor of authenticity. Authenticity is here understood as a complex of qualities that are essential to the cultivation of trust in media content, and fundamentally tied to the expression of emotion in a believable manner. As Gunn Enli put it, the "paradox of mediated authenticity is that although we base most of our knowledge about our society and the world in which we live on mediated representations of reality, we remain well aware that the media are constructed, manipulated, and even faked" (2015, p. 1). Because of this paradox, media organizations and platforms work hard to convince us of the authenticity of their content through a variety of means, ranging from lighting and post-production editing to the scripting of supposedly spontaneous interactions. Here, I'm particularly interested in tracing the role of authenticity in personalized stories across platforms and genres.

In one of the most influential definitions of mediated authenticity, Martin Montgomery suggested that there are three main ways in which authenticity could be understood in broadcast talk contexts, highlighting the complex of the cluster of meanings attached to the concept:

> First there is talk that is deemed authentic because it does not sound contributed, simulated, or performed but rather sounds natural, "fresh", spontaneous. Second, there is talk that is deemed authentic because it seems truly to capture or present the experience of the speaker. Third, there is authentic talk that seems truly to project the core self of the speaker – talk that is true to the self of the speaker in an existential fashion. (Montgomery, 2001, pp. 403–4)

These understandings show the paradoxical interaction between performativity and truthfulness-as-authenticity. Central to the performance of authenticity is the revelation of the self through emotional self-disclosure. For Theo van

Leeuwen (2001), media content is authentic when it is true to the essence of a phenomenon or, for an individual, a deeply felt sentiment. Indeed, questions of emotion are never far from the surface in discussions of authenticity. It has been a prominent theme in scholarly discussions of Reality TV, which since the 2000s has played an increasingly dominant role in our television schedules through its compelling manufacturing of authenticity (Enli, 2015; Hill, 2005). John Corner, in an influential piece about *Big Brother*, written shortly after its first series aired in the United Kingdom, suggested that the emergence of Reality TV represented a shift in the affective order underpinning documentary programming:

> Within this new affective order, this emerging "structure of feeling," a busy dialectic of attraction and dislike provides the mainspring of the entertainment. The very volatility of the feelings here allows for a viewing combination in which what are, for nonfictional formats, quite unparalleled modes of "getting close" become mixed with a remarkably cold, objectifying distance. (2002, p. 266)

For Enli, the performance of ordinariness is vital for a successful Reality TV participant – and to come across as ordinary requires careful emotional expression and management: "The authentic participant is [...] a person who adjusts his or her spontaneity and emotionalism to be compatible with the media format criteria, and is able to, when required by the public surroundings, control feeling" (Enli, 2015, p. 89).

The importance of the management of emotion for the authentic performance is not unique to Reality TV. While it might be one area where discussions of authenticity and its relationship to emotion have been foregrounded, Reality TV both contributes to and is reflective of a broader shift in the terms of emotional expression in mediated contexts. In what observers see as an increasingly emotionalized society, individuals are understood as more authentic if they are in touch with their feelings and able to talk about them openly. The ways in which such authenticity is discursively produced, however, vary according to the respective speakers and their intended publics, reflecting the complexities of a dynamic media ecology. In the following sections, the chapter considers, first of all, the ways in which authenticity, performed through emotional expression, is central to the appeal of political leaders because it establishes them as "ordinary." The chapter then turns to questions around how, by contrast, "ordinary people" are constructed as providing authentic emotive content to supplement the information-centered discourse of conventional news reporting. In the case of political leaders and "ordinary people" alike, authenticity through emotionality is a guarantor of trustworthiness.

Emotional ordinary as authenticity in political life

The importance of the performance of authenticity is well illustrated by debates over the believability of politicians (Coleman and Firmstone, 2017; Enli, 2015; Stanyer, 2013). As discussed in the Introduction and Chapter 1, this development can be seen as part of a broader trend of the "informalization" of politics (Manning et al., 2017; Wouters, 2007), whereby political leaders are increasingly compelled to communicate informally with voters to cultivate affective bonds. With a breakdown in institutional trust, it has become all the more important for politicians to come across as "real" and believable (Enli, 2015, p. 128). The quest for informality and authenticity generates further incentives for emotional talk and personal disclosure. As Stephen Coleman and Julie Firmstone (2017) have demonstrated through their study of political performance in the 2014 European Parliament elections, this requires a complex set of discursive maneuvers: political leaders must establish themselves as serious and authoritative personae while also coming across as "one of the people." This leads to hybrid performances which allow them to balance authority and authenticity.

However, the efforts of political leaders to construct an authentic persona are not a new phenomenon, and have long been a feature of US presidential rhetoric (e.g. Lim, 2002; Umbach and Humphrey, 2016). Franklin D. Roosevelt was widely recognized for his mastery of authenticity through his mediated performance of intimacy. His fireside chats "seemed authentic because he engaged emotionally and acted as if he was talking to his friends" – even if they were actually recorded in a White House office (Enli, 2015, p. 30). Although it has always been an ingredient for political success, winning the battle for hearts and minds increasingly means winning the battle for authenticity. Donald Trump has been described as generating a "cult of authenticity" (Hill, 2017) through his forthrightness and his use of spontaneous, unpolished language. Trump's spontaneity is also seen as an indicator of emotional engagement with his voters. For *Forbes* magazine's John Baldoni (2016), "Trump is skilled at connecting with an audience because he can read their mood and respond accordingly." When Arlie Hochschild (2016) referred to Trump as an "emotions candidate," she referred to his ability to authentically perform the emotions of his audiences (see Chapter 5), which was seen as essential to his electoral success.

Similarly, authenticity was a key battleground in the UK General Election in May 2017 (Wahl-Jorgensen, 2017a). The Labour leader, Jeremy Corbyn, had endured long-standing media vilification and delegitimization for his left-wing views (e.g. Cammaerts et al., 2016). However, once the campaign was underway, Corbyn turned around public perceptions, coming out ahead in the battle for authenticity. Indeed, Corbyn's authenticity was frequently contrasted to the perception of Prime Minister Theresa May as a cold and heartless control freak. Writing in the *Times* on June 3, Janice Turner (2017) observed, tongue-in-cheek: "'He's so authentic,' people cry, as he presents homemade jam to *The One Show* while condemning the low-wage economy, calmly, without artifice or spin. 'Bless! He seems so real!' And so he does, compared with Theresa May, a broken pull-string doll who can't even utter her five preprogrammed phrases." Marina Hyde (2017), writing in the *Guardian*, argued that May's "primary means of showing solidarity with workers is to deliver answers so robotic that they suggest even her own job has already been automated." Hyde's observation highlights how understandings of authenticity are tied to *emotional qualities* – an "authentic" politician is someone who is able to feel *compassion* for voters, to be able to deliver the policy changes they need (Umbach and Humphrey, 2016). The contrast between Corbyn's perceived emotional empathy and May's cold and remote performance was a common theme throughout the election campaign. It gained momentum after May's performance on a BBC *Question Time* election special. Here, she dismissed the concerns of a National Health Service nurse who had not received a pay rise since 2009, stating, "There isn't a magic money tree that we can shake that suddenly provides for everything that people want" (Sharman, 2017). As Brian May (2017) wrote in the *Mirror*, now "that the blinkers are off, we see Theresa May in her full glory – a ruthless insatiably ambitious woman with not a shred of compassion for man or beast." Miranda Sawyer (2017) claimed in the *Observer* that Corbyn's "appeal is not in his grasp of numbers but his understanding of emotion," reifying the distinction between reason and emotion to explain the Labour leader's success.

For political leaders, the performance of an emotional register which marks them as "ordinary," "normal" and "human" serves to cement their authenticity (Wood et al., 2016). Though articulated in distinctive ways, the emphasis on the mediated construction of authenticity is not unique to political leaders, but is central to the cultivation of trust in media content across genres, and has been for some time. In particular, journalists and audiences privilege "personalized storytelling" on the part of regular people caught up in unfolding stories as a way of manufacturing such authenticity.

Emotion, authenticity and personalized storytelling

In my research on how newspaper editors deal with letters to the editor, carried out in the mid-1990s, the valorization of personalized storytelling as a marker of authenticity emerged as a prominent theme (e.g. Wahl-Jorgensen, 2001). At the time, letters to the editor were the main way in which ordinary people were given a voice in public debate. And as I interviewed editors of newspapers of all types and sizes, their preference for personalized storytelling – ideally with a strong emotional component – became apparent. For example, one editor of a small weekly paper in an affluent community struggling to come to terms with issues of urban development and growth explained this preference for letters in the form of such personalized stories from local residents by contrasting them with lobbying groups and public relations practitioners using "political rhetoric":

> The resident tends to speak plainly and from the heart, more than some of the political rhetoric of some of these organizations. You see the same kind of rhetoric from some of these groups. It might be very heartfelt, but a lot of times you'll see things like 'and we appreciate all the many volunteers that can make this organization the organization that it is [...]. We've made many strides and much progress in achieving our goals.' And then they don't say what those goals are, or specifically how they've made strides. It's almost like they're out to attract more membership than do good deeds. [...] Individuals have something more specific to say, and they're usually more honest about saying it. [...] Here's Olinger's [anti-development letter writer] letter in the paper where he says that "from where I stand, there's no rural anymore", whereas a group like the Civic Association is going to be lambasting town government for its time-consuming process of granting applications to deserving home-owners who deserve to build their dream-home in the hills. [...] So you're not getting the truth and the whole truth out of them

> as an organization. You are getting the truth from this individual, in this letter, 'cause this is how he's feeling, and that's why he's written this letter. He's not mincing words, he's not shielding his true intentions in a bunch of mumbojumbo. [...] Olinger [...] how are you going to challenge him? Are you going to say, "I don't agree that there's no rural anymore"? You can't challenge his opinion.

Like many other editors, this one celebrates the "heartfelt" discourse of the regular citizen who openly talks about their feelings, juxtaposing it with the stale, rehearsed "boilerplate" rhetoric of the activist groups, a discourse that is "kind of manufactured, coming out of an assembly line," or "just like an ad," as other editors put it. This position emphasizes the authenticity of the "ordinary citizens" and their personalized storytelling. It is viewed as compelling because of its emotional integrity, associated with a cluster of features linked to authenticity (e.g. Enli, 2015), including sincerity, truth and concreteness.

The celebration of the perceived authenticity – and the closely related emotionally engaging nature of ordinary people's contribution – discussed in the case of letters to the editor also carries over into journalists' and audiences' views of user-generated content, as demonstrated by our research at the BBC, carried out through interviews, focus groups and ethnographic observation in 2007 and 2008 (see Wahl-Jorgensen et al., 2010). We found that both audience members and journalists valued user-generated content in the form of amateur footage on the basis of its perceived authenticity and emotional truth. For example, one regional BBC producer, in reflecting on his station's coverage of the UK summer floods in 2006, highlighted the search for emotional user-generated content as an indispensable resource for complementing facts-based conventional reporting:

> I think it is the insight that you get, the emotion you get, that is the great value and strength of user-generated content. Anywhere where you have a powerful story that has a human

angle to it, UGC [i.e. user-generated content] can help it. And it works especially well when you choose it as a complement to the traditional overview story that we would generally do anyway. [...] During the floods what we really wanted from UGC was the emotion, I guess. We wanted to be able to convey the experience of having a life turned upside down in a day because of this cataclysmic event. What was that like? And that's not something that needs any sort of balance, as it were. [...] The flooding doesn't matter because X number of buildings were damaged, because X millions of pounds will have to be spent. That's all just numbers. It matters because people's lives are changed by it, and we were able to portray that more successfully than we usually would do with user-generated content.

For this producer, the factual information of a "traditional overview story" was made to matter through the emotional resonance of user-generated content. Focus group members were more explicit in juxtaposing such user-generated content with the more objective and distanced, and hence less engaging, professional discourse of journalists. One focus group discussed the empathy invited in viewers by news packages which include footage of extraordinary events filmed by ordinary people – in this case a woman filming her living room as the floodwaters were pouring through it. They contrasted the poignancy of this footage with the cold detachment they imagined a professional journalist would bring to the same story:

> *June*: Well I think that a professional person couldn't feel like that woman, because it's her home, so she's giving a more accurate [...] she's bringing it home to you more than if it was a professional person in her house.
> *Juliet*: That's really important actually, I never thought of it like that. The person behind the camera is feeling all of those things, and you are seeing it literally through her eyes [...] what's important to them, like.
> *Christopher*: It's not as emotive by any stretch of the imagination if it's professional footage.

These audience members valued user-generated content over ostensibly "objective" news stories produced by professionals because it provided "emotive" information about what the person behind the camera was "feeling." This position represents a direct challenge to the journalistic paradigm of objectivity, and appears to draw on an epistemological vocabulary which equates truth with authenticity, emotional integrity and immediacy. Such a vocabulary both mirrors and draws on assessments of Reality TV genres (e.g. Hill, 2005). This view, which came up in many of our focus groups, suggests that conventional journalistic ways of knowing, based on ideals of objective reporting, may in fact be seen by audiences as less capable of encapsulating the "truth" than more emotive forms of storytelling. In this sense, the emotional authenticity performed through user-generated content served as a way of bolstering trust in media content.

In the context of social media, authenticity has taken on a new significance through their facilitation of personalized storytelling in public. For example, many trending Twitter hashtags enable exactly this sharing of personal experience relating to unfolding political debates. As Zizi Papacharissi noted, in her study of the intersection of the personal and political on Twitter:

> Autobiographical statements include the presentation of private thoughts to a public setting as a way of creating a bond of intimacy with an imagined audience and simultaneously affirming the authenticity of the performance. Thus, audiences validate the performance as authentic because the person has shared a truly private thought, no matter how uncomfortable and potentially compromising this disclosure may be. At the same time, the individual has employed performativity to stage a narrative that conveys authenticity, creates intimacy, and presents a political statement. (2015, p. 109)

When the personal becomes political through such performed authenticity, we create the grounds for compassion.

These, I will argue, are crucial elements in understanding the importance of emotion in mediated politics. The following section further develops the relationship between personalized storytelling and compassion by looking at how this relationship has been articulated differently in cases ranging from letters to the editor to Humans of New York Refugee Stories and feminist hashtag activism. The section shows that cultivation of compassion is oriented towards the creation of particular communities, and that these communities vary according to communicative contexts, and therefore shape the horizons for political action.

Compassion and personalized storytelling

Tales of personal experience have the capacity to generate compassion because they dramatize the large and small events that unfold around us by linking them to tales of emotions that others can understand, whether they be ones of pain, fear, happiness or love. As Hannah Arendt compellingly argued, the power of personalized storytelling lies in its ability to make connections between individual experiences and issues of the common good, to penetrate "the meaning of what otherwise would remain an unbearable sequence of sheer happenings" (1968, p. 104). Such stories generate a bridge between private and public realms because they

> cut through abstractions and other obscurities and focus on the everyday meaning of life and our dealings with it. Stories enable us to think creatively and imaginatively about our experiences and the experiences of others; they empower us to interpret and thereby comprehend the endless details of life. [...] [Stories have a] basic role in transforming individual and essentially private experience into a shared and therefore public reality. (Glasser, 1991, pp. 235–6)

Viewed through this lens, it becomes clear that the distinctive form of personalized storytelling – using a language that dramatizes concrete, emotionally inflected experiences, rather than drawing on abstract ideas – facilitates the generation of compassion. This is because it allows us to enlarge our worldviews, looking beyond our own narrow self-interest and towards the experience of others, even if they may be very different from us. As Daryl Koehn has argued, the mobilization of what she describes as "empathy" can transform our worldviews and moral standpoints:

> By attempting to understand what an action, opportunity, or benefit means to this other party on her own terms, we open ourselves to substantial shifts in the way in which we have thus far thought about these matters. Empathy allows someone else's experience and perspective to become a part of our moral baseline and therefore can function to help us overcome prejudices and misconceptions. (Koehn, 1998, p. 57)

This goes against the liberal tradition's emphasis on the dispassionate and disembodied ideal of public debate, suggesting that, instead, we can only appreciate the circumstances of the *concrete* and *embodied* other. Feminist scholars have noted an "epistemological blindness" in this search for the generalized other (Benhabib, 1992, p. 164). They argue that the understanding of rationality that underpins much political philosophy "cannot capture the moral features of particular interpersonal relationships in concrete situations" (Rehg, 1994, p. 3). To imagine the situations of others we must be able to put ourselves in their shoes without being overtaken by our own interest in the issue.

Indeed, the importance attached to bringing the personal into the realm of politics is a major contribution of the feminist movement, embodied in the widely circulated catchphrase "the personal is political" (Hanisch, 2000). This phrase originated out of the work of consciousness-raising groups in which women came together to discuss their experiences of patriarchy. As Carol Hanisch reflected, one "of the first things we discover in these groups is that personal problems are political problems. There are no personal solutions at this time. There is only collective action for a collective solution" (2000, p. 114). For feminists, then, the sharing of personal stories revealed larger shared experiences which, in turn, made possible collective political action – a theme explored in more detail in the next chapter.

The relationship between personalized storytelling, politics and compassion has been widely discussed in scholarly debates over the creation of cosmopolitan sensibilities through coverage of distant suffering (e.g. Beck, 2006; Boltanski, 1999; Chouliaraki, 2006, 2015, Kyriakidou, 2008, 2009; Ong, 2009). Although this literature tends to focus on how the media report global crises and disasters (Pantti et al., 2012), the arguments about the cultivation of a moral imagination (Tester, 2001) based on personalized storytelling apply more broadly. They provide useful resources for thinking through the role of such mediated storytelling around the small and everyday events that shape our experience, as well as momentous and disastrous ones that usually characterize reports of distant suffering.

The basic conviction behind this body of work is that media representations affect our engagement with the distant sufferer. Thus, there is a crucial link between representation and emotion/action or, conversely, indifference/non-action. Storytelling constitutes our prime collective resource for examining and understanding emotions that may otherwise arise out of fundamentally "unknowable" and "unshareable" experience (see Bleiker and Hutchison, 2008).

But not all mediated representations of suffering are created equal. Along those lines, Lilie Chouliaraki (2006) has pointed to the need to carefully distinguish between different ways of approaching suffering, and the emotional responses they solicit. To this end, she proposed a typology of three different forms of news of suffering, what she calls "adventure," "emergency" and "ecstatic" news. Adventure news is "news of suffering without pity," characterized by brief, factual reports represented by a "void of agency" because of the absence of any human actors from the story. As a result, "there is no possibility of human contact between the other and the spectator." By contrast, emergency news is "news of suffering with pity," which represents victims as individuals who can be helped by the action of distant others. Finally, ecstatic news, exemplified by coverage after the September 11 attacks, brings the sufferers as close to the spectators as possible, opening up a space for identification (Chouliaraki, 2006, pp. 10–11). For Chouliaraki, such ecstatic news has the capacity to open up spaces for identification through the cultivation of compassion, constructing "the sufferers as *sovereign agents* on their own suffering and in a relationship of *reflexive identification* between these sufferers and the spectators" (2006, p. 157). Ecstatic news tends to be reserved for the suffering of people who are "like us" – proximate others in geographical or cultural terms – while excluding the suffering of distant others (Chouliaraki, 2006, p. 181). Nonetheless, a truly cosmopolitan disposition can only be created if such reflexive identification is extended beyond proximate contexts. The cultivation of the "cosmopolitan disposition seems to depend [...] on contextualizing the intensely personal in the realm of the public and the political" (Chouliaraki, 2006, p. 215; see also Pantti et al., 2012).

Letters to the editor and the creation of a local community
These scholarly debates show us that personalized storytelling can generate compassion because it relates the concrete embodied experience of others, facilitating identification by placing us in their shoes. In doing so, it relies on the interjection of the personal and emotional into the public and political. In my research on letters to the editor, this theme came up repeatedly. For instance, one editor discussed her favorite debate, emerging in response to the closing of a popular bookstore, which could no longer operate profitably because of a rent increase:

> Everybody thought it was going to close, so they all wrote letters in and talked about how they remembered it. A high

school girl wrote about how she went there to study and drink coffee, and later to buy materials for her research projects. One guy wrote about how he would bike past the bookstore on his way home every day, and he would always stop, take a look, and never leave without buying a book. He just couldn't. People from nearby businesses wrote in and talked about how it would be a big loss to the community if the bookstore closed. So this was more personal because it was really affecting them. It was very moving to see people being so upset about this.

The editor thought the debate had brought attention to the issue and actually saved the bookstore: in the end, its employees took over the lease, inspired in part by community support. Writing letters was a way for members of the community to tangibly demonstrate the impact of the closing, to imbue what was to some an anonymous business with a deeper meaning. It thereby linked together the newspaper readers in this community in a bond based on shared emotions and experiences, creating the conditions for compassion through reflexive identification. In this instance, the community brought into being through personalized storytelling was a local one, constituted by newspaper readers. And the stories of individual attachments to the bookstore, through the cultivation of compassion, brought about tangible social and political change by securing the future of the store.

The mobilization of compassion through personalized storytelling is no longer solely in the hands of mainstream media organizations. The digital age and the rise of social media have opened up a wide variety of opportunities for bottom-up and hybrid forms of storytelling that have contributed to democratizing the cultivation of compassion (see Wahl-Jorgensen, 2014). Here, I will look at two examples of such forms of storytelling, each of which seeks to bring particular communities into being through the cultivation of compassion. I will begin by discussing the case of Humans of New York Refugee Stories, which sought to foster a cosmopolitan community based on compassion for the suffering of migrants. I will then contrast this form of mediated cultivation of compassion with feminist hashtag activism, which represents an attempt at mobilizing compassion within hybrid counterpublics.

Humans of New York Refugee Stories and the creation of a global cosmopolitan community

In the fall of 2015, at the height of attention to the global migrant crisis, New York photographer Brandon Stanton, best known for his Humans of New York project, documented the human stories behind the crisis.

Through Humans of New York, Stanton has catalogued the lives of ordinary New Yorkers, using photographs and interviews. He has gained popularity across an array of social media platforms, including Facebook (15.5m likes), Instagram (3.9m followers) and Twitter (356,000 followers), and his book documenting the project became a *New York Times* best-seller. On September 29, 2015, he announced that he would be sharing stories from refugees making their way across Europe:

> These migrants are part of one of the largest population movements in modern history. But their stories are composed of unique and singular tragedies. In the midst of the current "migrant crisis", there are millions of different reasons for leaving home. And there are millions of different hardships that refugees face as they search for a new home.

It is clear from Stanton's statement that the project wears its moral ambition on its sleeve: it aims to dig beneath the numbers, revealing the human stories that open up the door for audiences to empathize with the suffering of distant others. The cultivation of compassion takes place through the sharing of the lived experience of migrants, who are constructed as embodying universal emotions, in response to life-and-death moments which are, in turn, recognizable as universally terrifying and moving.

The Refugee Stories project was fostered in partnership with the UN Refugee Agency, the UNHCR, and therefore can be seen as part of a larger trend of humanitarian collaborations. Such collaborations have been developed between NGOs and news organizations, but have also involved new types of actors, like Humans of New York, to enlarge the global community which cares about the plight of distant sufferers through storytelling and thereby encouraging assistance and donations (Cooper, 2015). This agenda has unfolded in tension with conventional journalistic ideals of objectivity and impartiality. Nonetheless, like other successful humanitarian collaborations, it has used time-honored journalistic techniques associated with human interest stories, circulated to audiences through the facilitation of digital platforms and social media.

One typical Refugee Stories post, featuring a photograph of a crying woman, told the story of how she lost her husband at sea after their boat capsized: "The waves were high. I could hear him calling me but he got further and further away. Eventually a boat found me." Another post, featuring a photograph of a father and his daughter, recounted the father's lament:

> I wish I could have done more for her. Her life has been nothing but struggle. She hasn't known many happy moments. She never had a chance to taste childhood. When we were getting on the plastic boat, I heard her say something that broke my heart. She saw her mother being crushed by the crowd, and she screamed: "Please don't kill my mother! Kill me instead!"

In taking this approach, the Refugee Stories project aspires to the making of ecstatic news by turning the sufferers into sovereign agents in relation to their own suffering and generating identification through telling their stories (Chouliaraki, 2006, p. 157). This example highlights the power of emerging forms to bring compassionate communities into existence by telling stories that ground audiences in the lived experience of actual human beings. Refugee Stories show the audience that the personal and private stories of refugees represent a shared political reality, which we ignore at our peril.

Feminist hashtag activism and the creation of hybrid counterpublics

The creation of a shared political reality – and with it, the possibility of change – through personalized storytelling has been a key theme of research on feminist hashtag activism. This emerging research agenda examines, among other things, how such activism draws on personal accounts to dramatize a range of feminist issues, including domestic violence, sexism, racism and the safety of women in public places (e.g. Horeck, 2014; Khoja-Moolji, 2015; Loken, 2014; Rentschler, 2015; Stache, 2015; Thrift, 2014; Williams, 2015). Rosemary Clark (2016), who has been at the forefront of research in the area, suggested that the narrative logic of feminist hashtags is dependent on their ability to produce and connect individual stories. As such, it refashions the "personal is political" logic underpinning the consciousness-raising strategies of Second Wave feminism discussed above through a reliance on the affordances of social media. Clark is one of several scholars to study feminist attempts at resisting victim-blaming strategies through hashtag activism (e.g. Rentschler, 2015). One such prominent hashtag, #WhyIStayed, explored the motivations for victims of domestic violence to remain in the abusive relationship. As Clark observed:

> [T]he hashtag acted as an easily personalized storytelling prompt, which provided a particular narrative focus for survivors to frame their diverse experiences in a compelling manner in 140 characters or less. [...] Through the ritualistic repetition of a Twitter hashtag, the #WhyIStayed movement united a huge variety of abuse stories under a single counter-frame. (2016, p. 796)

Some of the most retweeted personal accounts shared under the hashtag included the following:

@galvanized: Because he managed the cash. #WhyIStayed. (September 8, 2014, 12:52 pm)

@SCrystal: Because he separated me from all my friends and family and I had nowhere to turn. #WhyIStayed. (September 8, 2014, 5:00 pm)

@megamay: Because I grew up in an abusive family, why would I expect the person I was marrying not to #WhyIStayed. (September 11, 2014, 6:50pm). (Cited in Clark, 2016, p. 796; user handles modified in original)

The hashtag brought the issue of domestic violence into public debate through shared experiences of abuse – but ones refracted through the lens of a multitude of individual experiences. In doing so, it offered new languages for understanding gendered violence (see also Thrift, 2014). This paved the way for the #MeToo hashtag, which in 2017 and 2018 has called attention to sexual harassment and assault experienced by women and men around the world, creating a "shared, global, voice to begin talking about the sexism that still underpins our society" (van Hensbergen, 2017). Although the phrase "Me Too" was first used in 2006 by activist Tarana Burke, it was revitalized and popularized by actress Alyssa Milano. On October 15, 2017, Milano sent a tweet suggesting that if "you've been sexually harassed or assaulted write 'me too' as a reply to this tweet." By the following morning, the tweet had received 55,000 replies and was trending on Twitter (Sayej, 2017). The campaign gained further momentum as celebrities joined men and women from all walks of life to call attention to the systemic problems of sexual violence. Allegations arising out of the movement ended the careers of Hollywood stars and high-profile entertainment industry figures including Harvey Weinstein, Kevin Spacey, Bill O'Reilly and Louis CK, as well as prominent politicians, academics and journalists. The campaign succeeded in making a radical intervention in public debate, and the "silence breakers" – those taking great risks to speak out in public about sexual assault – became

Time Person of the Year for 2017 (Zacharaek et al., 2017). As Kaitlynn Mendes and her colleagues (2018) have observed, the history of the #MeToo hashtag demonstrates both increased public willingness to engage with and take seriously claims of sexual harassment, and the building of networks of solidarity on the basis of sharing of individual stories. In so doing, the use of such hashtags makes survivors feel heard and creates the possibility for social change.

The strategy of drawing on personalized stories to reframe public debate through Twitter hashtags is not unique to English-speaking communities and has gained sustained currency around the world since the earliest years of the social media platform. In Sweden, the hashtag #prataomdet was used in 2010 to call attention to experiences of borderline sexual assault, following on from the rape allegations made against WikiLeaks founder Julian Assange. Johanna Koljonen (2010), who started the hashtag, explained her motivation by arguing that "if we can't tell the story, we commit violence against ourselves." Similar hashtags circulated in English, French, German and Russian. Following the 2012 Delhi gang rape case, when a young woman, Jyoti Singh, was beaten, gang raped and tortured in a private bus and subsequently died from her injuries, there has been significant mobilization against sexual violence. For example, the NGO Breakthrough – a global human rights organization – created the hashtag #BoardtheBus to provide a virtual community in which women could share their experiences on buses (Eagle, 2015).

If letters to the editor may foster the creation of *local* communities of compassion, while Refugee Stories seek out a *global cosmopolitanism*, feminist hashtag activism seeks out a different type of community, akin to a *hybrid counterpublic* (see also Sills et al., 2016; Subramani, 2013). Hashtags do not rely solely on personalized narratives. Rather, the hashtag activism facilitated by Twitter represents what might be at various times playful and humorous, cacophonous, collaborative and antagonistic "affective news streams" (Papacharissi,

2015). Given the bottom-up and individualized nature of contributions, however, and the fact that the affordances of Twitter tend to support identity formation and community creation among like-minded individuals (Papacharissi, 2015, p. 67), the compassion that is cultivated by hashtag activism is often tied to addressing social inequality and empowering marginalized groups. This, in turn, suggests the emergence of distinctive and culturally specific forms of storytelling and language characteristic of "counterpublics," or "parallel discursive arenas where members of subordinated social groups invent and circulate counterdiscourses to formulate oppositional interpretations of their identities, interests, and needs" (Fraser, 1992, p. 123). As Michael Warner has specified, such counterpublics incorporate both personal and impersonal address and thereby often "challenge modernity's social hierarchy of faculties" (2002, p. 85). However, the counterpublics brought into being by hashtag activism do not just orient themselves towards the organization of oppositional communities, but also aim for broader forms of social and political change beyond these communities. As such, they can be seen as *hybrid counterpublics* with multiple audiences and aims, reflecting the dynamic and sometimes contradictory complexities of "affective news streams." The creation of compassion in such hybrid counterpublics is contingent and fraught, as hashtags are often hijacked by opponents who seek to subvert, undermine or ridicule their political projects (e.g. Hagdu et al., 2013), as when the prominent #BlackLivesMatter hashtag was hijacked by political conservatives using the #AllLivesMatter hashtag (e.g. Damiani, 2016). As such, social media, while facilitating new and bottom-up ways of cultivating compassion, also always embody the dangers of negative affective behaviors. When emotional storytelling circulates in public in the era of social media, such circulation occurs with a new set of attendant challenges which ultimately mean that such storytelling is no longer a straightforward and finite act, but remains ever incomplete and open to contestation.

Conclusion

This chapter has charted the reasons why personalized story-telling is so central to political life. The chapter has made the argument that such storytelling (1) bolsters claims of authen-ticity, and (2) cultivates compassion oriented towards the creation of communities that seek social and political change. Looking beyond the award-winning journalism examined in Chapter 2, this chapter has focused on a range of different practices of personalized storytelling, in both conventional and emerging media forms. In doing so, it has analyzed how the manufacture of authenticity and compassion works in complex ways which depend on the contexts in which stories circulate. In its examination of authenticity, the chapter has made the point that for political leaders, the cultivation of authenticity takes place through the display of emotion in a way that establishes them as "ordinary." By contrast, when letters to the editor and user-generated content are valued by journalists and audience members alike, their celebration of authenticity is premised on the role of lived experience in dramatizing the impact of major unfolding news stories, thus making them come alive.

The discursive construction of authenticity is closely tied to the cultivation of compassion. The chapter has examined several different ways in which forms of media content call compassionate communities into being. It has argued that while personalized storytelling always solicits compassion oriented towards community creation, this is articulated differently across platforms and genres. While letters to the editor bring about *local communities*, and Humans of New York Refugee Stories foster *cosmopolitan compassion*, the communities created by feminist hashtags could be more accurately viewed as *hybrid counterpublics*, seeking to organ-ize like-minded groups and individuals while reaching out to broader publics for political change. Across these varied platforms and genres, personalized storytelling operates as a political strategy which is explicit about its use of emotionality to bring about change.

So far, the book has treated emotion in a general manner. However, it is important to make distinctions between emotions, and to understand how they do different work in different mediated contexts. For this reason, the book now turns to examining the workings of a particular emotion which has been seen as both vital and dangerous in political life: that of anger. In the next two chapters, I examine anger as political emotion, looking at its mediated performance through the lens of two related cases. Chapter 4 develops a typology of mediated anger by examining the routine coverage of protest. The chapter demonstrates that in media coverage, anger is always-already a political emotion which serves to explain and sometimes justify the actions of protesters, and that this anger is frequently described as legitimate because it comes about as the result of collective grievances. Chapter 5 builds on these insights by taking a closer look at the role of anger in coverage of Donald Trump following on from his election victory, suggesting that anger has become a viable explanatory framework for understanding political life, representing a shift in the "emotional regime" towards an emerging form of angry populism.

CHAPTER FOUR

Towards a Typology of Mediated Anger

If emotions are essential and inevitable components of mediated politics, and play a key role in fostering forms of engagement based on the cultivation of authenticity and compassion, it is important to attend to the ways in which different emotions are articulated by groups and individuals and circulate in the public sphere. This chapter therefore turns towards a closer examination of the role of mediated anger in shaping mediated politics.

The chapter opens by developing a typology of mediated anger as performative, discursively constructed, collective and political. It then applies this framework to routine coverage of anger in protest coverage in UK newspapers during a selected two-month time period in 2015, demonstrating that there is a *spectrum* of discursive constructions of the legitimacy of mediated anger.

Anger in public discourse

As this chapter will demonstrate, anger is crucial as a distinctly *political* emotion (Lyman, 1981, p. 61). It has been maligned in political thinking as a negative emotion, and one that potentially gives rise to aggression and violence and requires careful management (e.g. Hochschild, 1983). Philosophers since the Stoics have viewed the "civilized life as one that avoids anger" (Holmes, 2004, p. 127). Anger is recognized in social theory as a reaction to injustice, and therefore inherently relational (Holmes, 2004). This understanding of anger was articulated by Aristotle, in his *Rhetoric,* where he defined it as "an impulse, accompanied by pain, to a conspicuous revenge for a conspicuous slight directed without justification towards what concerns oneself or towards what concerns one's friends" (1968, pp. 1382–3). Scholars in disciplines such as psychology and philosophy have typically viewed anger as an *individual* emotion which is unavoidable and difficult to control, and ultimately destructive to social relations. For example, the legal philosopher Martha Nussbaum has provided a compelling articulation of the dangers of anger in her book *Anger and forgiveness: Resentment, generosity, justice.* Here, she argues that "anger is not only not necessary for the pursuit of justice, but also a large impediment to the generosity and empathy that help to construct a future of justice" (Nussbaum, 2016, p. 8). This is because individual anger is usually accompanied by a desire for payback or retribution, which is never normatively justified and is socially counterproductive. There is, in Nussbaum's view, one "borderline case of genuinely rational and normatively appropriate anger that I call *Transition-Anger*, whose entire content is: 'How outrageous. Something should be done about that'" (2016, p. 6). Transition-Anger is appropriate because it entails moving beyond the pure emotion of anger to think about possible ways out of it, towards the resolution of injustices. However, even if anger is rarely normatively justifiable – or rational – it has three roles that are valuable in *instrumental* terms:

> First, it is seen as a valuable signal that the oppressed recognize the wrong done to them. It also seems to be a necessary motivation for them to protest and struggle against injustice and to communicate to the wider world the nature of their grievances. Finally, anger seems, quite simply, to be justified: outrage at terrible wrongs is right, and anger thus expresses something true. (Nussbaum, 2016, p. 211)

While Nussbaum's detailed excursus into individual anger shows its moral and social inadequacy, her recognition of the usefulness of anger occurs in the context of collective anger; or anger expressed by groups of individuals, directed at a shared injustice.

Along the lines of the understanding of mediated emotion as a distinctively performative social construction, which is central to this book, this chapter sees *mediated anger* as a very different creature from the anger expressed by individuals who are, to use Nussbaum's (2016) example, angry with their partners, perpetrators of crimes against their friends, or irritating colleagues. Instead, the understanding of mediated anger developed here shares a series of features with the types of anger at work in social movements. Anthropologists and sociologists of emotion who have studied such movements share the assumption that anger is a political resource which is based on the public articulation of shared grievances (e.g. Holmes, 2004). Their analysis is premised on examining the constitution of emotion – and the domain of emotion itself – in discourse or situated speech practices (Katriel, 2015; Lutz and Abu-Lughod, 1990). Their work shows that any analysis of anger needs to make differentiations between types of anger, and that *collective anger articulated in public* may be a very different creature from *individual anger aired in private*.

Developing a typology of mediated anger

Here, I propose that mediated anger is distinctive because it is *performative*, *discursively constructed* through journalistic narratives, and usually *collective* and *political*. Through these features, some forms of mediated anger are discursively legitimated, and come to stand as exemplars of what Nussbaum (2016) refers to as "Transition-Anger," insofar as they are oriented towards claims to justice and social change.

First of all, mediated anger is *performative* in the sense that it is based on the performance of actors in the public sphere. As social movements scholars and anthropologists have noted, emotions are, in the first instance, culturally constructed (Katriel, 2015), but the ways in which these cultural

constructions take on meaning through their public articulation matters greatly, and is frequently highly strategic. When
we speak of mediated anger as performative, this also reflects
the fact that the authenticity of the emotions that circulate in
mediated public discourse is impossible to ascertain, and that
it is both more relevant and more interesting to consider *which*
emotions do gain purchase in the public sphere, *why* and *with
what consequence.* The ways in which we speak about anger in
public matters hugely precisely *because* they are performative.
And this performative construction of emotion that springs
to life through mediated discourses also has significant ideological consequences. Such discourses provide an emotional
compass that we – as audience members and citizens – can
use to orient ourselves and distinguish between more or less
legitimate and rational forms of anger.

2 Secondly, mediated anger is *discursively constructed* through
the narrative of journalists. That is to say, when we speak of
anger as it appears in news coverage, it represents not the
emotion as felt in an individual, but rather journalists' interpretation of behavior of actors with reference to the emotion
of anger as situated within the narrative of the journalistic
text (see also Wettergren, 2015). But if journalism is one of
the key vehicles used for both establishing and perpetuating
particular emotional regimes, it also facilitates the sharing of
particular legitimate ways of talking about our feelings and
hence the conditions of possibility for shared action, as discussed in the Introduction. As Julia Eksner has suggested,
emotion "displays in language may be employed as tools of
hegemony by dominant groups and state institutions, and as
vehicles of resistance by non-dominant groups" (2015, p. 193).

On the basis of this key tension in the understanding of the
role of anger as a political emotion, I am here interested in
how it is constructed in media coverage of protest. Scholarly
work on the media coverage of protests finds that they are
largely framed, through reliance on a "protest paradigm,"
as disruptive to the social order (Boyle et al., 2012; McLeod,

2007). This is precisely because of the irrational behavior of angry protesters who threaten to turn violent. The extent of public anger is, in turn, often used as a means of predicting participation in protest, and therefore the potential for violence and other forms of disorder (Greer and MacLaughlin, 2010). Describing protesters as "angry" has frequently served as a strategy for discrediting a movement and its tactics. However, mediated anger is also contextual, as interpretations of anger are inherently ideological. This is well illustrated in Kevin DeLuca and his colleagues' work on blog debates over the Occupy Wall Street movement. Their study found that when right-leaning blogs described protesters as angry, it "was usually identified as a cause for concern – that is, protesters' anger was seen as illegitimate and potentially dangerous." By contrast, left-leaning bloggers viewed the anger of the protesters as legitimate and therefore *not* dangerous (DeLuca et al., 2012, p. 494). In this case, commentators across the political spectrum identified anger as an important explanatory framework – but the discursive construction of this anger depended on the political vantage point of the writer. That is to say, the same expressions of anger can be seen as simultaneously disruptive and productive; destructive and empowering. As the chapter will demonstrate, the ideological construction of protest is central to the political complexities of mediated protest, and frequently reflects not just positionings on the political spectrum, but also broader geopolitical contexts.

3   Finally, mediated anger is usually *collective* and therefore ultimately *political*. Though anger is in the first instance an individual emotion, it comes to matter politically when it is articulated by collectives in public, towards a shared objective of addressing an injustice. In media coverage, emotions are often described as belonging to or articulated by collectives, in marked contrast to how emotion discourse operates in everyday talk (e.g. Wahl-Jorgensen, 2013a; see also Chapter 2 in this book). This is not to say that individual emotions do not make an appearance in media coverage, but that collective

emotions – particularly anger – appear to be both more frequent and more newsworthy. This should not be surprising:
while individual emotions are frequently relegated to the private sphere, collective emotions – particularly anger – serve as
a marker of importance, highlighting possibilities for disruption of the social order and the emergence of transformative
political projects.

The ways in which anger operates in the context of social
movements have become a matter of interest in recent years,
as scholars studying oppositional and marginalized groups
have begun to recognize anger as an important resource of
collective empowerment (e.g. Goodwin et al., 2001; Jasper,
2011). Indeed, the feminist slogan "the personal is political"
speaks precisely to the significance of making public, collective and hence political the shared but discursively privatized
experiences of women – in terms of varied challenges that are
marked with gender, including those of child care, domestic
violence and housework, which would otherwise be relegated
to the private sphere. Deborah Gould (2010, 2012) studied the
role of anger in queer and feminist movements. She took a
particular interest in the potential of political empowerment
through the labeling of emotions – as when lesbians "feeling bad" collectively relabeled their emotion as anger (Gould,
2012). By naming and articulating the negative affect of "feeling bad" about the consequences of patriarchy as "anger," it
becomes a public and collective emotion which empowers the
angry group to take action. Similarly, in work on the AIDS
activist group Act Up, Gould (2010) examined how anger, as
a collective emotion, was encouraged as a positive resource,
whilst despair was discouraged. Frances Shaw demonstrated
that Australian feminists used blogging to give "form and
shape to the dissonance they felt in their own lives, and to
share the discourses that enabled them to turn it into policies
claims" (2014, p. 221). The expression of feelings of anger
then contributed to the creation of a political community.
This work shares a recognition that collective anger can be a

particularly useful resource for oppositional political life (see also Holmes, 2004), and that it is readily recognized as an expression of shared injustice. As Peter Lyman put it, "[A]nger is an indispensable political emotion – for without angry speech the body politic would lack the voice of the powerless questioning the justice of the dominant order" (2004, p. 133). This, in turn, points us in the direction of what Nussbaum (2016) refers to as Transition-Anger: an anger which is normatively legitimate because it involves claims for justice and social change; not merely voicing and explaining the emotion, but also raising the question of what should be done about it. When mediated anger is collective and political, it has the potential to transcend the narrow self-interest and retributive orientation of individual anger.

Studying mediated anger in protest coverage

I carried out a small study of mainstream media coverage of anger in protest to better understand how emotion is discursively constructed in that context. First, I conducted a Nexis UK search on stories in UK newspapers with the word "protest" or "demonstration" in the headline during the two-month period between July 1 and September 1, 2015, which yielded a total of 1,914 stories. This initial search provided a baseline for understanding the frequency of stories about demonstrations or protest. I next narrowed down the search to examine stories that discussed anger and protest, by adding the search terms "anger" OR "angry" anywhere in the text. This yielded a sample of 262 stories during the same time period. The selected time scale was based on an interest not in looking at the coverage of one particular protest, but rather in examining the routine ways in which mediated discourse constructs the relationship between anger and protest. For this reason, I selected periods without major protests which might skew the coverage. Instead, I aimed to examine a variety of different forms and contexts of protests.

The initial set of searches reveal that anger is a prominent, but not exclusive, framework for discussing protest, insofar as the phrase was used in just under 14% of stories. I deliberately did not search for related emotion words, such as "outrage," "fury" or "rage," as for the purposes of this study I was interested only in mediated discourses that explicitly invoked anger. A closer examination of the sample of 262 stories revealed that 16 of them were not relevant, as they dealt with topics such as the death of a protest singer, or language use in the EU, or because they reflected onlookers' anger with protesters, rather than the anger of the protesters themselves.

Many of the protests covered over these two time periods occurred outside the United Kingdom – that is to say, in national and political contexts that were unfamiliar to newspaper audiences and therefore required explanation and domestication (Claussen, 2004). In this context, coverage of demonstrations in Morocco over the trial of a woman wearing a skirt to market, and in Bangladesh over the lethal beating of a young boy, matters not just because it tells us about what is going on elsewhere in the world, but also because it signals, through journalists' discursive construction, how domestic audiences should interpret it. This enables us to investigate the complexities of the cultural politics of anger, to paraphrase Sara Ahmed (2004), and to understand how mediated constructions of anger are tied into larger global contexts. Nonetheless, there were also a significant number of stories that dealt with domestic protests within the United Kingdom – including frequent mentions of widespread protests by farmers over their treatment by supermarkets, but also encompassing Cardiff residents taking to the streets to complain about new council rubbish bins and Rotherham taxi drivers protesting against a new licensing law.

Regardless of the location of protests, coverage did not offer simple or unitary constructions of the anger of demonstrators. Rather, the ways in which the protests and the role of anger within them were described in the coverage appeared to be shaped by several factors. First of all, there was what we might call a geopolitics of protest coverage at play, which means that "globalized power relations shape the view from the nation state" (Pantti et al., 2012, Chapter 3). Journalists may be more likely to provide extensive coverage of protests in countries that are viewed as significant to domestic interests, just as opinionated journalism may privilege causes that are aligned with such interests. At the same time, the ideological orientation of newspapers matters in the context of a highly politically polarized journalistic field in the United Kingdom (Benson and Neveu, 2005, p. 5). Right-leaning newspapers may be more interested, for example, in reporting favorably on concerns about immigration on the continent, while left-leaning newspapers may have greater editorial sympathy for anti-austerity protests in Greece. This demonstrates the complexities of the discursive construction of mediated anger, and how the same expressions of anger may be refracted rather differently depending on the political lens through which they are interpreted.

The analysis shows that there is a *spectrum* of discursive constructions of the legitimacy of mediated anger. At one end sits *rational and legitimate anger*, which forms the basis for comprehensible projects for social change. Along the spectrum sits *aggressive and/or disruptive anger motivated by rational and legitimate concerns*. Finally, at the other end of the spectrum lies *illegitimate and irrational anger*.

Rational and legitimate anger

What is particularly striking is that in the vast majority of cases – 211 out of 246 stories, or 86% – the anger of protesters was described as both rational and legitimate. The role of anger in these stories was to provide an *explanatory framework* for understanding the protests. As such, the media came to frame a variety of different protests as being driven by, and giving voice to, politicized forms of anger which may be legitimate.

The *Bristol Post* was one of many newspapers to report on

farmers protesting against dairy import policies introduced by supermarkets, and led their story as follows: "Dairy farmers angry about the importing of milk to make cheese, yoghurt and other products have held peaceful protests at supermarket depots" (August 18). This lead is particularly interesting in its suggestion that the dairy farmers, despite their anger, staged peaceful protests. The story continued by providing details of the farmers' grievances and the broader retail and policy context, including changes in EU regulations. As such, although anger was an important theme in the article (the word "angry" was repeated in a later section), the anger was both substantiated and legitimated by a more detailed explanation of the substance of their opinions, suggesting rational argumentation rather than unrestrained passion and the possibility of violence, which are so often seen as a theme of protest coverage.

This was, indeed, a typical pattern in stories that constructed anger as rational and legitimate. For example, a *Sunday Times* article about protests in the Ukraine linked the actions of protesters to generalized feelings of anger over a public appointment: "An anti-government protest took place last week outside the central bank and there was anger among critics of the government over the appointment of a state prosecutor thought to have close links to Russia" (July 5). In this segment, the emotion of anger is associated with, but not described as causing, the protest. The anger described here is one which is aimed at a highly specific – but also potentially rational – grievance: that of the appointment of a "state prosecutor thought to have close links to Russia." Here, then, anger appears to provide a necessary framework which legitimates the protests, rather than framing them as disruptive, aggressive or violent. For the center-right *Sunday Times* newspaper, it also provides an opportunity to report on opposition to the Russian government, frequently targeted for its repressive and anti-democratic practices in the British press. More broadly, this story exemplifies a range of coverage in which protesters or their actions were not specified as being angry, but the narrative implied that the anger of specific populations – critics of the Ukrainian government, some Greeks, German villagers, Welsh library users and South African students – helped to explain the protests. In this sense, anger becomes a barometer of public opinion: it functions as a measure of the seriousness of the underlying social issues raised by the protest. In doing so, it operates as an injunction to care through the journalists' mediated witnessing (Cottle 2013; Pantti et al., 2012): it calls for news audiences to pay attention to these stories precisely *because* groups and collectivities are angry. For example, a story in the *Western Daily Press* about the farmers' protest first established the legality of farmers' actions before suggesting that their anger indicated the need to take their claims seriously:

> The farmers in these protests are not breaking the law. They are at worst causing inconvenience to some shoppers and some extra work for supermarket shelf-stackers.
>
> But no-one should under-estimate their anger or their need for support. They need to be taken seriously and their voices need to be heard. (August 1)

In several cases, articles made distinctions between justified anger, on the one hand, and aggression and violence, on the other. A *Bedford Today* article about a group of women demonstrating at the treatment of refugees at Yarl's Wood immigration removal center specified that although "people were angry and upset it wasn't an aggressive atmosphere, it was incredibly supportive" (August 11).

This demonstrates a common discursive construction whereby the politicized expression of anger appears legitimate precisely because it is occasioned by rational claims oriented towards social justice, and is expressed in a peaceful manner. However, even if this was a common way of situating anger as controllable and therefore constructive, there were also a number of instances where anger was understood as legitimate despite causing disruption and/or violence.

Aggressive and/or disruptive anger motivated by rational and legitimate concerns.
The construction of anger as legitimate, even if accompanied by aggression, disruption or violence, occurred in a total of 14 stories, representing just under 6% of the sample. In this small number of stories, violence and disruption were mentioned – often in passing – while significant attention was devoted to explaining the substance of the underlying grievances. For example, a *Telegraph* story about a demonstration calling for a "yes" vote in the Greek referendum over whether to accept the EU bailout package mentioned threats against journalists but framed the discussion in the context of a broader public mood of anger at media coverage:

> At a demonstration calling for a "yes" vote, journalists and camera crew deemed to be left-wing were threatened with violence. There has been growing anger among some Greeks over the coverage of the referendum, according to German news website Focus, with one of the main gripes being that private broadcasters are too biased in their reporting. (July 5)

Here, the protest is only very briefly described – and in terms that recall conventional understandings of protesters as violent (in this case, against perceived left-wing journalists and camera crews). The context, however, provides an explanation for this behavior in terms of anger at media coverage of the referendum – anger that may be grounded in legitimate grievances.

This discursive construction is also at work in a *Telegraph* story about student protests in South Africa:

> The South African president, Jacob Zuma, agreed to a freeze on university fees last night after thousands of protesting students surrounded his offices and fought pitched battles with riot police. The protests, in which demonstrators ripped down security fences, set fire to portable buildings and hurled bricks at police, were the latest in a week of disturbances prompted by anger at inflation-busting fee hikes. (October 24)

Some of these stories also cautioned that the disruptive behavior was characteristic only of a minority of protesters, with the vast majority being peaceful. For instance, a story reflecting on the 10-year anniversary of the G8 summit in Edinburgh contrasted images of rioters with those of the enormous anti-poverty protest:

> The most graphic images of the events surrounding the G8 summit ten years ago show angry rioters clashing with baton-wielding police officers on the streets of the Capital.
>
> But just as dramatic are the pictures of a quarter of a million people filling the city centre as they march through Edinburgh in bright sunshine, calling on the world leaders to "Make Poverty History". (*Edinburgh Evening News*, July 6, 2015)

However, despite this small number of stories which recounted instances of disruption or violence as part of a normatively justified protest, there were also instances where disruptive violent behavior was seen to discount the legitimacy of particular demonstrations.

Illegitimate and irrational anger
Anger was discursively constructed as both illegitimate and irrational in a total of 21 stories in the sample, representing just under 9% of the sample. The small number of stories constructing anger in this way is, in a sense, surprising, given the fact that such treatment reflects the "protest paradigm," which focuses on conflict and violence as a way of discrediting protesters and describing them as irrational (Boyle et al., 2012; McLeod, 2007).

A significant number of these articles appeared in the right-wing *Mail Online*, accounting for a total of eight articles, representing 38% of all stories which constructed protest in this way. In one such story, the journalist described the "shocking behavior" of participants at San Francisco's monthly Critical Mass bike ride, as evidenced in a video recording obtained by the media organization: "Shocking video shows mob of bicyclists attacking female motorist in a rental car during cycling safety protest. [...] The angry mob stopped the car's progress and wouldn't let the driver move" (*Mail Online*, September 1). The irony of participants in what was allegedly a "cycling safety protest" behaving in an unsafe and violent manner here serves to underscore the irrationality of the protesters, and to undermine any substantive message associated with the actions.

Indeed, describing protesters as angry and disruptive was sometimes used as a strategy to discredit them. Such a strategy was, for example, used by politicians to denigrate protesters. As elite sources, they serve as the "primary definers" (Hall et al., 2013), determining the framework through which the story is interpreted. In an *Essex Chronicle* report, Priti Patel, Conservative Member of Parliament for Witham, complained about a group of elderly disabled constituents in handing in a petition to protect the National Health Service (NHS) from the Transatlantic Trade and Investment Partnerships (TTIP) between the United States and the European Union. She described them as engaging in "appalling harassment and thuggish behaviour":

> "They [...] came to the Conservative office unannounced, created a disturbance by banging on windows, the office door, taking pictures of the office and frightened the lady working in the office.
>
> "By their own admission they arrived there in an 'angry' state." She added: "This campaign has nothing of any substance to say about the NHS and the organisers are more interested in twisting and misrepresenting my comments on this matter rather than engaging constructively about local health services" (*Essex Chronicle*, August 5)

In this account, the anger of protesters rendered them irrational and therefore disturbing and frightening, while having "nothing of any substance to say about the NHS." Against this framework, the article went on to interview the protesters and discuss the substance of their concerns: "The People's

NHS fear the TTIP deal could mean multinational corporations privatising huge swathes of publicly owned assets, including the NHS, with the British Government unable to stop them."

Some of the stories explicitly described anger as harmful to social cohesion, and juxtaposed it to more positive affective responses such as compassion. For example, a report on protest against large-scale migration in Germany, published in the *Sunday Times*, analyzed a perceived shift in the emotional climate of politics as follows: "In Sumte, across Germany and indeed throughout continental Europe, compassion for foreigners fleeing war and barbarism in their homeland has given way to anger and fear, boosting support for populist parties and raising the prospect of a violent backlash" (October 25). Here, the emotions of anger and fear are marked as destructive, in clear opposition to "compassion for foreigners fleeing war and barbarism in their homeland," and potentially giving rise to violence. This points to the ways in which mediated anger cannot be seen in isolation, but is discursively co-constructed with other political emotions, and gains meaning through these associations.

This is further complicated by questions of *who* the protesters are, and *what language* they use in articulating their grievances. Along those lines, several of the protests that were constructed as illegitimate involved openly racist language and groups known for extremist views, as in this *Mail Online* account of a video detailing tension between the Ku Klux Klan and the New Black Panther Party:

> Angry clashes erupted between members of the Ku Klux Klan and the New Black Panther Party.
>
> And in the same video, a white man in a light blue top threatens the black people in attendance by saying "I'll hang your black *ss," while another angry white supremacist shouts at the crowd: "You come here and I'll knock you on your black *ss muthaf*ker."
>
> Meanwhile, a man holding the Confederate flag told

another African American that they were "the color of excrement," Raw Story reports. (July 22)

The openly racist behavior of Klan supporters was juxtaposed with the compassionate actions of a police officer on the scene at the demonstration:

> As hatred and racial intolerance engulfed a rally over the Confederate flag in South Carolina, a poignant picture of a black police chief helping a man who was wearing a swastika T-shirt emerged on Twitter.
>
> The sick man, according to reports, had suffered from heatstroke and was being helped by Leroy Smith, the director of the South Carolina Department of Public Safety.
>
> Smith's ability to show compassion to the man draped in clothes bearing the insignia of racist intolerance has gone viral and been retweeted over 2,000 times since it was shared on Twitter.

Here, again, anger is constructed as normatively undesirable, illegitimate and exclusionary through its juxtaposition with the desirable pro-social emotion of compassion. In stories that rely on this juxtaposition, it appears that compassion serves as an antidote to exclusionary anger, establishing "feeling rules" (Hochschild, 1983) that tell us how we ought to behave in the company of others.

A final category of illegitimate anger was premised on establishing the protest as arising from the irrational conduct of a small group or just one aberrant individual, as in this story about a man demonstrating against parking tickets by driving a horse and cart into a town center:

> The driver of a horse and cart that brought town-centre traffic to a standstill in an extraordinary protest has threatened to repeat it "every day".
>
> Ray Beecham blocked High Street, Croydon, with his horse and carriage for 20 minutes as part of a bitter dispute with the council over parking tickets.
>
> He caused a queue of buses and cars stretching to

Wellesley Road before being moved on by police on Thursday afternoon. (*Croydon Guardian*, August 5)

Here, the protest is marked as "extraordinary," and the police involvement is noted, serving to underscore the ways in which Beecham's behavior is both irrational and illegal. In addition, this story and other similar ones implied that for one person to cause such disruption on the basis of their individual grievances was normatively undesirable. This, once again, points to the importance of mediated anger as collective and therefore political: to count as legitimate, media constructions of anger require a shared cause which is always-already directed towards social change. It is therefore a species of what Nussbaum (2016) refers to as Transition-Anger. But, counter to the allegedly rare occurrence of Transition-Anger in everyday life (Nussbaum, 2016, p. 36), mediated constructions of anger appear to be dominated by this form.

Interpreting mediated anger

Overall, then, anger is used as an overarching framework explaining the motivation to engage in collective action. Mediated anger is legitimate when it provides a means to express collective, rather than individual, grievances. So, typical of newspaper discourse more broadly, anger is expressed on the part of groups, rather than individuals, and is central to the formation of their claims and grievances in the public sphere. However, the *consequences* of protesting in anger, which in turn impact on the horizons for political action, are dependent on context, and often articulated in conjunction with other emotions, like compassion. What this implies is that there is a broad discursive "common sense" agreement on the role of anger as a mobilizing emotion. But there is also a recognition that anger can be channeled into more or less constructive forms of political action. This analysis also demonstrates that it is not simply the case that an emphasis on anger in protest serves to discredit protesters or neglect their message. Rather, journalistic discourses suggest that people protest *because* they are angry, but this anger is, in the majority of cases studied here, both rational and legitimate. This complicates dominant scholarly accounts of the construction of protest, even if some scholars have noted a move towards a more nuanced representation of activists emerging over time (Di Cicco, 2010).

It should be noted that the distinctive patterns detected in this study are based on routine coverage of a range of protests over an extended period. This, in turn, implies that the kinds of demonstrations studied here may be distinctive from those that form the basis of most studies of protest coverage, which focus on large-scale discrete events that are often, by their very nature, more extensive and therefore more disruptive than the demonstrations dominating the sample analyzed here, which frequently either occur outside the United Kingdom, or are small-scale and localized. These features, in turn, require journalists to contextualize the protests by explaining the substantive concerns animating them in the first place – a practice that contributes to their legitimation. This highlights the need for more extensive research on routine coverage of smaller-scale protest, which might serve to further refine the protest paradigm.

What is clear is that in the examples given here, journalists contribute to the discursive construction of the meaning of the protest – and the role of anger within it. Yet protests are, by their very nature, performative and public acts which are often carefully orchestrated, particularly with respect to the display and management of emotions, whether positive or negative (Juris, 2005). Here, it is interesting to note that the use of anger, disruption and violence as an explanatory framework for constructing protest has been strategically resisted by non-violent social movements. This is particularly important in a time of "image politics" designed to create "critique through spectacle" (DeLuca, 1999), but has long been a feature of social movement approaches. For example, the tactics of the anti-war protests of the 1960s, including placing flowers in soldiers' guns and the injunction to make love not war, were particularly striking because they were both consistent with the message of the movement and contested dominant media constructions of protest. More recently, Occupy has constructed itself as a horizontal, egalitarian, creative and strategically non-violent movement (e.g. DeLuca et al., 2012). Hong Kong's "umbrella revolution" in 2014 garnered sympathy around the world precisely because its participants, predominantly described as "gentle" and "polite" and brandishing only umbrellas, were met by disproportionate – and violent – police violence (Hui, 2015). What these movements share, then, is a deliberate and strategic reversal of the presumption of political theory that collective action is necessarily predicated on anger and therefore causes violence. This suggests that despite the importance of anger as an explanatory framework, it is also one which is contested by the movements themselves. Anger, then, is a complex and inherently ideological discursive resource.

[handwritten margin notes: "not in my case"; "intentionally adopt anger/aggressive frame to disturb journalists"]

Conclusion

This chapter has sought to recover the importance of anger as a political emotion through its examination of protest coverage. The chapter opened by developing a typology of mediated anger, suggesting that we should view such anger as distinctive because it is performative, discursively constructed, collective and political. Examining a sample of UK newspaper stories featuring routine protest coverage, the chapter has suggested that the idea of anger as a cause of engagement and a barometer of the intensity of public feeling is central to media discourses around protest, and ultimately forms an injunction to care. Mediated anger is variegated and complex, depending on its articulation with other narrative elements: although, in a majority of cases, it appears to be rational and legitimate, and even disruptive or violent protests may be counted as such, there are also exceptions. Anger in protests is more likely to be constructed as illegitimate when it results in violence; when it is associated with intolerance or extremism; and when it is associated with very small groups or individuals, rather than collectives articulating shared grievances. This, in turn, suggests that protesters can be simultaneously angry *and* rational, peaceful and legitimate. Discourses on protest construct a common-sense theory of political motivation, whereby anger explains the desire for political engagement, but only occasionally brings about other negative emotions or actions. This anger, in turn, stems from collective and publicly articulated grievances, usually against larger injustices that no individual can address on their own. Through these stories, then, anger is always-already political and has the potential to change the world, for better or worse. To illustrate this insight, and anchor it within the context of significant contemporary transformations in the prevailing "emotional regime" (Reddy, 2001), the next chapter takes a closer look at the role of anger in Donald Trump's populist discourse. It suggests that in our current historical moment, anger has become a central framework for understanding political life, ushering in an era of "angry populism."

CHAPTER FIVE

Shifting Emotional Regimes: Donald Trump's Angry Populism

This chapter builds on the insights around the nature of mediated anger to examine a particularly important contemporary transformation in the prevailing "emotional regime" (Reddy, 2001) heralded by the rise of Donald Trump. Having established that anger is widely viewed as a significant collective and political emotion, the chapter suggests that Trump's ascent is powered by the emergence of "angry populism." Adopted as an interpretive framework in media coverage, it suggests that the anger of Trump, his supporters and his opponents is both salient and relevant to political life.

Theorizing populism and political anger

The changes in the emotional regime charted here should, first of all, be understood in the context of contemporary forms of populism. As a political project, populism tends to be premised on the mobilization of the people around an opposition to shared enemies (Laclau, 2005). Contemporary populisms are based on discursively generating collective identities based on oppositions between "the pure people" and "the corrupt elite" and usually involve affective allegiances to a charismatic leader (Mudde, 2007, p. 23; Mudde and Kaltwasser, 2012, p. 7). Because of the structuring role of such oppositions, populist identities are often exclusionary (Laclau, 2005, p. 195).

For the purposes of this chapter, I focus on the right-wing populism that Trump exemplifies, which draws on such exclusionary solidarities to target resentment at the most vulnerable members of society, including immigrants and ethnic minorities (see Ost, 2006). As such, Trump's appeal is organized around a particular negative affective constellation representing the coalescence of longer-standing practices and trends (see also Berry and Sobieraj, 2014). Yet it also appears to be distinctive – and distinctively angry; premised on the discursive construction of shared grievances. First, Trump's electoral victory has been widely connected to broader patterns of economic anger. The prominent economist Ann Pettifor is one of many observers to link the election result to the economic consequences of globalization. She has argued that it should be understood as part of a global pattern of response:

> In a "counter-movement" to globalisation and recognising the failure of democratic governments to protect societies from the depredations of self-regulating markets, [these societies] have reacted by electing "strong men" (and women) that do offer protection. Donald Trump posed as a strong protector, and won the support of those Americans "left behind" by globalization. (Pettifor, 2017, p. 53)

Secondly, Ronald Inglehart and Pippa Norris, in their analysis of cross-national survey data, argue that support for Trump is the result of a "cultural backlash": it is a reaction "by once-predominant sectors of the population to progressive value change" (2016, p. 3) – particularly salient among older, white male, religious and less educated parts of the population. This "cultural backlash" thesis also casts votes for Trump as made in anger, if for slightly different reasons. What these theories share is the idea that the decision to vote for Trump arises from forms of reactionary anger, born out of longer-standing exclusion from privilege, whether economic or cultural. This chapter makes the case that understanding the circulation of anger in public discourse around the rise of Trump is, in fact, vital to understanding the phenomenon.

Of course, political anger is not reserved for the actions of marginalized groups or social movements. Instead, grievances and disaffection should rightly be understood as permanent features of political life (Oberschall, 1973, p. 298). Anger serves a productive role because it generates bonds of emotional solidarity and forms the basis for collective action. As David Ost puts it in the opening of his book *The defeat of solidarity: Anger and politics in postcommunist Europe*:

> Anger, solidarity and democracy have traditionally gone together. Democracy has usually been advanced when people angry about their exclusion from wealth and power join together in solidarity. This does not mean just mass demonstrations or disruptive action. From New Deal America to Keynesian Western Europe, liberal and socialist parties resuscitated democracy in the West by organizing the anger of those long deprived of social protection. (Ost, 2006, p. 1)

Anger has always been central to the strategic appeals of mainstream political parties (see also Higgins, 2008), and should be recognized as a key ideological resource: "Politics does not become angry only when non-elites shout. Anger is built into politics through the everyday activities of political parties, which continually both stoke and mobilize anger in order to gain and maintain support" (Ost, 2004, p. 229).

There are two key reasons why anger is so important to mainstream politics, according to Ost. First of all, there is widespread anger because of economic inequalities, and capturing "economic anger" is central to popular appeal, which is particularly successfully harnessed by illiberal populist political actors (Ost, 2006, p. 9). Secondly, political parties need to cultivate solidarity to maintain their base: "This requires creating an emotional connection with supporters, the establishment of an 'us' against the 'them' of other parties, an emotional bond that can best be maintained when the other is cast negatively as an object of aversion" (Ost, 2004, p. 229). For political parties and the politicians who represent them, anger must be organized, channeled and harnessed in particular ways, and the organization of anger is vital to the construction of political narrative.

The context for angry populism

However, the current mobilization of anger merits analysis as a distinctive formation. Historically, the successful management of emotions has been vital to successful presidential candidacies, while poor control has derailed campaigns. The Democratic primary candidacy of Howard Dean in 2004 collapsed after the infamous "Dean Scream." At the end of his spontaneous speech reacting to his third-place result in the Iowa Caucus, Dean made a high-pitched scream, which he later attributed to a sore throat. This moment was captured by several media organizations and then circulated widely. Following on from the media frenzy, Dean was denounced as unpresidential. His display of odd non-verbal language served as a marker of uncontrollable emotionality, and effectively put an end to his race.

By contrast, Trump's outbursts and gaffes have been too numerous to count. During the election campaign, they attracted attention when they fit into a broader narrative around his candidacy, as in his mocking of the disabled reporter Serge Kovaleski; when he appeared to call for the assassination of Hillary Clinton; and when his "grab them by the pussy" interview came to light. The blatant disregard for "emotion rules" – or rules governing displays of emotion in particular situations (Hochschild, 1983) – might have terminated any other candidate at any other time. Instead, Trump sailed onward, constantly emoting in socially inappropriate ways.

The theme of Trump's anger has been picked up by journalistic and scholarly observers to explain the anger both of Trump voters and of Trump himself. It was a prominent refrain in journalists' attempts at making sense of Trump's appeal to voters disenchanted with the political process. Chris Cilizza (2017) explained Trump's rise in the *Washington Post* with reference to polling data. He argued that it should be understood as the result of a confluence of circumstances, including the hollowing out of the economy, the loss of faith in institutions, unrest within the Republican Party and anger with the federal government. Similarly, an *Atlantic* article linked Trump's ascent to divisions in the Republican Party, powerfully embodied in the Tea Party movement: "Was it any wonder, then, that a candidate came along whose anger was even more consuming and less constructive, whose disregard for political norms was even more flamboyant, whose appeals to racial resentment were even more overt, whose disregard for fact and fondness for conspiracy was even more pronounced?" (Ball, 2016).

These observations reflect the broader resonance of anger as a political resource for the projects of populist politicians. Writing in the *New Yorker* about the president's first 100 days in office, David Remnick described Trump's ascent as part of a broader global trend of a rebellion against liberal democracy, linking it to anger:

> The Trump presidency represents a rebellion against liberalism itself – an angry assault on the advances of groups of people who have experienced profound, if fitful, empowerment over the past half century. There is nothing about Trump's public pronouncements that indicates that he has welcomed these moral advances; his language, his tone, his personal behavior, and his policies all suggest, and foster, a politics of resentment. It is the Other – the ethnic minority, the immigrant – who has closed your factory, taken your job, threatened your safety. (2017, p. 20)

Such observations highlight not only the prominence of an emotional politics of anger in contemporary politics, but also Trump's ability to tap into that anger (see Hochschild, 2016).

Angry populism and a changing emotional regime

Even if much of the analysis of the rise of Trump has been based on observations about distinctive cultural, historical and economic circumstances in the United States, there is reason to think that these trends may reflect broader developments. Along those lines, as noted in the Introduction, Pankaj Mishra (2017) has suggested that we may be seeing the rise of a global "age of anger," fueled by violent dissatisfaction with social and political institutions and their inability to deliver improved life circumstances to marginalized groups.

The argument around the emergence of an "age of anger" suggests a change in the ways we perform and interpret our emotions in public, centrally tied to political practices inside and outside – as well as against – institutions of governance. For the historian William Reddy (2001), we need to see practices of governance as driven in part by the way we speak about emotions in public. He introduced the term "emotional regime" to refer to the "set of normative emotions and the official rituals, practices, and 'emotives' that express and inculcate them" (Reddy, 2001, p. 129). Along similar lines, Michael Delli Carpini has suggested that the rise of Trump is linked to a broader set of transformations in the "media regime," associated with political, economic, cultural and technological changes. The transformation in the media regime result in the normalization of "a new set of rules, norms, institutions, and expectations" (Delli Carpini, 2018, p. 18). The emerging media regime is one where conditions allow for the president to consistently "make statements that are verifiably false, be called out on these misstatements and pay (to date at least) no political price for them" (Delli Carpini, 2018, p. 20). While Trump has successfully exploited the conditions of the media regime, these were already firmly in place before he emerged on the political scene. This, in turn, means that "the competing narratives emerging from [the] combination of beliefs, opinions, and alternative facts – rather than the material conditions underlying them – become the basis for political discourse and action" (Delli Carpini, 2018, p. 21).

We can see the change in the media regime as intricately linked to, and enabling, a shift in the emotional regime. If emotional regimes coalesce through the public expression of emotives, the media play a key role in facilitating their emergence and their transformation (see also Pantti and Wahl-Jorgensen, 2011). By studying changes in the use of emotional language in media coverage of a comparable event over time (and presidential administrations), we can therefore trace changes in the emotional regime. In this case, I am studying shifting emotional regimes by looking at expressions of anger in post-election and inauguration coverage of Barack Obama's first election and inauguration in 2009, as well as Donald Trump's election and inauguration in 2017. In taking this approach, I am following the lead of journalism historians who have looked at changes in coverage of, for example, the President's State of the Union Address (Schudson, 1982) and Thanksgiving (Brennen, 2008) to understand transformations in journalistic practice. The purpose of my analysis, however, is not to offer a detailed historical exploration of emotional regimes, but rather to provide a snapshot of a particular critical moment of change, represented by the election of Trump. Such an analysis cannot establish whether Trump's populist anger represents a unique emotional regime. But it can point to shifts in the relative prominence of particular emotions, and highlight what this tells us about horizons for public discourse and political change.

Trump's populist anger cannot be understood as simply constructed through the discourses of mainstream media, but rather must be seen as emerging within a hybrid media system (Chadwick, 2013). Trump, like other populist politicians, has been highly successful at mobilizing support through his use of Twitter (Engesser et al., 2017), and his tweets have, in turn, attracted extensive media coverage. The increasing prominence of social media shapes not just the content of mainstream media, but also their affective style. According to a number of observers, the affordances of Twitter facilitate a discursive climate which is more extreme, divisive and polarized (Shepherd et al., 2015). Trump appears to be a beneficiary of this affective shift by crafting his charged messages on Twitter in a way that spills over into mainstream media (Karpf, 2017).

This chapter suggests that the ascent of Trump is a reflection of a shift towards an emotional regime of "angry populism" – a rhetoric which seeks broad appeal through the deliberate expression of anger and which feeds a journalistic narrative that understands anger as central to political life. Its findings indicate that this anger is sometimes directed at specific targets, including the political establishment and other cultural and economic elites, women, migrants, ethnic minorities and anyone perceived as a threat to American interests (see also Newmyer, 2017). At other times, however, the anger does *not* have a target, but instead seems to be more diffuse and ill defined – a form of anger which is politically consequential in its own right.

Studying the rise of angry populism

To illustrate this emerging emotional regime, the chapter examines the occurrence of the phrases "anger" and "angry" in the period between Trump's election in November 2016 and the day following his inauguration in January 2017, contrasting it with the period between Obama's first election victory in November 2008 and his first inauguration in January 2009. It then takes a closer look, through a qualitative textual analysis, at the more manageable sample of the day following the inauguration for each of the two presidents.

The chapter focuses on this particular period to avoid tapping into anger surrounding conflicts associated with the campaign, instead focusing on the language of anger surrounding the election and inauguration of the two presidents. This period is critical in both establishing and contesting the reputation, vision and public image of a new president (Mansch, 2005). Inaugurations seek to cement the dominant narrative around the president. They are mediated public rituals building consensus around the spectacle of affirming the new incumbent and the shared values he or she represents

(Bajc, 2007; Bormann, 1982; Kertzer, 1989). They represent moments when the nation is often represented as coming together, with divisions set aside. This makes the study of anger in inauguration coverage all the more interesting: if anger is viewed as an uncontrollable and dangerous emotion, it is anathema to the ideological consensus of the inauguration ritual, where we might expect it to be largely suppressed or invisible (Beasley, 2001). At the same time, the inauguration coverage also frames the presidency by providing an interpretive context for understanding key debates surrounding the new president, and therefore provides a sense of the emotional regime s/he embodies.

Using Nexis UK, coverage in US newspapers and newswires were searched for major mentions of Trump (November 6, 2016–January 21, 2017) and Obama (November 4 2008–January 21, 2009), and mentions of "anger" or "angry" anywhere in the text. This basic quantitative examination does not tell us anything about the *substance* of the coverage of anger, but merely detects the presence of this particular emotion word, or its correlate, "angry." It does, however, provide a useful indication of the relative salience of anger in mediated debates over the two candidates. It should be noted that the analysis deliberately steers clear of examining similar or related emotion words such as "indignation," "fury" or "frustration." The reason for this decision is to maintain a clear focus on what are explicitly identified as public articulations of anger as a central political emotion.

A clear pattern emerges from this analysis. Following Trump's election and up until the day after his inauguration, there were 3,828 stories using the terms "anger" or "angry," contrasted with 1,449 for Obama. This gives an indication that anger was much more salient in post-election coverage of Trump than following Obama's first presidential victory. If we then look at the shorter time period of the inauguration and the day after in each of the two cases, we get a smaller and more manageable sample of the role of anger at this critical moment of establishing the interpretive framework through which the presidency is understood. To locate such a sample, the search detailed above was repeated, adding "inauguration" as a search term anywhere in the text, looking only at the period of January 20–1, 2009, for Obama, and January 20–1, 2017, for Trump. For Obama, the search yielded a total of 47 relevant stories, whereas for Trump, there were almost twice as many – 90.[1] It should be noted that the sample period for Trump's inauguration also included some coverage of the Women's Marches in Washington and around the United States, which had been timed to coincide with the inauguration and were framed with reference to it.

To better understand how this smaller sample constructed anger, the analysis looked, first of all, at the target of anger across all the stories: that is to say, at *what* or *whom* is the anger directed? This provides us with a sense of how the anger is explained – and, in some cases, legitimated. If anger is a way of addressing a shared sense of injustice, the nature of the injustice matters hugely to the framing and interpretation of the anger. Table 5.1 shows the targets of the anger in the respective inauguration stories. The table includes all instances accounting for more than 7% of references to the targets of anger.

Table 5.1: Targets of anger in coverage of Obama's first inauguration (2009) and Trump's inauguration (2017)

Obama's inauguration ($n = 47$)		Trump's inauguration ($n = 90$)	
Target	*Percentage (raw figure)*	Target	*Percentage (raw figure)*
Historical racism	19.1 ($n = 9$)	Donald Trump	53.3 ($n = 48$)
Overcrowding at inauguration	17 ($n = 8$)	Unspecified anger	20 ($n = 18$)
War in Gaza	10.6 ($n = 5$)	The economy	10 ($n = 9$)
George W. Bush	8.5 ($n = 4$)	Washington establishment	7.8 ($n = 7$)
Delay in attorney general appointment	8.5 ($n = 4$)		

When anger was referenced in coverage of Obama's inauguration, this was almost never directed at Obama himself. There was, in fact, only one instance where he was the implied target. This occurred in an *Atlanta Journal-Constitution* news story in January pointing to the anger of the gay community directed at the choice of evangelical pastor Rick Warren, known for making homophobic statements, to deliver the invocation at the inauguration. Instead, the most frequent mention of anger was as a response to the historical experience of racism among African-Americans, who were celebrating the Obama victory as an opportunity for overcoming racist discrimination. Interviewed for a news story in the *Bakersfield-Californian* (January 20), local African-Americans recalled their own personal experiences with segregation, and celebrated the inauguration as a new beginning:

> "My president has proved that in America, all things are possible," [one interviewee] said.
> "Success requires participation," she said. "It's out there. You gotta go out and get it."
> "The guys in the 'hood who are angry and upset?" [another interviewee] added. "They can't complain any longer that there's a ceiling for black people."

This story – along with numerous others – drew on references to anger as a way of generating a contrast between a difficult past, and a hopeful present and future.

The second most frequent target of anger was overcrowding at the inauguration, which made it difficult for some citizens to participate, as in this article from the *South Bend Tribune* (January 21):

> Some people got angry and another woman became exhausted and needed help from paramedics, Johnson said. Once inside, though, people forgot about their feet hurting and the long waits, she said. Everyone was happy to be there, including an elderly woman in a wheel-chair, wrapped in a shiny silver blanket.

Table 5.2: Subjects of anger in coverage of Trump's inauguration

Subject of anger	Percentage (raw figures)
Opponents of Trump/Demonstrators	55.5 $(n = 50)$
Trump	23.3 $(n = 21)$
Supporters of Trump	13.3 $(n = 12)$
Other	7.8 $(n = 7)$

Here, the anger of being unable to participate fully in the historic event of Obama's inauguration is juxtaposed with the transformative effects of being present. These examples, then, tell the story of a journey from anger to happiness and hope, represented by the rise of Obama.

By contrast, the anger expressed in coverage of Trump's inauguration overwhelmingly targeted Trump himself (see Table 5.2 above). This was true for more than half of all references to anger in the sample, and was based on extensive coverage of protesters gathering for the inauguration itself, as well as the Women's March on the day following the inauguration. Trump's opponents also represented the majority (55.5%) of the *subjects* of anger – those represented as angry in stories. If we look more closely at these subjects of anger in the case of the Trump inauguration, what is particularly interesting is the relatively small number of different types of actors accounting for the vast majority: Trump, his opponents and his supporters account for more than 90% of angry actors.

This is in sharp contrast to the Obama inauguration coverage, where the subjects of anger are identified as representing a wide variety of actor types – to mention just a few, they include Kenyan citizens, Gaza activists, African-American community leaders, domestic politicians and Bush supporters. This also reflects the wide variety of targets of anger in the case of the Obama inauguration. It implies that discord and conflict have an inevitable place in narratives of political events, and that Obama's inauguration provided the opportunity for reflection on a wide variety of long-standing political grievances. This may be a common pattern for inauguration coverage given its role as an opportunity to establish the contextual framework for the presidency (Mansch, 2005).

In many of the stories on the Trump inauguration, the anger of the protesters was described as energizing a new social movement. For example, the *Rocky Mountain Collegian* (January 21) reported on the positive spirit amongst local protesters on election day, who were united in their anger at Trump: "'This is so heartwarming,' said 77-year-old Geoff Bruce, who marched alongside his wife, Harriet Hall, wearing a gray and pink cat-eared hat. 'Isn't it marvelous how one person who hates has unified so many people?'"

The anger of protesters was frequently legitimized with reference to the substance of their grievances. A widely syndicated Associated Press article (January 21) observed that "Trump's call for restrictive immigration measures, religious screening of immigrants and his caustic campaign rhetoric about women and minorities angered millions." Similarly, a news story in the *Eureka Times-Standard* (January 21) quoted an anti-Trump protester stating: "My feelings are beyond anger. It's a deep-seated nauseous feeling in my gut that we have a person that's racist, homophobic, classist and everything basically un-American." Here a protester's feelings "beyond anger" were legitimated with references to widely shared grievances about Trump and his behavior.

Trump's supporters, however, were also described as angry, accounting for 13.3% of the subjects of anger. The anger of Trump supporters – often directed at a perceived decline in economic opportunities – was used to explain their voting decisions, as in this Associated Press news story (January 21):

> Trump's victory underscored that for many Americans, the recovery from the Great Recession has come slowly or not at all. His campaign tapped into seething anger in working class communities, particularly in the Midwest, that have

watched factories shuttered and the certainty of a middle class life wiped away.

Expressions of anger at the Washington establishment was another common target, accounting for 7.8% of references – consistent with understandings of populism as oriented around an opposition between "the pure people" and "the corrupt elite" (Mudde, 2007). It was most prominent in coverage of Trump's inaugural speech, as in this report from the *Los Angeles Times* (January 20): "His 16-minute speech – the shortest since President Carter's inaugural in 1977 – lacked specific policy. In its place was a sense of anger at what he defined as a ruling political class that had raided America for its own benefit."

However, what is perhaps most striking about the construction of anger in stories about Trump's inauguration is that a high proportion of references to anger did *not* identify a target. As the literature on anger suggests, it is highly unusual for anger, as expressed in political coverage, not to have a target. Rather, anger normally *requires* a target for it to matter politically (Pantti and Wahl-Jorgensen, 2011). By contrast, in stories about Trump's inauguration, anger appeared to become newsworthy in its own right. As Table 5.1 shows, 20% of expressions of anger in that sample had no clear target. And in the vast majority of cases, this unspecified anger was that of Trump himself:

> The 16-minute inaugural address that President Trump delivered was Trumpism distilled to its raw essence: angry, blunt-spoken and deeply aggrieved. (*Los Angeles Times*, editorial, January 20)

> Donald John Trump intends to govern as the same fiercely angry man who inspired the discontented but aroused the worries and fears of so many other Americans. (E. J. Dionne, syndicated column, January 21)

Describing anger as having a particular target both explains the anger and contributes to legitimizing it. By contrast, the unspecified anger of Trump and his supporters suggests that they are angry for no particular reason or cause. Instead, the image that emerges from the media coverage is that anger is essential to their identity and their worldview. This essentializing of anger is central to understanding the place of angry populism as the emotional regime of the Trump era. It suggests that the particular brand of exclusionary populism cultivated by Trump depends on the performance of anger as a way of dramatizing grievances. Analysts suggested that Trump appealed to voters in large part because he saw the utility of a new and angrier form of political discourse. As CNN noted in an inauguration update (January 20):

> Donald J. Trump identified, long before anyone else did, the anger and desire for change that millions of Americans craved. He addressed that in frank, blunt terms that deeply resonated with millions who were fed up with Washington's political class and felt left behind in the globalizing economy.

Through his astute reading of the Zeitgeist, Trump became an emotional performer, acting as the advocate of the people and the impersonator of their anger. His anger mattered because it became a political force in its own right. As Michael Wolff wrote in a *Hollywood Reporter* column (January 21):

> Even if it is a teleprompter speech – an unfortunate concession to liberal manners – the determination or, if you will, truculence, or golf face, angry and pissed off, is written in, or cemented, as he practices it. [...] Trump, shoulders hunched, arms swinging, brow furled, lips pursed, is the medium of his message.

The first 100 days of angry President Trump

If we look at the coverage following on from Trump's inauguration and up to the end of his first 100 days in office,[2] we see frequent references to his anger. This is particularly prominent in the period immediately following his inauguration, as well as in reflections on his first 100 days in office. Just like the inauguration, the landmark of the first 100 days in office provided an opportunity to make broader statements about the character of the new president. In a widely syndicated column, published on May 1, 2017, Jennifer Rubin argued that "President Donald Trump remains an angry, irrational figure, someone who still must stir up hatred against the press, against immigrants, against Democrats to enliven his base." The president is here constructed as fundamentally and essentially angry – though the anger is directed at particular actors.

The media coverage after the inauguration also frequently pointed to specific targets of Trump's anger, including the media, elites and attempts to block his travel ban:

> President Donald Trump is angry at all the news coverage about the people who stand to be hurt because of the Republican plan to repeal and replace the Affordable Care Act. (Creators Syndicate, March 20)

> The legal and legislative pushback has left the White House frustrated and angry. Trump slammed the court orders on his travel ban as "unprecedented judicial overreach." (*Chicago Daily Herald*, March 19)

> The US has a robust, free, and fair media. No wonder that makes Donald Trump angry. (*Eureka Times-Standard*, March 12)

Over the course of Trump's first 100 days in office, his anger was established not only as an essential feature of his character, but also a guiding force in policy decisions:

> Donald Trump's election was propelled by the wave of anti-globalization anger that is sweeping the United States and other Western advanced economies. Trump has echoed that anger in his rhetoric. And now he is responding to that anger with policy. (*Washington Post* column, February 5)

Further, Trump's anger was represented as having a contagion effect, as it spread across the population – sometimes for what was described as legitimate reasons, at other times for no reason at all:

> Before last year's presidential election, Donald Trump was
> solidly the candidate of anger. [...] Now Trump and his motley
> crew have taken over the White House and those who were
> angry before are no longer quite so. [...] Thus the mantle of
> anger has passed to the left. The Women's March and the
> protests against the immigration ban fiercely demonstrated
> the resistance Trump can expect to his blundering policies.
> (*Cornell Daily Sun*, February 27)

Other observers highlighted how Trump has driven a shift
towards generalized public anger, amongst both his supporters and his opponents. Political scientist Michael Berkman,
writing in the *Daily Cardinal* on February 13, suggested: "His
tweets show his supporters what he is thinking, directly and
unvarnished. Less well appreciated, but apparent in our
research based on new polling, is how Trump's anger and its
targets are quickly adopted and internalized by large numbers
of his followers."

The widespread emphasis on Trump's performative
anger, and his appeal to an aggrieved public through this
anger – alongside the interest in the anger of protesters and
opponents – has had significant consequences in shaping
public debate over the presidency. It suggests the salience
of angry populism, implying that anger is a viable interpretive framework for understanding political discourse and its
performance, along with the motivations of political actors.
More than that, Trump's populism works *because* of the anger
it expresses: anger is foundational to his appeal and his political project. But it also appears to be what we might call an
umbrella emotion: one which covers a wide variety of grievances and disaffections.

What is also important to note is that not all anger is created
equal. The media coverage implied that the anger of Trump's
supporters and opponents alike is caused by legitimate
grievances, and might give rise to new forms of solidarity
– embodied, for example, by the positivity of protesters. By
contrast, the anger of Trump himself is largely viewed as

opportunistic, illiberal and dangerous. As the Massachusetts *Telegram and Gazette* (January 21) reported:

> Carol Sarafconn, a member of [Jewish congregation] Agudat Achim, said the past year frightened her as she believed anger and hate took center stage and bigotry and intolerance became the norm.
>
> "It frightens me that the intuitions I treasure are criticized and scrapped," Ms. Sarafconn said. "[...] When social contracts are weakened, anti-Semitism isn't that far behind. When hate and anger become acceptable, anti-Semitism does, too."

What this implies is that Trump's populist anger is dangerous not, as political theorists might have it, because it is uncontrollable or violent, but because it fosters other negative feelings (bigotry, intolerance, hate) which are incommensurate with democracy (see also Cilizza, 2017; Ott, 2017). This, indeed, might be another reason why Trump's anger is newsworthy in and of itself: it is seen as closing down constructive debate and inviting in fascism through the back door.

Conclusion

This chapter has made the case for the importance of considering emotion as a factor in mediated politics. The chapter has proposed that we need to look at the role of anger as a mobilizing emotion in explaining the rise of Trump. It has demonstrated a shift in the "emotional regime," represented by media discourses following Trump's inauguration, comparing them to coverage of Obama's first swearing in. In particular, it has argued that media coverage suggests a shift towards an emotional regime of angry populism. The new emotional regime heralds a broader change in public discourse and the terms of public life, spurred on in part through the affordances of the hybrid media system. The regime renders anger a viable framework for interpreting political life, and suggests that its performance is essential to the brand of populism represented by Trump. Given the prominence of anger in contemporary politics, then, the chapter has sought to sketch out some of the complexities of expressions of anger. It has suggested that it is not just a tool of political opportunists like Trump. The anger of Trump supporters as well as protesters against him is given voice and represented as legitimate and pertinent.

Even if anger has long been denounced as a negative and dangerous emotion, it is also important to consider the ways in which protesters against Trump are seen to view it as positive and mobilizing. But this alone does not offer a way out of angry populism. It may be helpful to look at examples of contexts where related emotional regimes – like those of Geert Wilders in the Netherlands and Marine Le Pen in France – have been defeated by appeals to more inclusive solidarities. Such examples remind us that collective and political emotions are dynamic and ever-changing, perhaps none more so than anger.

CHAPTER SIX

The Politics of Love: Political Fandom and Social Change

The previous two chapters of this book have focused on what is perhaps the most powerful negative political emotion of all: anger. However, the attention to the complex ways in which anger is constructed in mediated politics should not blind us to the role of positive emotions in mediated contexts, as well as the complicated ways in which such emotions circulate in the hybrid media ecology (Chadwick, 2013).

This chapter takes us down this road by looking at what happens if citizens are driven by love. Scholars of emotion have studied the social construction of love and its circulation through public discourse in a variety of different contexts, ranging from the love of multiculturalism (Ahmed, 2004, Chapter 6) to narratives of love in early modern autobiographies (Jarzebowski, 2015), to mention just two examples. This chapter focuses on a very particular kind of love which is closely tied to forms of political discourse and action. It compares two recent cases of political fandom: fan discourses around former British Labour leader Ed Miliband on Twitter and US President Donald Trump on Reddit.

The chapter suggests that these fandoms articulate in diverse ways, shaped by the affordances of the media platforms on which they circulate, and the broader communities to which participants belong. Ultimately, the chapter shows that the position of the political fan creates a distinctive subjectivity that both facilitates and legitimates political engagement.

Fandom and politics

Fandom is defined by the affective attachment to a particular figure or text (Hills, 2002). This affective engagement often takes the form of love for a particular text or figures (Gray, 2007; Gray et al., 2007; Lewis, 1992), even if fans also experience conflictual and contradictory emotions around the object of their fandom (Alters, 2007; Ang, 1985; Click, 2007; Sandvoss, 2013). Fandom is discursively performed and involves the construction of individual identity and interpretive communities (e.g. Gray et al., 2007; Hills, 2002). Scholarly accounts of fandom have tended to focus on the fans of popular culture texts and figures (e.g. Hills, 2002; Sandvoss, 2013). However, in the past decade, scholars have begun to pay attention to "political engagements in popular culture" (e.g. Sandvoss, 2013, p. 253). Work has traced how fans have used their affective communities as the basis for efforts to "address civic or political issues through engagement with and strategic deployment of popular culture content" (Brough and Shrestova, 2012, Section 2.3). The Harry Potter Alliance (no date) represents one of the most prominent recent examples of such practices, calling attention to problems of social justice and human rights on the basis of fan allegiances (see also Jenkins and Shrestova, 2012, Section 1.8). Similarly, the pop star Lady Gaga has served as a powerful activist for human rights and equality because she "appears to reach those who have never participated in the philanthropy/activism realm before, with many making their first powerful connections with political figures and witnessing the change they can make as citizens" (Bennett, 2014, p. 138). These examples suggest that practices of fandom – even if often dismissed as marginal, pathological or deviant (Dayan, 2001; Jensen, 1992) – may have strong connections to forms of political action.

Attention to such practices takes place against the backdrop of the recognition of an increasingly close relationship between politics and popular culture (e.g. Jones, 2005, 2010; van Zoonen, 2005; see also Chapter 1 in this book). This has entailed the emergence of the celebrity politician, or a politician who becomes a celebrity in their own right (Cardo, 2014; Corner and Pels, 2003; Street, 2003; Wood et al., 2016). Recently, political leaders such as Barack Obama and Justin Trudeau have gained global recognition. Following on from the end of his presidency in January 2017, Obama retains the position in the top three of most-followed Twitter accounts in the world, trailing Katy Perry and Justin Bieber, just ahead of Taylor Swift and Rihanna, and is viewed as a global political celebrity (Kellner, 2010; Sandvoss, 2012).

At the same time, we have seen the increasing involvement of popular culture figures in forms of mainstream politics, as well as activism. Since Hollywood B-movie actor Ronald Reagan was first elected to governor of California in the late 1970s and then President of the United States in the 1980s, the world has seen a slew of celebrities entering electoral politics. For example, the Pakistani cricket star Imran Khan launched a successful career in opposition politics in the 1990s by starting the Tehreek-e-Insaf party, organized around an anti-corruption platform, and he was elected prime minister in 2018 (Soldani, 2016). In India, Bollywood star Jaya Bachchan was elected to Parliament in 2004, and gained widespread public support following her condemnation of the 2012 Delhi gang rape (Soldani, 2016; see also Chapter 3). Midnight Oil lead singer Peter Garrett served as Australian Labour MP for almost a decade, while actress Glenda Jackson served as an MP in the UK for 23 years. Perhaps needless to say, the most prominent recent example is that of Reality TV Star Donald Trump winning the election as President of the United States in 2016.

With this increasingly close relationship between politics and popular culture comes a shift in the understanding of citizens. As discussed in previous chapters, this book is premised on the assumption that political engagement is motivated by both passion and rational decision-making. This assumption is shared by scholars of fan studies, who have turned to take seriously the political energies of fandom, as well as the practices of political fans. These scholars have observed that the subject position of the fan shares key features with that of the citizen – including forms of emotional engagement. For example, Henry Jenkins has argued that activists "generate the same levels of emotional energy challenging the current Powers That Be in Washington that fans routinely direct against the current Powers That Be in Hollywood" (2006, p. 245), while Cornel Sandvoss has proposed that both citizens and fans engage in "regular, emotionally involved consumption of a given narrative or text" (2005, p. 8). For Liesbet van Zoonen, key shared features between the subject position of the fan and the citizen suggest that we may benefit from drawing on the mechanisms of fandom to rethink engagement with politics:

> The behavior of fans in relation to soaps, popular music, and other entertainment genres is not fundamentally different from what is required of citizens. Fans and citizens [...] come about as the result of performance: of artists on the one hand, and of politicians on the other. (2005, p. 16)

Despite the widespread recognition of this kinship, there have been only a small number of studies of political fandom (e.g. Gray, 2007; Sandvoss, 2012, 2013). These studies have highlighted the role of political fandoms in establishing forms of engagement and trust, and facilitating more active forms of participation in the context of emerging digital platforms.

This chapter builds on that emerging body of work by investigating two very different recent examples of political fandoms: the Milifandom movement around former UK Labour leader Ed Miliband as it circulated on Twitter; and those posting about their love for Donald Trump on Reddit. As such, it starts from an interest in individuals and groups deliberately declaring love as the affective basis of their attachment to a political figure. The chapter explores what it means for politics when fans declare their love for a politician: What forms of political expression, action and community does it make possible? How does it construct the subjectivities of participants? In short, what does it mean to love a politician?

There is no straightforward answer to this question. The position of the political fan borrows from the conventions both of particular fan cultures – as in the case of the Milifandom – and of subcultures formed by political affinities – as in the case of the Trump lovers. Further, the forms of expression and engagement are shaped by the affordances of the respective platforms inhabited by the fandoms. While the affordances of Twitter facilitate virality, playfulness and irony, those of Reddit facilitate community affirmation and consolidation.

Milifandom and the energization of young voters

When the UK Labour leader Ed Miliband became the object of an adoring teenage girl fandom in the run-up to the 2015 general election, it was probably the last thing that any pundits, observers and fellow politicians would have expected. Ever since Miliband had won the Labour leadership contest against his charismatic older brother David in September 2015, he had suffered negative media coverage, stuck with the moniker "Odd Ed" (Gaber, 2014) and ridiculed for everything from his robotic delivery to his inability to elegantly consume a bacon sandwich (Broersma, 2015). He was widely seen as uncomfortable in the spotlight and compared unfavorably to his opponent, the slick and media-savvy Conservative prime minister, David Cameron (Langer, 2011).

It was therefore a surprise to everyone – including the Labour Party and Miliband himself – when the Labour leader became the subject of fan adoration. Miliband's sudden rise to fan prominence made headlines and gave the Labour Party a boost in the polls. Indeed, as Matt Hills pointed out:

> It is this still-powerful discursive separation of "fans" and "citizens" that made Milifandom newsworthy. Here was something that seemed to violate deeply held cultural categories. "Fan likes Ed" was a variant on "man bites dog", a quirky story that could break up the monotony of predictable, professionalized media-controlling spin, and a locked-down election campaign. (2015, p. 89)

The emergence of Miliband as a fan object was not the result of concerted spin or party campaigning. Instead, it was the result of a grassroots initiative from a group of young women. The 17-year-old Abby Tomlinson initiated the #milifandom hashtag to start a movement against the negative media portrayal of Miliband in April 2015. In an interview with the *Guardian*, Abby explained her motivations as follows:

> Ed Miliband is often presented quite badly in the media [...] I think that's really unfair, because no one actually looks at his policies. They just look at a picture of him eating a bacon sandwich and think, "I don't want that guy." I want to change that. (Weaver 2015)

What is interesting about Tomlinson's motivation is its insistence on engagement with the substance of policy, while retaining its grounding in tropes of fandom (Hills, 2015; Sandvoss, 2015). This duality was reflected in the "affective news streams" emerging around the hashtag (Papacharissi, 2015). #Milifandom quickly trended on Twitter, as thousands of people (mostly young women) shared their admiration and desire for the Labour leader. Drawing on fan culture practices of play and affectivity, they posted photoshopped images of Miliband as James Bond, Harry Potter and David Beckham.

While the Milifandom was heavily premised on such visual memes, posters also verbalized their affective attachments to the Labour leader. One member of the Milifandom, Aisha, wrote: "i love ed miliband so much it is painful." Another,

identified as Chloe, asked: "why is ed miliband slowly turning into the love of my life," while a third Milifan mused on
how she had "a strong unexplainable emotional connection
to a 45 year old politician." Members of the Milifandom also
expressed desire, using language borrowed from vocabularies
of fandom. For example, Mel wrote: "I've sent a screenshot of
an Ed Miliband life size cutout (available on Amazon!) to at
least three people tonight, hinting, desiring, wanting." Ellie,
in a post that was widely retweeted and cited in media reports
on the Milifandom, exemplified the playful fan practices that
straddled irony and adoration (Sandvoss, 2015). As she wrote,
"this all started out as a joke but now i think i legitimately
fancy ed Miliband." Ellie's post is particularly interesting
because it highlights what Sandvoss (2015) has described as
the neutrosomy of texts associated with political fandom:

> In voting, as elsewhere in the consumption of popular cul-
> ture, we are asked to make choices; choices which we make
> through a mixture of consideration and affect. Such affect, in
> turn, is rooted in the appropriation of texts and on fans' abil-
> ity to make a given text their own, to rework it into a space
> of immense textual significance, a transitional object, or a
> space of self-reflection. The more polysemic given texts, the
> greater the number of fans with varying appropriative needs
> – i.e. backgrounds, experiences and beliefs – it can attract.

For Sandvoss, textual formations can be so polysemic that
they turn "neutrosomic" – empty of any meaning in and of
themselves. This is just what happened to Miliband in the
hands of his fandom: he was "textually poached" (Jenkins,
2012), remixed and recirculated freed of conventional contexts, opening up new spaces for reflection and engagement.
Through his neutrosomy, members of the Milifandom were
able to invest their own meaning in their object of adoration.
And while the playful, ironic and creative acts of photoshop-
ping Miliband's head onto the bodies of iconic popular culture
images may have "started out as a joke," they gained their own
momentum precisely because these activities served as a way

of energizing audiences that may not otherwise have been enthused by politics. This was demonstrated as members of the group tweeted not just about Miliband's desirability, but also about his policies. Abby Tomlinson implored voters to support Labour by tweeting: "You've seen the trend #milifandom. Now #VoteLabour *http://www.labour.org.uk/manifesto.*" Other members of the group highlighted particular party program positions, as Lia tweeted: "Labour are apparently prioritising mental health so I'll probably vote for them so the funding goes up and I get my help! #milifandom," and Jemima Rose took note of Labour's anti-austerity stand: "am happy to become a fan so long as he upholds his promises, does not cut our services as austerity will never clear deficit #milifandom" (cited in Sanghani, 2015).

The Milifandom phenomenon also gained purchase outside of the world of social media, with media observers widely seeing the phenomenon as a harbinger of youth political engagement. As Chris York (2015) put it in the *Huffington Post*, a "simple hashtag has done what every spin doctor has tried and generally failed to do for years – engage young people in politics."

More than anything, the Milifandom phenomenon shows us that the tools of fan cultures – including the social sharing of your feelings and thoughts about and images of the object of your infatuation – can be a highly effective instrument in political life as well.

Even if fans were assumed to be irrational, emotional and overwrought, the attachment to Miliband was both emotional – based on his alleged "hotness" – *and* rational – based on the group's conviction about the merits of Labour's policies. The Milifandom moment arose out of a particular historical moment, and served as an important precursor to the subsequent surprise electoral showing of the Labour leader who followed him, Jeremy Corbyn (as discussed in more detail in Chapter 3), widely ascribed to the energization of young voters through social media. The Milifandom drew on the affordances of Twitter in two main ways. Most fundamentally, it relied on the ability of the hashtag to organize discussions amongst like-minded individuals. In doing so, it facilitated the creation of an affectively based hybrid counterpublic (as discussed in Chapter 3) that both formed a distinctive political community and reached out to broader audiences for political change. Secondly, given the visual display affordances of Twitter – the ability to share images and videos – the hashtag also facilitated a virality premised on both the political and the affective. As Rosie put it, "So turns out people stop taking your political views seriously if your selfies with a jokey caption are in a buzzfeed article, thanks" (cited in Sanghani, 2015). As such, the Milifandom relied on the paradoxical political impact of their joking appropriation of fan culture. For Matt Hills, such examples drove home the point that "fan-citizens can perform their identities and their 'affective intelligence' via social media in ways that have left the old(er) guard uncertain whether to interpret all this as ironic, earnest, or semi-ironic" (2015, p. 89).

The emergence of the "Corbynistas" as a movement rallying around the leadership of the unconventional Labour leader relied in large part on a narrative established by the Milifandom: the idea that unconventional and unpolished politicians may be both easier to relate to and more trustworthy than their slicker counterparts. Such a political persona may construct them as both "one of the people" and capable of understanding the concerns of ordinary voters – characteristics vital to emerging notions of authenticity (Coleman and Firmstone, 2017). Informed by the fan practices of the Milifandom, Corbyn supporters created ironic viral memes which styled the Labour leader as a fashion icon and a hero of the grime music scene, to mention just two examples (Parkinson, 2017).

Trump fans on Reddit and the creation of political community

By contrast to the Milifandom movement, which was predicated on using the languages and practices of fan cultures through the affordances of Twitter, fans of Donald Trump did not converge on just one platform, but rather used a variety of sites. This made it more difficult to isolate a particular site to examine for evidence of the practices of Trump fans. There were multiple hashtags used by his supporters and the alt-right movement associated with his rise (e.g. Milner and Philips, 2016). His campaign and its supporters were active across social media sites. For example, empirical evidence indicates that Trump was the clear winner of the Twitter campaign, as tweets from him and his supporters were far more likely to go viral than those in support of Hillary Clinton (Rossman, 2017). Trump has several Facebook-based fan clubs with large numbers of members, although these are organized around the posts of the site owners, and therefore offer little space for discussion by self-identified fans. However, Trump supporters also used a wide variety of news sites, as well as dedicated online forums and discussion sites. Here, Reddit was chosen to locate individuals explicitly identifying as Trump fans. Reddit is a large and swiftly growing online community which hosts a range of discussion forums, or "subreddits" (Singer et al., 2014). Although it has been historically credited as a radically "open" site which billed itself as the "Front Page of the Internet" and exercises little editorial control and censorship (Miller, 2015), research has also suggested that it is an "increasingly self-referential community that focuses on and reinforces its own user-generated image- and textual content over external sources" (Singer et al., 2014, p. 517). It has proven to be particularly hospitable to the alt-right movement and supporters of Donald Trump, especially through its subreddit, r/The_Donald, which is one of the most active communities on the site (e.g. Lagorio-

Chafkin, 2016; Wray, 2017). Chris Miller explains the structure of Reddit as follows:

> The basic elements of reddit can be quickly explained to any digitally literate individual today: registered site members submit content, either in the form of text hosted by reddit or a link to externally hosted content (images, videos, articles, etc.), which is then voted on by the user community. Submissions that receive the most votes move to the top of the "front page," the home page of reddit that all users (members and non-member "lurkers") first see. (2015, p. 2)

Because of Reddit's ranking algorithm, through which popular posts and comments are recognized by prominent placement, particular practices and forms of expression are structurally bolstered, and may strengthen community cohesion and insularity (see also Chapter 7). Given the fact that the site has been widely used by the alt-right community, its affordances have given this community a chance to develop a distinctive language and set of cultural practices. These include its use of language such as "Cuck" for emasculated opponents (derived from cuckold), "Snowflake" for entitled individuals, "shitposting" for the alt-right's oppositional social media activities, "God Emperor" for Trump and "centipedes" for Reddit Trump supporters, to mention just a few examples (e.g. Roy, 2016a, 2016b).

To locate self-identified fans of Trump, I searched the r/The_Donald subreddit for posts on the topic of "I love Donald Trump," and selected the most relevant of these. Two top-ranked posts mentioned love of Donald Trump, and were highly ranked by the Reddit community. The one which received the most comments (338) was titled "Why we love Donald: because he is really just a regular Joe!" Submitted on December 26, 2016, by birdlady4trump, the post title was accompanied by an image of Donald Trump about to eat a taco bowl, which was originally posted on Twitter by Trump himself. This image had also circulated widely in mainstream media, as well as on other social media sites.

The post featured several types of responses. First of all, many posters commented on the appealing taco bowl, posting "dat tacobowl" (osoo), "damn, now I want a taco bowl" (6-PackorWine) and "My wife and I went to NYC and stopped in Trump tower to get a Taco Bowl as a joke. Turned out to be one of the tastiest things I've ever had" (oumad). Secondly, the post occasioned a number of policy-related comments around Trump's and Clinton's respective attempts at appealing to the Hispanic community, as well as Trump's campaign promise to build a wall with Mexico. For example, one poster commented, "I like the rolls of construction plans in the corner. Build the wall!" (bleh19799791). Others analyzed the taco bowl image as a clever strategy for appealing to Hispanic voters and dispelling views of Trump as racist:

> Love this tweet so much. You know Trump did it on purpose knowing he would trigger a bunch of lefties for simply eating a taco bowl and saying he loved Hispanics.
> The best part is that fucking grin. He knows exactly what he's doing. (Qa2)

Many of these participants juxtaposed Trump's taco bowl image with Hillary Clinton's attempts at "pandering" to Hispanic voters by hiring a Mariachi band for a rally or professing to carry around hot sauce:

> That tweet was just fucking hysterical. Like, when Hillary wants to pander she goes "I keep hot sauce in my purse!" Trump buys a fucking taco bowl and says "I love Hispanics!". Could not get any more direct lmao [laughing my ass off]. (Pickel_Weasel)

A small number of contributors posted comments critical of Trump. For example, one such reply challenged the assumption of the original post, countering that Trump is "an average joe worth 10 billion and lives in a golden penthouse in his own skyscraper" (cynicsrising). This post was met with a number of replies, which played on the irony of the billionaire-as-average-Joe, constructing it as a sign of the strength and appeal of Trump. At the same time, they compared Trump's extraordinary ordinariness and his ability to connect with citizens to Clinton's awkward and manufactured interactive style:

> We have the best average Joes don't we folks? (oneUnitUSA)

> **WE LOVE OUR BILLIONAIRE AVERAGE JOE!** (wow_man MAGA)

> We have the best average joe billionaires don't we folks? (PurplePoloPlayerKEK)

> a man who literally lives in a giant tower with his name in gold-printed letters was able to connect to the former middle-class better than Hillary "my dad was a small business" Clinton

> L M F A O
> M
> F
> A
> O [Laughing my fucking ass off] (oneUnitUSA)

These responses were reflective of the sentiment pervading most of the comments: while they recognized Trump's extraordinary status as a billionaire businessman who exemplified the fulfillment of the American Dream, they reinforced the original poster's sentiments by stating their affective engagement with Trump on the basis of his ordinariness and his ability to connect with ordinary Americans. This, in turn, tied into a "deep story" circulating amongst Trump supporters, based on their emotional reading of political life. This "deep story" is, among other things, premised on an individualist belief in progress and prosperity through hard work, a feeling of betrayal by elites and political classes who are seen to have "jumped the line" to advance their own fortunes, and who, in turn, vilify and ridicule the poorly educated, Christian, conservative and rural populations who went for Trump in large numbers (Hochschild, 2016):

A regular Joe, who worked his ass off without excuses to create 8 billion dollars in wealth, thousands of jobs, and became President of the United States. Quite the role model if you ask me. (Lad_Status_Wewd)

He really is probably as close as you can get to someone who is on the average level and capable of being President.

He doesn't hold that elitist mentality that they all have. even the ones who claim they don't. looking at fuckboy Bernie [Sanders]. (ItsLightMan)

The theme of ordinariness, is, as discussed in Chapter 3, central to the performance of politicians' authenticity. At the same time, as Chapter 5 suggests, for Trump's supporters, his appeal is strongly tied to the perception that he constitutes an authentic anti-establishment voice, speaking up for "The People." This should also be understood in the context of the demographics of Trump voters, who tend to be older, less educated, male and overwhelmingly rural, and therefore identify strongly with the outsider narrative of Trump (Cramer, 2016; Gould and Harrington, 2016; Hochschild, 2016). The anger of Trump and his supporters is premised on creating a community against the elitism of the mainstream political establishment. Indeed, several comments on the post were explicitly directed at reinforcing the community of Trump fans. One, for example, likened it to a family:

God, remember when THIS caused "outrage" in the msm [mainstream media]? Got THEIR asses! Merry Christmas centipedes, it's been a wonderful year shi[t]posting with all of you, and we get 8 more years to grow closer as a family! (steveryans2CA)

The analysis of this post highlights, first of all, that the r/ The_Donald community engage in numerous practices that characterize fan communities, including the Milifandom: Through shared affective connections to the object of their fandom, they actively maintain a community characterized not just by common ideological commitments, but also by collaboratively created forms of language, jokes and images. The post highlights the dynamic interactions between ongoing political events and the discourse of fan communities, as community members used the post not just as an opportunity to declare their love for Trump, but also to articulate – often in ironic and playful ways – their commitment to his policy agenda and their opposition to Clinton ("$hilary,"), as well as "leftists," "Obama" and "fucking phony motherfuckers," to mention just a few named targets. This, in turn, meant that the positive emotional expression in support of Trump was frequently accompanied by negative and exclusionary discourses aimed at his opponents. The expression of love, then, clearly does not operate in discursive isolation, but may instead be central to the formation of exclusionary identities and communities.

The other top post dedicated to declaring love for Trump was based on more abstract ideological observations, rather than tied to a particular political event, and attracted 39 comments. The original poster, Steady Dividents, posted in October 2016, just before the election:

> Why I love Donald J. Trump: he identifies as an AMERICAN not a Republican or Democrat. He tells us what we NEED to hear NOT what we want to hear. He's taking the most criticism out of anyone in History, but HE LOVES US MORE.

The post was headlined with an image of Trump waving.

This post invited a range of comments and replies in which community members reflected in more general terms on their allegiance to Trump, often justified in terms of features which exemplified his selflessness and courage in the face of the elitist establishment:

> Publicly speaking uncomfortable truths Spending your own fortune Withstanding the constant barrage of a biased and adversarial media Having attempts made on his life Having his name dragged through the mud
>
> And people say he does it just for his own ego – classic leftist projection.

> Thank you, President Trump, for putting your life and reputation on the line on behalf of the American people! (MrRobotVSTheWorldVA)

For other commenters on the post, their love for Trump was justified through his image as a father figure and family man – a common theme in discourses on presidential masculinity (e.g. Khan and Blair, 2013). As feminist scholars have argued, in patriarchal societies, candidates must affirm their hegemonic masculinity by establishing themselves as good fathers and husbands, with these subject positions serving as metaphors for the role of head of state (Khan and Blair, 2013). For some posters, idealized representations of Trump's fatherhood served to cement their general view of his character, while for others, it was linked to his perceived genuineness and ability to lead the nation:

> He's a good dad, the kind everyone should have. Only the good dads tell you what you need to hear rather than what you want to hear. No wonder he has such great kids. (lurking4trumpUSA)

> I have gone from hating the man to a loyal centipede in less than a year. Donald Trump seems to be a genuine person who cares about his family and his country.
> I swore I would never vote again after 2012, but Mr. Trump has changed my mind. Libertarians for Trump!
> MAGA [Make America Great Again]! (PrangleDrangle)

The Reddit members commenting on this post justified their affective commitment to Trump with references to broadly circulating discourses on Trump in particular and political leaders more generally. That is to say, although the r/ The_Donald subreddit shows evidence of insularity in its distinctive language and practices of community affirmation, as well as in its consistent identification of particular ideological opponents, it also speaks to wider cultural values and assumptions associated with national identity. The affordances and culture of Reddit appear to have advanced this insularity, but do not foreclose contestation and engagement with events, languages and communities outside the site.

Conclusion

If "fandom is an aspect of how we make sense of the world, in relation to mass media, and in relations to our historical, social, cultural location" (Jensen, 1992, p. 27), the examples of the Milifandom movement and Trump lovers dramatize the differential locations of members of these respective fan communities, and the consequences of the affordances on the platforms where they circulate. The Milifandom movement rose to prominence through the circulation of photoshopped images of Miliband which went viral and helped to spread substantive political messages, helped by the visuality and shareability of Twitter posts. By contrast, the affordances and culture of Reddit facilitated the creation of a shared language and the affirmation of community. Even if both communities engaged in fan practices by articulating their affective commitment to the object of their fandom, their discussions were also shaped by ongoing political events and developments. They were oriented not just towards the affirmation of fan identities, but also towards social and political change.

Although both communities were motivated by love, this positive emotion was put to very different uses in the two contexts. For the Milifandom, it served as a way of ironically subverting dominant constructions of Ed Miliband, and was more or less uniformly associated with other positive forms of emotional expression, including desire and political interest. For the Reddit r/The_Donald posters, their love of Trump served to mark their allegiance to a community which was, in line with the tenets of angry populism discussed in Chapter 5, often defined in opposition to particular enemy "Others." This meant, in turn, that Trump's fans combined the expression of the positive emotion of love with the denunciation of enemies, with Hillary Clinton the most frequent target. In the case of the Trump fans, love articulated with anger and hate in complex ways to facilitate the formation of exclusionary identities.

If the communities created by particular platforms are in part shaped by technological affordances, it is also important to consider the ways in which such affordances are grounded in what we will describe as an "emotional architecture" – a set of deliberate design decisions intended to direct the emotional tenor of interaction. The next chapter turns to examining exactly this issue by examining the emotional architecture of Facebook, taking a particular interest in the reactions emoji.

CHAPTER SEVEN

The Emotional Architecture of Social Media

This chapter builds on the investigation of the relationship between platform design and affordances and emotional expression by tracing the political consequences of the emotional architecture of social media. As with the architecture of other public spaces, design decisions around the affordances of social media are sometimes *intended* to structure forms of expression, whereas in other cases, the consequences of decisions are coincidental and unexpected by-products. Increasingly, a great deal of thought goes into tailoring emotional architectures towards more positive and pro-social forms of expression – in part as a result of the greater potential to monetize positivity and commodify users' emotional labor. On this basis, the chapter detects a dynamic and ongoing negotiation of the emotional affordances of social media which is vital to our formation of networked identities. It considers the case of Facebook's reactions emoji, which exemplifies the ways in which the emotional architecture of social media contributes to the shaping of public debate.

The idea animating this chapter is that the design of public spaces – and the forms of emotional interaction enabled within them – has a concrete impact on the conditions for public debate. Architects, urban planners and philosophers are among those who have argued that the design of space shapes the public life of communities in the way that, for example, the presence of playgrounds and green urban spaces allows for children to play outside and adults to meet and interact; while the monumental buildings and sweeping avenues of Fascist states signal the authority of absolute power. The social dynamics of public space enable particular social, political and cultural formations and forms of agency while discouraging others (Harvey, 2000). For example, Kevin DeLuca (2011) has written about the "architecture of oppression." Analyzing the experience of the Occupy movement, he suggested that with "private shopping malls having replaced public squares and restrictive laws governing the remaining public places, the people's right to assemble has been dramatically diminished" (DeLuca, 2011). David Brain is one of several scholars calling for engagement with processes of architectural production on the basis of their consequences for public life, arguing that "the discipline of design has also played a key role in constructing the symbolic vocabularies and representational practices which shape the experience and interpretation of meaning in the built environment" (1997, p. 240).

In the same way, information architecture, or the architecture of information systems, including virtual environments, has wide-ranging consequences (whether intentional or not) for the types of public interaction and participation possible (e.g. Raboy, 1997). Often, this is referred to as an "information infrastructure."[1] Other metaphors for the interactions between the structuring of space and place and emotional responses call to mind the natural environment. They emphasize complex interactions between the architectures, social visions and sometimes haphazard decisions that shape the spaces we inhabit. Here, I prefer the term "architecture" because of the connotations of the deliberate design of public space with the intent of encouraging certain kinds of interaction and discouraging others.

All spaces for mediated public participation have particular emotional architectures. For example, the letters to the editor section, one of the most long-lived participatory formats within conventional media, has been characterized by an emphasis on relatively formal contributions written in the language of rationality (e.g. Wahl-Jorgensen, 2007). Newspapers have sought to construct letters sections as a civic and civil public space in which participants are radically accountable for their statements owing to the very publicness of their contributions. Contributions which do not conform to norms of civility, rationality and other key deliberative ideals are excluded from publication by the gatekeepers, who make constant decisions which are, among other things, designed to sanitize and improve the neighborhood of public discourse (Wahl-Jorgensen, 2007).

This chapter views emotional architecture as a key factor in shaping engagement with and participation through social media, looking more closely at Facebook. While social media vary in their functionality and focus (Kaplan and Haenlein, 2010), they emphasize an "injunction to share" material, views and information – personal, social and political – with others in the network (Hermida, 2014; van Dijck, 2013). In the United States, upwards of 80% of the population use social media (Statista, 2017b), while in the United Kingdom, 59% of the population do so (Think Digital First, 2018). Globally, social media sites account for the majority of time spent online, with a penetration of 37% in 2017 (Kemp, 2017). In this chapter, much of the attention focuses on the emotional architecture of Facebook as the social media site which is most prominent as a news source, and also the one which has most successfully monetized its activities through the careful architectural policing of emotional expression. As of February 2017, Facebook had close to 2 billion users on a global basis (Fiegerman, 2017), with 214 million users in the United States alone (Statista, 2017a). Close to half of people in the United States use Facebook to access news, and for the vast majority of these audiences, the social media platform is their most important news source (Lichterman, 2016). Industry analysts believe that the site is only increasing its emphasis on news (Read, 2016). What this means is that Facebook now needs to be taken seriously as a major news organization which is shaping our shared conversations – as well as the knowledge we bring to these conversations. The architecture underpinning these conversations – whether visible, through reactions emoji and other affordances, or invisible, through algorithmic curation – is shaped by an explicit concern for managing the emotions of users in a positive and pro-social direction.

I am not alone in taking an interest in how the architecture of social media shapes public debate and interaction. Ian Goodwin and his colleagues (2016) have argued that Facebook's architecture promotes particular forms of sharing behavior online, compelling young people to enact a "precarious popularity" through the sharing of images of social alcohol consumption. For Goodwin et al., "[T]his expanded imperative to share is a governing dimension of Facebook's overall architecture." Similarly, Zizi Papacharissi has researched what she refers to as the virtual geographies of social media, specifying an interest in "the underlying structure or architecture of these sites, on the premise that it may set the tone for particular types of interaction" (2009, p. 199). For her, the architecture of social media "is defined as composite result of structure, design and organization" (2009, p. 205). It does not overdetermine behavior online, but rather creates particular parameters for interaction which can then be modified, challenged or resisted by users. As Papacharissi cautions:

> [O]nline social networks simultaneously suggest genres of behavior through their architectural elements and submit the same architectural elements to the behavioral idioms of their users, who customize them to connect better their offline and online interactions. So, while the architecture of social networking sites is suggestive, it does not have to be inherently limiting, depending of course on the culture and orientation of the online social network. (2009, p. 203)

This observation provides a useful reminder of the interaction between human agency and technological architecture. The range of expression is not overdetermined by the affordances of the emotional architecture, but particular forms might be structurally encouraged. Here, it is worth acknowledging that social media architectures are not narrowly *emotional* but also have a series of other, often closely related consequences, including political, economic and social ones. Decisions about whether to enable advertising on a site, whether to allow comments and whether such comments may be anonymous all contribute to shaping the types of interaction encouraged in the virtual environment.

The increasing ubiquity of social media, the ease of participation and the varying degrees of publicness and political action associated with them raise important questions about the changing nature of public participation in the networked age. In today's "media life" (Deuze, 2012), where we do not merely *consume* media, but increasingly live our lives *through* the media – and social media in particular – the complexity of emotional management regimes online increasingly mirrors that of those prevailing in the offline world. However, social media are far more ontologically complicated than conventional media. Social media challenge conventional divides between the private and the public, the individual and the collective, and the personal and political.

Social media are heavily predicated on deliberate identity construction and self-branding (e.g. Marwick, 2013; Seargent and Tagg, 2014; Thumim, 2012). In the era of the networked self, moreover, "to be authentic to yourself, one must first be authentic to others" (Banet-Weiser, 2012, p. 80). The presentation of a desirable self is a key preoccupation of social media participants (Kaplan and Haenlain, 2010). This self-presentation takes place through "public displays of connection," which "serve as important identity signals that help people navigate the networked social world, in that an extended network may serve to validate identity information presented in profiles" (boyd and Ellison, 2007, p. 219). This, in turn, means that emotional architectures of social media – ranging from our emotional reactions to news from our private and public life, to our performative alignment with particular causes – are central in facilitating the identity construction of networked selves.

Unlike "old" or "conventional" media, social media are frequently discussed in terms of emotion – both positively and negatively. They represent an emerging set of venues in which the elicitation of emotional expression and reaction is explicitly discussed and encouraged by information architects and others involved in crafting their discursive parameters. And these architectural decisions have a profound impact on the potential for political discussion and action.

The emotional life of the virtual world

In the early days of the internet, there was substantial optimism about, and emotional investment in, the potential of the virtual world to bring about democratized forms of public participation. A generation of "cyberoptimists" proclaimed the possibilities that new "virtual communities" could generate "electronic agora" enabling new and liberating forms of participation (e.g. Rheingold, 1993). Early enthusiasts celebrated the creation of a *community* of like-minded individuals – connecting on issues ranging from parenting, health, politics and gaming through a fairly basic information architecture facilitating the formation of groups exchanging text-based information – in deliberately emotional terms, contrasting their own strong attachment to the coldness and inhumanity usually associated with computers. As Howard Rheingold wrote:

> The idea of a community accessible only via my computer screen sounded cold to me at first, but I learned quickly that people can feel passionately about e-mail and computer conferences. I've become one of them. I care about these people I met through my computer, and I care deeply about the future of the medium that enables us to assemble. I'm not alone in this emotional attachment to an apparently bloodless technological ritual. (1993, p. 2)

Rheingold's position captures the emotional tenor associated with the excitement over the democratizing potential of networked modes of participation and forms of community available online, invoking "passion" and "care" – deeply embodied emotions that contrast with the understanding of interactions with "cold" and "bloodless" machines. It also represented an early articulation of what many now take for granted: that the machines, cold, bloodless, inorganic and dispassionate though they may be, are tools for connecting us with distant others in the virtual world for whom we can care as deeply and intimately as for those in our immediate physical surroundings.

However, as empirical research began to demonstrate the limitations of the online environment, scholars became more pessimistic about the liberating and empowering potential of the virtual world. An alternative set of arguments emerged, rejecting early cyberoptimist perspectives. The critiques suggested that new media technologies, rather than inevitably bringing about democratic and social utopia, might instead be subject to the same problems that characterize "real-world" encounters, and that these problems might, in fact, be exacerbated by the emotional architecture of the online world.

The anonymous and disembodied nature of interactions online – enabled by the minimally restrictive and "open" architecture of early forums for public participation – appeared to allow participants to dispense with behavioral norms of civility and respect, and engage in uncivil behavior through verbal aggression, hostility and attacks. Observers were particularly interested in investigating anti-social behaviors associated with the expression of negative affect. Drawing on the term "flaming," or "the hostile expression of strong emotions and feelings," scholarly and popular discussions expressed concern about the discursive environments generated by the emotional disinhibition and lack of social control of the online world. Early internet scholars thus observed that participants, unmoored from the strictures of social convention, were swearing, name-calling, attacking and just being plain rude to others whose views they found offensive (Lea et al., 1992).

If anything, these preoccupations have only increased with the emergence of social media, particularly in the light of high-profile examples of online hate speech, such as the #gamergate incident, which entailed the harassment of women working in the video game industry (Shepherd et al., 2015). This has further intensified in the increasingly polarized political climate following on from the rise of Donald Trump in the United States, and closely related forms of populism in other countries around the world (Karpf, 2017).

Flaming and trolling have been broadly viewed as destructive and anti-social affective behaviors – and are often punished with exclusion and social sanction by virtual communities. They are seen as detrimental to the communities in which they occur because they constitute deliberate attempts at disrupting communicative norms which ensure pro-social behavior (e.g. Bishop, 2014; Gurău, 2013).

The preoccupation with bad emotional behavior online is not merely reflected in scholarly debates, but also reverberates in contemporary popular discourse. If anything, the narrative of the online world as a "bad neighborhood" of public participation – an irrational environment dominated by negative affect – is well entrenched. Underpinning popular and media interest is the assumption that such behavior is on the rise. The past few decades have seen growing attention to problems of cyberbullying, especially amongst young people (e.g. Snakenborg et al., 2011). In the United Kingdom, for example, the Crown Prosecution Service issued new legal advice in 2016 on the prosecution of cyberbully cases, including the proliferating use of fake profiles for harassment (Osborne, 2016), and by 2017, police had stepped in to intervene in nearly 6,300 cyberbullying cases in one year, following more than 19,000 reports (Cole, 2017). In the United States, research has found that more than a quarter of middle and high school students experienced cyberbullying between 2007 and 2016, with figures rising to over a third since 2014.[2] Melania Trump made cyberbullying her key cause as First

Lady during the presidential campaign, even if there has subsequently been little evidence of her plans coming to fruition (Puente, 2017). Concerns about the closely related practice of hate speech online have also increased, with new legislative frameworks emerging across the world (Banks, 2010).

The commodification of emotional labor: encouraging positive and pro-social expression

As a result of such concerns about the detrimental consequences of anti-social affective expression online, issues around the expression of emotion have been central to the generation of social media architectures. At stake here is the attempt at understanding how the complex motivations and behaviors of individuals map onto the discursive opportunities and restraints constructed in networked environments. The philosopher Michael Walzer (1986) coined the term "open-minded" public spaces to describe areas designed for multiple and sometimes unforeseen purposes, and in which users "are prepared to tolerate the broad utility of the space" (Fernback, 1994, p. 38). He contrasted these to single-minded public spaces, designed for distinctive purposes and therefore less likely to encourage diverse uses. Early environments for online interaction were characterized by open-mindedness, and came with both dangers and opportunities for particular affectively charged interactions. As Jan Fernback observed:

> Cyberspace has this "open-minded" quality; users of all stripes flock here, with only the rules of social propriety and "netiquette" to guide them, and engage with one another. Flaming and virtual harassment in cyberspace, like the Spanish Inquisition's *auto-da-fé* ceremony of public torture, illustrate the dark character of CMC's [i.e. computer-mediated communication's] public arena, but this darkness is often the price exacted for the tolerance required to realize and maintain truly open-minded public space. (1994, p. 38)

The vocabulary of open-mindedness versus single-mindedness is problematic in several respects. It gives agency to technologies of space by granting them a mind of their own, and generates a dichotomous opposition between open-mindedness and single-mindedness. Further, in Fernback's reading, it implies a necessary trade-off between enabling the expression of negative affect and creating the conditions for open discussion and tolerance. At the same time, the distinction is helpful in calling attention to the architecture of virtual worlds, and the ways in which it shapes behavior in public spaces.

Here, I will suggest that even as popular discourses have focused on the expression and elicitation of *negative* emotion online, decisions around the emotional architecture of social media are made to ensure the preponderance of *positive* and *pro-social* emotions, and that this development has palpable consequences for the types of public debate made possible. In an environment where there is increasing pressure for users to express positive emotions, the space for conflict, contestation and argument is structurally limited.

The historian of emotion William Reddy (2001) proposed that our expression of emotion may be "overlearned" insofar as we learn to channel our emotional reactions into socially acceptable forms through socialization. Sociologist Arlie Hochschild (1983), in her study of airline stewardesses, developed the concept of "emotional labor" to describe the ongoing work that we engage in to maintain relationships (see also Chapter 2). Emotional labor entails the "handling of other people's feelings and our own" (Hochschild, 1983; see also Baym, 2015[3]). Social media both enable and require emotional labor, just like the face-to-face interactions they mimic. But unlike the emotional labor of the stewardesses that Hochschild studied, social media users are encouraged to engage in unremunerated forms of emotional labor (see also van Dijck, 2013). The idea that media audiences participate in various forms of unremunerated labor is not a new one. Ever since Dallas

Smythe (1981) first discussed the notion of the "audience commodity," scholars have been aware of the fact that audiences/ users are actively engaged in the production of value.

Maurizio Lazzarato (1996) has discussed what he refers to as "immaterial labor" – activities which contribute to producing the cultural content of particular commodities. These forms of labor are not necessarily recognized as work – instead they constitute activities "involved in defining and fixing cultural and artistic standards, fashions, tastes, consumer norms and, more strategically, public opinion" (Lazzarato, 1996, p. 137). Drawing on Lazzarato's work, Michael Hardt describes this as "affective" immaterial labor which involves the production and manipulation of affects and requires "human contact and proximity" (1999, p. 93). Hardt and Lazzarato thus call attention to the ways in which emotional labor plays a central role in adding value to cultural artifacts. What is distinctive about the emotional labor carried out by social media users is not just its contribution to performative self-branding in public, but also the ways in which it is harnessed by social media organizations for financial gain (Gilroy-Ware, 2017). As a result, particular forms of emotional expression are structurally encouraged, while others are discouraged. This occasions careful architectural management by those seeking to profit from it. As the chapter will now discuss, in the case of Facebook, the emphasis of the architectural management is on the expression and elicitation of positive and pro-social emotion, towards the cultivation of an emotional economy that benefits the social media organization.

The commercialization of emotional labor on Facebook

The emotional architecture of Facebook is a direct result of the site's commercial orientation. As Rob Heyman and Jo Pierson (2015) have noted, through a variety of features, on Facebook, "the private space is subsumed under the commercial space and [...] the colonization reconfigures the public space." This "colonization" has several concrete consequences. Mark Andrejevic has pointed to the relative flexibility of Facebook – the way it "can constantly change its capabilities and affordances, and frequently does." It does this to facilitate greater activity by its users, only to exploit that activity by "capturing a broader spectrum of information about user activity" (Andrejevic, 2011, p. 280). This allows the site to market products to users more effectively, as well as to sell information about audiences to corporate clients. Andrejevic points out that offering a plethora of interactive opportunities and structures, while empowering users to engage in gratifying forms of virtual socializing, also represents a somewhat sinister development. This is because this strategy is premised on compiling, aggregating and classifying information shared by users, to sell it on to companies. It engenders a form of commodified "instrumentalized hypersociality" (Andrejevic, 2011, p. 280) whereby mediated social interaction is exploited for commercial means.

Along those lines, Facebook – like other social media sites – directs social interaction in particular directions designed to maximize user engagement and therefore profits. There is growing pressure to move away from the "open-minded" architecture of early virtual public spaces, and towards a more "single-minded" model. In her examination of the architectures of social media, Zizi Papacharissi argued that Facebook

> [E]merged as the architectural equivalent of a glass house, with a publicly open structure which may be manipulated (relatively, at this point) from within to create more or less private spaces. Looseness of behavioral norms obliges users to construct their own, but the network provides tools with which individuals may construct and leave behavioral cues for each other. (2009, p. 215)

The affordances of Facebook may facilitate varied forms of participation, but the site also structurally encourages particular forms of engagement organized around the mobilization of positive and pro-social forms of engagement. For Tim Berners-Lee (2010), Facebook is a "walled garden" whose principles go against the universality and openness so central to the normative premises underpinning the World Wide Web. As Carolin Gerlitz and Anne Helmond put it, "Facebook's very definition of the social web falls together with an increasingly structured, preformatted and traceable web. Being social online means being traced and contributing to value creation for multiple actors including Facebook and external webmasters" (2013, p. 1359). The history of Facebook's reactions emoji highlights the deliberate ways in which the platform has sought to direct its users towards positive and pro-social forms of expression.

Emotional architectures and public debate: the history of Facebook's reactions emoji

I am here focusing on Facebook's reactions emoji as an example of a particularly influential emotional architecture which has significant structuring consequences for public debate online. As Luke Stark and Kate Crawford (2015) have noted, emoji should be seen as "conduits for affective labor in the social networks of informational capitalism." Their incorporation into devices and platforms exemplifies "techniques of computational control." As such, their use is restrained by the commercial orientation of "informational capital":

> Emoji offer us more than just a cute way of "humanizing" the platforms we inhabit: they also remind us of how informational capital continually seeks to instrumentalize, analyze, monetize, and standardize affect. Representations of feeling in general, and happiness in particular, are often painted across the exterior of money-making ventures. Emoji are an exuberant form of social expression but they are also just another means to lure consumers to a platform, to extract data from them more efficiently, and to express a normative, consumerist, and predominantly cheery world-view. (Stark and Crawford, 2015)

The distinctive history of Facebook's reactions emoji shows how the site's emotional architecture generates a commodified affect control structure which calls for universalized expressions of emotion which can, at the same time, be easily aggregated (e.g. Pariser, 2011). Facebook's first step towards structuring reactions towards positive and pro-social forms of emotion took place when the Like button was introduced. The button was rolled out on Facebook in February 2009, and across the internet from 2010 (Gerlitz and Helmond, 2013). With the introduction of the button, it became possible to "Like" "status updates, photos, links or comments. Initially only available within the platform, the Like button came with a counter showing the total number of likes as well as the names of friends who clicked it" (Gerlitz and Helmond, 2013, p. 1352). It was presented "as a shortcut to commenting in order to replace short affective statements like 'Awesome' and 'Congrats!'" (Gerlitz and Helmond, 2013, p. 1352). Indeed, Facebook's Like button feature was, for a month during the design process, known as the "Awesome" button until the design team decided on "Like" as a more universal expression of positive affect (Pariser, 2011, p. 149).

Following on from its introduction, the button had a major impact on the online business environment, occasioning widespread discussion of how to make money from the "Like economy" (e.g. Carter, 2013), which also involves the labor of users as both a social activity and one which produces value for the company (Gerlitz and Helmond, 2015).

The universalizable positivity of the Like button was celebrated among social media marketers. For example, Ayelet Noff (2011), the CEO of social media PR company Blonde 2.0, argued that "Facebook is a social community and in order to survive there needs to be positivity in the air. Negative energy can only lead to negative content which in turn would harm such a network." When media architectures and content are first and foremost designed to facilitate consumption, there is a strong pressure for light-hearted and positive content which creates a "buying mood" (Baker, 1995).

The Like button reflects the dominance of what Eli Pariser

referred to as a "friendly world syndrome." Pariser suggested that "the stories that get the most attention on Facebook are the stories that get the most Likes, and the stories that get the most Likes are, well, more likable" (2011, p. 149). These observations highlight how the emotional architecture of Facebook has concrete consequences for the tone of public discourse by generating an environment where light-hearted, positive content is emphasized over weightier "bad news" stories which might involve important social, political and personal issues. Other scholars studying the phenomenon across social media have detected a prevalent "positivity bias" (e.g. Reinecke and Trepte, 2014), which means that social media users are overwhelmingly likely to share posts expressing positive emotion as they seek to construct desirable networked selves (Utz, 2015). The picture of the online world of public interaction drawn by these observations is a very different place from the hostile, uncivil neighborhood discerned in earlier analyses of online public participation. It suggests that if audiences increasingly use Facebook as a news source, they will view the world through glasses tinted by emotional positivity.

The dominance of the Like button – and the positivity it encouraged – generated significant critical debate. In 2012, a campaign on Facebook to add a Dislike button garnered three million signatures. The idea of a Dislike button was rejected by Facebook "on the grounds that it would sow too much negativity" (Frier, 2016), reflecting the company's concern with maintaining a discursive neighborhood of positivity. Nonetheless, the company continued to grapple with the problem of ensuring that its architecture facilitates the measurement and expression of user emotions as accurately as possible, while directing these emotions in a positive direction. Since 2009, Facebook has hosted "Compassion Research Days" where programmers have considered how best to tinker with the site's features to facilitate the expression of compassion. At the 2013 meeting, programmers proposed introducing a "Sympathize" button (Meyer, 2013). *Atlantic* technology editor

Robinson Meyer (2013) speculated that "Facebook may be reluctant to add too many buttons that signify specific emotions. Give users options – Like, or *sympathize?* – and they may feel like neither gets at their feelings."

Despite such concerns, Facebook made it a priority to build into its architecture a more nuanced palette of human emotions. In September 2015, it announced the decision to roll out "a technical way to express regret or sympathy in a situation" (Meyer, 2015). As *Slate's* Will Oremus (2015) observed:

> [I]t makes sense for Facebook to consider some alternatives, because understanding when users are expressing things like sympathy, outrage, or laughter rather than approval will help Facebook fine-tune its news-feed algorithms. More nuanced responses means more data for Facebook to mine and monetize – and if you dislike that, then you're on the wrong social network.

This observation points to the fact that Facebook has been a key driver of the emergence of an "emotional economy," where emotional engagement serves as a commercial currency, and its accurate elicitation and measurement translates into commercial gain. As *Forbes'* Amit Chowdhry (2016) noted:

> If Facebook offers an ideal mix of content for its users, then it would be able to ensure that users spend more time on the social network. And users that spend more time on the social network will see more ads, thus generating additional revenue.

Facebook's decision to roll out additional reactions was based on the aim of giving

> users more authentic ways to quickly and easily respond to posts, whether they are sad, serious, funny or happy. Before emoji "Reactions," users were often put in the awkward position of resorting to "liking" a post about a death or one that expressed frustration or disappointment, without distinction from how one would "like" an engagement photo. (Chaykowski, 2016)

Extensive research went into the design of the reactions emoji. Facebook worked with linguistics scholars to analyze the sentiments expressed most frequently by users in their comments in stickers, emoji and one-word reactions, seeking to distill this range of reactions into a manageable set of universalizable emoji (Stinson, 2016).

> People used the hearts-in-the-eyes emoji more than any other. They were also prone to expressing humor, sadness, and shock through visual means. The team took a subset of reactions that cut across the emotional spectrum and removed redundancies like sympathy and sadness, and joy and love. Then they tested them with users. [...] Reactions needed to fulfill two main criteria: universality and expressivity. (Stinson, 2016)

The reactions emoji were rolled out in February 2016 and included, in addition to the existing "Like" button, "Love," "Haha," "Wow," "Sad" and "Angry," as shown in Figure 7.1.

The reactions emoji share a pro-social orientation: Although they do enable negative emotions ("Sad" and "Angry"), they function first and foremost to facilitate the easy expression of sympathy for the poster in response to "bad news" disclosures – whether personal or political. Further, they were introduced into a particular expressive environment whose architecture was premised on positive and pro-social emotional expression. And the algorithmic curation of user timelines ensures that the posts with the most likes continue to figure most prominently (Bucher, 2012). This facilitates the persistence of the "friendly world syndrome," while enabling a more

Figure 7.1: Facebook's reactions emoji

nuanced regulation of the diversity of content based on emotional reactions.

Facebook is not the only social media organization to erect emotional architectures for commercial gain, but the prominent example of its reactions emoji highlights the fact that the "positivity bias" of social media has been carefully engineered. It operates alongside the algorithmic curation of content to profoundly shape the horizons for public debate and networked identity construction.

The evolution of reactions emoji is the most prominent example of the ways in which Facebook has sought to direct the emotions of its users. Other high-profile – and perhaps more controversial – examples include the large-scale "emotional contagion" experiment that Facebook carried out in 2014 on almost 700,000 users without their knowledge or consent. In this experiment, they demonstrated an emotional contagion effect by manipulating user newsfeeds:

> When positive expressions were reduced, people produced fewer positive posts and more negative posts; when negative expressions were reduced, the opposite pattern occurred. These results indicate that emotions expressed by others on Facebook influence our own emotions, constituting experimental evidence for massive-scale contagion via social networks. (Kramer et al., 2014, p. 8788)

More recently, Facebook has been granted a patent to use smartphone cameras and webcams to monitor user feelings and use it to deliver content and advertising tailored to their moods (Billington, 2017). These examples illustrate how Facebook's architectural practices – as well as future plans – foreground emotions as the driver of user engagement. But it also shows us that the social media organization, as one of the most influential news platforms in the world, has little hesitation in the manipulation of users – in terms of the news they are exposed to, and the emotions they experience as a result – for the purpose of commercial gain. Along those lines, our networked selves also constitute emotional selves.

And these networked emotional selves, it seems, are shaped by the platform architecture to afford only a limited range of emotion.

Conclusion

If Facebook is now the world's most important news medium, the ontology that underpins the architecture of the platform matters hugely to the public sphere. The centrality of emotion in directing the architecture of Facebook shows a paradigm shift in thinking about public debate as it takes place through social media. While this book has shown that emotion has long been vilified as an enemy of rationality in the public sphere, it is now at the forefront of the concerns of the architects designing the social media platforms through which so many of us now get our news.

The history of Facebook's reactions emoji highlights the commodification and marketization of public emotion, or what we might characterize as the emotional economy of our mediatized world. In particular, the privileging of pro-social positive emotion has coincided with the colonization of the public sphere by corporate interests. These corporations are more interested in targeting and tailoring content to interested consumers than in creating the conditions for a diverse public debate which has inevitable affective components that come in both positive and negative forms. If our news consumption increasingly takes place in environments predicated on the architectural management and algorithmic manipulation of our emotions, it is more important than ever to take emotion seriously as an object of study, and to understand its central place in public life.

Conclusion:
Nine Propositions about
Emotions, Media and Politics

Having journeyed through the varied landscapes that play host to the dynamic interactions between emotions, media and politics, I want to close by offering a series of propositions based on the contributions of the book. These propositions have conceptual, methodological and epistemological dimensions and should also be seen as invitations to future research: they open up new ways of seeing emotions, media and politics, and therefore new avenues of inquiry, development and contestation. In the following, I will propose that: (1) emotions matter to mediated politics; (2) emotionality and rationality are not mutually exclusive; (3) mediated emotions are performative; (4) emotions are everywhere in mediated politics; (5) emotional storytelling may cultivate authenticity and compassion; (6) anger is the essential political emotion; (7) love motivates us to engage in politics; and (8) the circulation of emotion is shaped by the affordances and architectures of platforms. On the basis of these propositions, I ultimately argue that: (9) research agendas in media and politics must consider the role of emotion.

(1) Emotions matter to mediated politics

At the core of the book is the proposition that emotions, long vilified and rendered invisible in mediated politics, are in fact essential to it. This idea was developed in the Introduction and Chapter 1. These chapters made that case that, first of all, citizens are motivated to participate in political life because of their affective engagement with politics – because they care. Political participation is predicated upon emotion and could not exist without it. Second, mediated discussion of the matters that affect us all is profoundly shaped by emotional appeals and language. As a result, emotion could be seen as an epistemological elephant in the room – the massive unspoken presence that hovers over everything but that we have for so long refused to see, talk about and engage with. The book has sought to render the elephant visible by pointing to a variety of ways in which we can locate emotion in mediated politics.

(2) Emotionality and rationality are not mutually exclusive

As Chapter 1 showed, liberal democratic theory has relied on the opposition between emotionality and rationality as a key structuring feature. Coming out of a history of opposition to authoritarian governance and, conversely, a normative invest-ment in the rationality of citizens, it has tended to understand emotion as the enemy of good citizenship – a force that is an inevitable part of social life but needs to be carefully man-aged and controlled so that rationality and reason can reign supreme. As a result, it has viewed emotionality and rational-ity as mutually exclusive.

However, in recent years, scholars from a range of social sciences and humanities fields have questioned this binary opposition, instead seeing the two as necessary ingredients of public life. For our purposes, the most central of such contributions include insights from political communication scholars on the increasingly close relationship between poli-tics and popular culture – and the role of emotion in shaping this relationship – as well as work in journalism studies on how emotions shape professional practices, news texts and audience responses. The close relationship between emotion-ality and rationality is, indeed, a key theme throughout the book. For example, while Chapters 2 and 3 revealed that the best of storytelling draws on both "rational" information and emotional personalized storytelling, Chapter 6 showed that political fan practices such as the Milifandom combined emotional engagement with rationally based appeals to political engagement.

(3) Mediated emotions are performative

When we talk about emotions in the context of mediated politics, we are dealing with a particular form of emotionality: the emotions that we encounter in mediated politics are discursively constructed through media discourses, based on political contexts, prevailing emotional regimes and emotion rules. They provide us with an emotional compass against which to orient ourselves, while staking out the horizons for political action. As such, emotional discourse is also inherently ideological, and emotion is therefore central to all of our political battles as they play out through mediated discourse. This, however, means that emotionality in media cannot be evaluated or judged on a par with emotions circulating in individual bodies. Emotions are both imbued with meaning *by*, and invest meaning *in*, the contexts where they appear and are solicited. They are integral to our accounts of ourselves and our surroundings, helping to form the "deep stories" (Hochschild, 2016) through which we make sense of everything that happens around us.

(4) Emotions are everywhere in mediated politics

Given the centrality of emotions to our collective sensemaking, it is not surprising that they are, in fact, omnipresent in the storytelling that informs our mediated politics. This was first established in Chapter 2, where we looked more closely at the "strategic ritual of emotionality" in Pulitzer Prize-winning journalistic stories. The chapter showed that through compelling personalized storytelling, journalists establish the meaning of the complex and often abstract events that unfold around us. Such storytelling does not occur at the expense of conventional practices of objectivity, but rather operates in tandem with these practices, as a "strategic ritual" which enhances the power of the stories because of their ability to cultivate compassion or feeling *with* others.

Once we accept the omnipresence of emotion in mediated politics, it allows us to take a more nuanced approach to understanding the work that they do, as well as the ways in which we seek to contest, regulate and channel emotion – projects that reverberate throughout this book.

(5) Emotional storytelling may cultivate authenticity and compassion

The interest in what emotions *do* was picked up in Chapter 3, where we looked at the ways in which the telling of emotional stories based on personal experience contributes to the cultivation of authenticity and compassion. The chapter drew on a range of cases, ranging from letters to the editor and vox pops, to user-generated content, social media hashtag campaigns and new forms of online hybrid storytelling represented by Humans of New York. It showed that personalized storytelling helps to bring neglected topics into the public sphere, and, in the process, call into being communities oriented towards political action. However, the forms of authenticity and compassion cultivated through emotional storytelling are not uniform. They are, instead, complicated by the platforms on which and genres in which they circulate, the subject positions of those telling their stories, and the kinds of authenticity and compassion that the storytelling solicits.

(6) Anger is the essential political emotion

While the Introduction and the first three chapters established the importance of emotion in mediated politics, subsequent chapters took a closer look at the distinctive ways in which *particular* emotions circulate. Along those lines, Chapters 4 and 5 focused on the role of anger as a political emotion. Anger is perhaps the most important political emotion, these chapters argued, because it energizes groups of individuals towards a collective response to shared grievances, for better and for worse. Drawing on the insight that mediated emotions are performative, Chapter 4 defined mediated anger as discursively constructed, collective and political. In its analysis of the routine coverage of protest, it demonstrated that anger serves as a cause of engagement and a barometer of the intensity of public feeling, ultimately forming an injunction to care. Chapter 5 further nuanced the analysis of anger as a political emotion by taking a look at the changing emotional regime represented by the rise of Donald Trump's angry populism. Based on an analysis of anger in coverage of Trump following his election, the chapter suggested that anger became a central explanatory framework for making sense of the motivations of the president and his supporters. This, in turn, has rendered anger both salient and relevant for political life. However, the chapter also indicated that not all anger is created equal. Instead, some forms of anger are discursively constructed as legitimate and justified, while others are seen as potentially dangerous and divisive.

(7) Love motivates us to engage in politics

If anger as negative emotion operates in complex ways in political life, Chapter 6 moved towards the examination of a complex *positive* emotion – that of love. By focusing on affective attachments of fans of Ed Miliband and Donald Trump, the chapter investigated the interactions between the fan cultural practices of these distinctive groups, and the affordances of the respective platforms where the fandoms circulated – Twitter and Reddit. The chapter showed that this particular kind of love builds affective communities that are oriented towards political change. Fan love can provide a powerful incentive for political engagement, as in the case of the Milifandom, but may also serve as the underpinning of exclusionary identities, as in the case of the Trump fans. Political fandom, then, powerfully illustrates that whether in love or war, we can never view emotions as purely positive or negative in their operations. Instead, we must understand how they are used strategically and performatively, and will always be both coopted and contested as resources in political life.

(8) The circulation of emotion is shaped by the affordances and architectures of platforms

Given the political significance of the management and channeling of emotion, and widespread concerns about incivility online, social media organizations have made concerted efforts at designing their *emotional architectures* and the affordances of their platforms to facilitate pro-social interactions. As Chapter 6 pointed out, the love of political fans was articulated in ways that were coproduced by the cultures of their communities and the affordances of the platforms. While Twitter facilitated the creation of a Milifandom hybrid counterpublic that both facilitated community formation and mobilized broader communities in the interest of political action, Reddit enabled the Trump fans to build a community premised on shared values and language. Chapter 7 built on this theme by investigating the emotional architecture of Facebook's reactions emoji. It suggested that Facebook has made deliberate attempts at directing the emotions of users towards positivity and pro-social behavior. The most prominent example of its emotional architecture is its reactions emoji buttons. By examining the history of this feature, the chapter demonstrated that Facebook has invested considerable resources in the management and manipulation of user emotions, and that this is in fact essential to its commercial success. However, by encouraging users to express particular types of emotions while making it more difficult to share others, Facebook has a significant impact on our shared conversations.

If our news consumption increasingly takes place in environments predicated on the architectural management and algorithmic manipulation of our emotions, it is more important than ever to take emotions seriously as an object of study, and to understand their central place in public life.

(9) Research agendas in media and politics must consider the role of emotion

Together, these propositions suggest that theories of media and politics must consider the role of emotion. Charting what such an intervention may look like would be a daunting project in its own right, and cannot be achieved within the confines of this brief concluding chapter. However, the conceptual frameworks that have influenced this book offer some clues about what such an endeavor might entail.

First of all, far from taking for granted the desirability of a rational approach to politics which leaves aside our embodied and emotional subjectivities, we must accept that political life is inevitably shaped by such subjectivities. Emotions fuel and direct our political energies and inform our rational decision-making. This means that political theories must make room for emotion – not as an undesirable opponent, nor as an inevitable complement to rationality, but rather as an integral part of any explanation of what it means to be engaged by, participate in and make decisions about politics. Any analysis of political life must be informed by the concrete conditions of possibility within actually existing democracies (Fraser, 1992). As Axel Honneth (2014, pp. 4–6) has argued, theoretical models of political life ought to be underpinned by normative claims developing within existing social, economic and political practices (see also Stemplowska and Swift, 2012). These, however, must take as a starting point the fundamentally agonistic and emotional nature of politics (e.g. Mouffe, 2000, 2005) which has formed the backdrop for this book.

Secondly, the book has shown that, *a priori*, emotions are neither inherently good nor inherently bad. Instead, they are deeply textured and knotted in ways that are difficult but important to unravel (Ahmed, 2004). As we have seen, they include angry, hateful and antagonistic feelings that may both energize and alienate, as well as positive ones that may foster both compassion and exclusion. For those interested in studying how emotion circulates through mediated politics, this implies the need for multi-method approaches that combine the bird's-eye view of quantitative methods with the granularity and specificity of qualitative methods.

Thirdly, a theoretical approach that takes seriously the role of emotion in mediated politics must take it for granted that such emotions are rarely uncontrolled, raw and undirected. Instead, mediated emotions gain their significance from their performative construction and their role as a strategic resource. Politicians, journalists, activists and citizens alike are engaged in continual contestation of the meaning of emotions as they circulate through mediated politics. Projects for social and political change and continuity, and for progressive and reactionary projects, are fueled by emotion. As mentioned in the Introduction to this book, the performative and discursive construction of mediated emotion calls for the need to pay attention to underlying power relations. For Michel Foucault (1980), whose insights were essential to this project, claims to rationality and knowledge ought to be understood as a regime of truth, predicated on dynamic power relations. Or, as Bent Flyvbjerg put it, "[P]ower defines what counts as rationality and knowledge and thereby what counts as reality" (1998, p. 319). In the same way, we must conceive of discursively constituted emotional claims as regimes of truth, intimately connected to and constituted through power relations.

Finally, with the emergence of online and social media

platforms, any theory of media and politics must also pay attention to how emotions are not merely performed and constructed through the discourses of groups and individuals, but also shaped by technological architectures and affordances. They emerge, develop and travel through words and images of politicians, journalists, citizens and activists, across the multiplicity of media genres and platforms that constitute our complex media landscape, and are molded by both the forces of the actors and the landscape they inhabit. This landscape, in turn, is comprised of both naturally evolving media ecologies and built environments. Conventional approaches have seen political life as shaped by the interactions between the triad of journalists, politicians and citizens (e.g. McNair, 2012, p. ix). Recognizing the increasing role of technologies and platforms in constructing our political reality – and the way emotion figures into this construction – we now have to contend with an environment which encompasses both human actors and non-human technological actants (Lewis and Westlund, 2015).

These few ideas represent a starting point for a reconceptualization. They highlight the need for rethinking theories of politics and media on the basis of a recognition of the vital role of emotion, for better and for worse. Taking seriously the role of emotion in mediated public life opens up new vistas for research in ways that can only enhance our inquiry, even if it also renders it more complicated than ever.

Notes

INTRODUCTION: UNDERSTANDING EMOTIONS IN
MEDIATED PUBLIC LIFE

1 While I sometimes distinguish between emotion (as singular)
   and emotions (as plural) when discussing concrete phenomena,
   at other times I use these two phrases interchangeably when
   discussing more abstract ideas around emotionality.

CHAPTER 2 EMOTIONS ARE EVERYWHERE:
THE STRATEGIC RITUAL OF EMOTIONALITY IN
JOURNALISM

1 This means that the analysis excludes the categories of editorial
   writing, commentary and criticism, which are *not* expected to
   adhere to the ideal of objectivity.
2 The archive can be accessed online here: *http://www.pulitzer.org/
   bycat*. "Hard news" categories which have not been drawn on
   for the study include breaking news (awarded only since 1998)
   and local reporting (awarded continuously only since 2007). On
   occasions when more than one award was given, the first listed
   award winner has been selected so as to avoid over-representing
   particular categories in the sample, with the exception of the 2008
   prize for investigative reporting, where the first story of the first
   listed winner, the *Chicago Tribune*, did not appear in the archive,
   and the *New York Times* was selected as the second winner. No
   award was given for feature writing in 2004 and 2014. Given
   that the prizes vary in terms of whether they are awarded for an
   individual story, a series or a larger body of work, the study focuses,
   for the sake of consistency, on the first entry appearing in the list
   of winning stories in each category. It means that if it is part of a
   series, it will be the first piece, the one which frames the narrative
   of the series as a whole. Overall, this sampling strategy yielded a

total of 136 stories, which also provided a rich body of qualitative
material for the examination of the range of strategies used in
embedding emotion within journalistic storytelling.

3   Where there are expressions of affect and judgments, the first
expression of these as they occur in the story, from the journalist
and from the source, is examined. This is because the stories in
the sample vary greatly in length – from fewer than 400 words to
more than 7,000 – and an exhaustive examination of all emotional
expression would over-represent the longer stories, which may
well be structurally different from shorter ones. Following an
informal piloting process, 51 stories (37.5% of the sample) were
coded by a second coder, and this intercoder reliability test resulted
in agreement ranging from 83 to 100% across the variables. Full
(100%) intercoder agreement was reached on basic variables
including story category, paper, year, topic, and lead type, whereas
the lowest percentages of agreement related to the variables
determining the object of appreciation for journalists (85%
agreement) and sources (83% agreement).

4   All quotations from the winning stories and citations concerning
them can be found at *http://www.pulitzer.org/bycat.*

5   A correlation analysis demonstrated that this association was
statistically significant at the 0.01 level.

6   There were no statistically significant differences among categories
for these variables. However, there were statistically significant
associations between different forms of appraisal as expressed by
journalists and sources.

7   This was more commonly the case in the feature category than any
others.

Chapter 5   Shifting Emotional Regimes: Donald Trump's Angry Populism

1   Note that these figures reflect the sample size after the exclusion
of non-relevant or repeated stories. The Trump sample contained a
much larger number of repeated stories, given the wide syndication
of particular wire stories across many newspapers.

2   I did this by carrying out a Nexis UK search on US newspapers
and wires in the period January 21, 2017, to May 1, 2017. Trump's
first 100 days in office ended on April 29, 2017, and by including
the two following days, I captured reflections on this traditional
landmark period. I used the search terms "Donald Trump" (major

mentions) and, within five words, "anger" (major mentions) or "angry" (major mentions). This yielded a total of 234 articles. By contrast, a search on Obama's first 100 days in office yielded only 84 articles. Other, less narrow searches (e.g. removing "Within 5 words" or major mentions for any of the keywords) yielded results too large to display in Nexis.

Chapter 7 The Emotional Architecture of Social Media

1 In comparison to "architecture," the notion of "infrastructure" is far more strongly connected to ideas of transportation and efficiency.
2 *http://cyberbullying.org/statistics.*
3 For Baym (2015), relational labor is distinctive from emotional labor, as stipulated by Hochschild (1983), because it is ongoing and tied to economic contexts. However, these features could be seen as central to Hochschild's original conception of emotional labor.

References

Ahmed, S. (2004). *The cultural politics of emotion*. Edinburgh: Edinburgh University Press.

Alters, D. (2007). The other side of fandom: Anti-fans, non-fans and the hurts of history. In: J. Gray, S. Sandvoss and L. C. Harrington, eds., *Fandom: Identities and communities in a mediated world*. New York: NYU Press.

Andrejevic, M. (2011). Surveillance and alienation in the online economy. *Surveillance & Society*, 8(3), pp. 278–87.

Ang, I. (1985). *Watching Dallas: Soap opera and the melodramatic imagination*. New York: Routledge.

Arendt, H. (1968). *Men in dark times*. New York: Harcourt Brace Jovanovich.

Aristotle (1968). *The rhetoric*, trans. W. Rhys Roberts. New York: Random House.

Back, T. B. (2017). How does it make you feel? An ethnomethodological study of the negotiation of emotional moments of 'change' on the Danish live televised talk show *Aftenshowet*. In: PhD conference on the "Softening of Journalism." University of Copenhagen, February 21–2.

Bajc, V. (2007). Surveillance in public rituals: Security meta-ritual and the 2005 US Presidential Inauguration. *American Behavioral Scientist*, 50(12), pp. 1648–73.

Baker, C. E. (1995). *Advertising and a democratic press*. Princeton, NJ: Princeton University Press.

Bakshy, E., Messing, S. and Adamic, L. A. (2015). Exposure to ideologically diverse news and opinion on Facebook. *Science*, 348(6239), pp. 1130–2.

Baldoni, J. (2016). Is Donald Trump a role model for authenticity? *Forbes*, January 2. *https://www.forbes.com/sites/johnbaldoni/2016/01/02/is-donald-trump-a-role-model-for-authenticity/#1a82a72933bc*

Ball, M. (2016). Is the Tea Party responsible for Donald Trump? *The Atlantic*, May 10. *https://www.theatlantic.com/politics/archive/2016/05/did-the-tea-party-create-donald-trump/482004/*

Banet-Weiser, S. (2012). *Authentic: The politics of ambivalence in a brand culture*. New York: NYU Press.

Banks, J. (2010). Regulating hate speech online. *International Review of Law, Computers & Technology*, 24(3), pp. 233–9.

Barnes, L. (2016). Journalism and everyday trauma: A grounded theory of the impact from death-knocks and court reporting. PhD, Auckland University of Technology.

Barrett, L. F. (2014). The conceptual act theory: A précis. *Emotion Review*, 6, pp. 292–7.

Baym, N. (2015). Connect with your audience! The relational labor of connection. *The Communication Review*, 18, pp. 14–22.

Beasley, B. (1998). Journalists' attitudes toward narrative writing. *Newspaper Research Journal*, 19(1), pp. 78–89.

Beasley, V. (2001). The rhetoric of ideological consensus in the United States: American principles and American pose in Presidential Inaugurals, *Communication Monographs*, 68(2), pp. 169–83.

Beck, U. (2006). *Cosmopolitan vision*. Cambridge: Polity.

Beckett, C. and Deuze, M. (2016). On the role of emotion in the future of journalism. *Social Media + Society*, 2(3).

Ben-David, A. and Matamoros-Fernandez, A. (2016). Hate speech and covert discrimination on social media: Monitoring the Facebook pages of extreme-right political parties in Spain. *International Journal of Communication*, 10, pp. 1167–93.

Benhabib, S. (1992). *Situating the self: Gender, community and postmodernism in contemporary ethics*. New York: Routledge.

Bennett, L. (2014). "If we stick together we can do anything": Lady Gaga fandom, philanthropy and activism through social media. *Celebrity Studies*, 5(1–2), pp. 138–52.

Benson, R. (2006). News media as a "journalistic field." *Political Communication*, 23(2), pp. 187–202.

Benson, R. and Neveu, E., eds. (2005). *Bourdieu and the journalistic field*. Cambridge: Polity.

Berger, C. and Calabrese, R. (1975). Some explorations in initial interaction and beyond: Toward a developmental theory of interpersonal communication. *Human Communication Research*, 1(2), pp. 99–112.

Berlant, L. (2007). Nearly utopian, nearly normal: Post-Fordist affect in La Promesse and Rosetta. *Public Culture*, 19(2), pp. 273–301.

Berlant, L. (2011). *Cruel optimism*. Durham, NC: Duke University Press.

Berners-Lee, T. (2010). Long live the Web: A call for continued open standards and neutrality. *Scientific American*, December. *https:// www.scientificamerican.com/article/long-live-the-web/*

Berry, J. and Sobieraj, S. (2014). *The outrage industry*. Oxford: Oxford University Press.

Billington, J. (2017). Facebook wants to secretly watch you through your smartphone camera. *International Business Times*, June 9. *http://www.ibtimes.co.uk/facebook-wants-secretly-watch-you-through -your-smartphone-camera-1625061?utm_source=social&utm_medi um=facebook&utm_campaign=%2Ffacebook-wants-secretly-watch-you- through-your-smartphone-camera-1625061*

Bird, S. E. and Dardenne, R. (1988). Myth, chronicle, and story: Exploring the narrative qualities of news. In: J. W. Carey, ed., *Media, myths, and narratives*. Beverly Hills, CA: Sage.

Bird, S. E. and Dardenne, R. (2009). Rethinking news and myth as storytelling. In: K. Wahl-Jorgensen and T. Hanitzsch, eds., *The handbook of journalism studies*. London and New York: Routledge.

Bishop, J. (2014). Representations of "trolls" in mass media communication: A review of media-texts and moral panics relating to "internet trolling." *International Journal of Web Based Communities*, 10(1), pp. 7–24.

Blaagaard, B. B. (2013a). Shifting boundaries: Objectivity, citizen journalism and tomorrow's journalists. *Journalism*, 14(8), pp. 1076–90.

Blaagaard, B. B. (2013b). Situated, embodied and political: Expressions of citizen journalism. *Journalism Studies*, 14(2), pp. 187–200.

Bleiker, R. and Hutchison, E. (2008). Fear no more: Emotions and world politics. *Review of International Studies*, 34, pp. 115–35.

Boehner, K., DePaula, R., Dourish, P. and Sengers, P. (2007). How emotion is made and measured. *International Journal of Human- Computer Studies*, 65(4), pp. 275–91.

Boiger, M. and Mesquita, B. (2012). The construction of emotion in interactions, relationships, and cultures. *Emotion Review*, 4(3), pp. 221–9.

Boltanski, L. (1999). *Distant suffering: Morality, media and politics*. Cambridge: Cambridge University Press.

Bormann, E. G. (1982). A fantasy theme analysis of the television coverage of the hostage release and the Reagan Inaugural. *Quarterly Journal of Speech*, 68(2), pp. 133–45.

Bourdieu, P. (2005). The political field, the social science field, and the journalistic field. In: R. Benson and E. Neveu, eds., *Bourdieu and the journalistic field*. Cambridge: Polity.

boyd, d. and Ellison, N. (2007). Social network sites: Definition, history, and scholarship. *Journal of Computer-Mediated Communication*, 13(1), pp. 210–30.

Boyle, M. P., McLeod, D. M. and Armstrong, C. L. (2012). Adherence to the protest paradigm: The influence of protest goals and tactics on news coverage in US and international newspapers. *The International Journal of Press/Politics*, 17(2), pp. 127–44.

Brader, T. (2006). *Campaigning for hearts and minds: How emotional appeals in political ads work*. Chicago: University of Chicago Press.

Brain, D. (1997). From public housing to private communities: The discipline of design and the materialization of the public/private distinction in the built environment. In: J. Weintraub and K. Kumar, eds., *Public and private in thought and practice*. Chicago: University of Chicago Press.

Brennen, B. (2008). From religiosity to consumerism: Press coverage of Thanksgiving, 1905–2005. *Journalism Studies*, 9(1), pp. 21–37.

Broersma, M. (2015). Hot dog politics: Why comfort food makes politicians uncomfortable. In D. Jackson and E. Thorsen, eds., *UK election analysis 2015: Media, voters and the campaign*. The Centre for the Study of Journalism, Culture and Community, Bournemouth University. *http://www.electionanalysis.uk/*

Brough, M. M. and Shresthova, S. (2012). Fandom meets activism: Rethinking civic and political participation. *Transformative Works and Cultures*, 10.

Bucher, T. (2012). Want to be on the top? Algorithmic power and the threat of invisibility on Facebook. *New Media & Society*, 14(7), pp. 1164–80.

Bucy, E. (2003). Emotion, presidential communication, and traumatic news: Processing the World Trade Center attacks. *Harvard International Journal of Press/Politics*, 8(4), pp. 76–96.

Burkitt, I. (2014). *Emotions and social relations*. London: Sage.

Cammaerts, B., DeCillia, B., Viera Magalhães, J. and Jiménez-Martínez, C. (2016). Journalistic representations of Jeremy Corbyn in the British press: From watchdog to attackdog. Media@LSE Report, London School of Economics. *http://eprints.lse.ac.uk/67211/1/CAmmaerts_Journalistic%20representations%20of%20Jeremy%20Corbyn_Author_2016.pdf*

Cardo, V. (2014). Celebrity politics and political representation: The case of George Galloway MP on *Celebrity Big Brother*. *British Politics*, 9(2), pp. 146–60.

Carlson, M. (2016). Metajournalistic discourse and the meanings of journalism: Definitional control, boundary work, and legitimation. *Communication Theory*, 26(4), pp. 349–68.

Carter, B. (2013). *The Like economy: How businesses make money with Facebook*. Indianapolis, IN: Que Publishing.

Cepernich, C., (2016). Emotion in politics. *The international encyclopedia of political communication*. Wiley Online Library.

Chadwick, A. (2013). *The hybrid media system: Politics and power*. Oxford: Oxford University Press.

Chalaby, J. (1998). *The invention of journalism*. Basingstoke and New York: Macmillan.

Chaykowski, K. (2016). Facebook no longer just has a "Like" button, thanks to global launch of emoji "reactions." *Forbes*, February 24. *https://www.forbes.com/sites/kathleenchaykowski/2016/02/24/face book-no-longer-just-has-a-like-button-thanks-to-global-launch-of-emoji-reactions/#44635689692d*

Chouliaraki, L. (2006). *The spectatorship of suffering*. London: Sage.

Chouliaraki, L. (2010). Ordinary witnessing in post-television news: Towards a new moral imagination. *Critical Discourse Studies*, 7(4), pp. 305–19.

Chouliaraki, L. (2015). Digital witnessing in conflict zones: The politics of remediation. *Information, Communication & Society*, 18(11), pp. 1362–77.

Chowdhry, A. (2016). Facebook emoji "reactions": Are there ulterior motives? *Forbes*, February 29. *https://www.forbes.com/sites/amitchowdhry/2016/02/29/facebook-reactions/#5c920fe31a62*

Cilizza, C. (2017). The dangerous rage of Donald Trump. *Washington Post*, March 6. *https://www.washingtonpost.com/news/the-fix/wp/2017/03/06/the-dangerous-anger-of-donald-trump/?utm_term=.391ac1 8aao1f*

Clark, R. (2016). "Hope in a hashtag": The discursive activism of #WhyIStayed. *Feminist Media Studies*, 16(5), pp. 788–804.

Clausen, L. (2004). Localizing the global: "Domestication" processes in international news production. *Media, Culture & Society*, 26(1), pp. 25–44.

Clay-Warner, J. (2014). Comment: Status, power and emotion. *Emotion Review*, 6(4), pp. 315–16.

Click, M. (2007). Untidy: Fan response to the soiling of Martha Stewart's spotless image. In: J. Gray, S. Sandvoss and L. C. Harrington, eds., *Fandom: Identities and communities in a mediated world*. New York: NYU Press.

Clough, P. T. and Halley, J., eds. (2007). *The affective turn: Theorizing the social*. Durham, NC: Duke University Press.

Cole, H. (2017). Throw the book at them. *The Sun*, May 7. *https://www.thesun.co.uk/news/3502815/police-called-to-step-in-into-nearly-6300-cy*

ber-bulling-incidents-on-facebook-last-year-prompting-fresh-fears-social-media-giants-not-doing-enough-to-tackle-abuse/

Coleman, S. (2013). *How voters feel*. Cambridge: Cambridge University Press.

Coleman, S. (2017). A tale of two narratives. In: M. Ekström and J. Firmstone, eds., *The mediated politics of Europe: A comparative study of discourse*. Basingstoke: Macmillan.

Coleman S. and Firmstone, J. (2017) The performances of mainstream politicians: Politics as usual? In: M. Ekström and J. Firmstone, eds., *The Mediated Politics of Europe: A Comparative Study of Discourse*. Houndmills, Basingstoke: Macmillan.

Coleman, S. and Ross, K. (2010). *The media and the public: "Them" and "us" in media discourse*. Malden, MA: John Wiley & Sons.

Connell, I. (1998). Mistaken identities: Tabloid and broadsheet news discourse. *Javnost/The Public*, 5(3), pp. 11–32.

Cooper, G. (2015). Unlocking the gate? How NGOs mediate the voices of the marginalised in a social media context. In: H. Savigny, ed., *Media, margins and civic agency*. London: Palgrave Macmillan.

Corner, J. (2002). Performing the real: Documentary diversions. *Television & New Media*, 3(3), pp. 255–69.

Corner, J. and Pels, D., eds. (2003). *Media and the restyling of politics: Consumerism, celebrity and cynicism*. London: Sage.

Costera Meijer, I. (2013). Valuable journalism: A search for quality from the vantage point of the user. *Journalism*, 14(6), pp. 754–70.

Cottle, S. (2013). Journalists witnessing disaster: From the calculus of death to the injunction to care. *Journalism Studies*, 14(2), pp. 232–48.

Coward, R. (2013). *Speaking personally: The rise of subjective and confessional journalism*. Palgrave Macmillan.

Cramer, K. J. (2016). *The politics of resentment: Rural consciousness in Wisconsin and the rise of Scott Walker*. Chicago: University of Chicago Press.

Crossley, N. (1998). Emotions and communicative action. In: G. Bendelow and S. Williams, eds., *Emotions in social life: Critical themes and contemporary issues*. London: Routledge.

Dahlberg, L. and Siapera, E., eds. (2007). *Radical democracy and the internet: Interrogating theory and practice*. Basingstoke: Palgrave Macmillan.

Dahlgren, P. (1995). *Television and the public sphere: Citizenship, democracy and the media*. London: Sage.

Dahlgren, P. (2009). *Media and political engagement: Citizens, communication and democracy*. Cambridge: Cambridge University Press.

Damiani, J. (2016). Every time you say "all lives matter" you are being an accidental racist. *Huffington Post*, July 15. *https://www.huffington post.com/jesse-damiani/every-time-you-say-all-li_1_b_11004780.html ?guccounter=1*

Davidson, J. and Milligan, C. (2004). Embodying emotion sensing space: Introducing emotional geographies. *Social and Cultural Geography*, 5(4), pp. 523–32.

Dayan, D. (2001). The peculiar public of television. *Media, Culture & Society*, 23(6), pp. 743–67.

De Castella, K., McGarty, C. and Musgrove, L. (2009). Fear appeals in political rhetoric about terrorism: An analysis of speeches by Australian Prime Minister Howard. *Political Psychology*, 30(1), pp. 1–26.

Delli Carpini, M. X. (2018). Alternative facts: Donald Trump and the emergence of a new US media regime. In: P. Boczkowski and Z. Papacharissi, eds., *Trump and the media*. Cambridge, MA: MIT Press.

DeLuca, K. M. (1999). *Image politics*. New York: Guilford Press.

DeLuca, K. M. (2011). The architecture of oppression. *Salt Lake Tribune*, November 4. *http://archive.sltrib.com/article.php?id=527528 39&itype=CMSID*

DeLuca, K. M., Lawson, S. and Sun, Y. (2012). Occupy Wall Street on the public screens of social media: The many framings of the birth of a protest movement. *Communication, Culture & Critique*, 5(4), pp. 483–509.

Dennis, E. E. and Merrill, J. C. (1984). *Basic issues in mass communication: A debate*. London: Macmillan.

Deuze, M. (2012). *Media life*. Cambridge: Polity.

Di Cicco, D. T. (2010). The public nuisance paradigm: Changes in mass media coverage of political protest since the 1960s. *Journalism & Mass Communication Quarterly*, 87(1), pp. 135–53.

Dixon, T. (2012). "Emotion": The history of a keyword in crisis. *Emotion Review*, 4(4), pp. 338–44.

Dori-Hacohen, G. and Shavit, N. (2013). The cultural meanings of Israeli Tokbek and their relevance to the online democratic public sphere. *International Journal of Electronic Governance*, 6(4), pp. 361–79.

Duffy, E. (1934). Is emotion a mere term of convenience? *Psychological Review*, 41, pp. 103–4.

Duncan, S. (2012). Sadly missed: The death knock news story as a personal narrative of grief. *Journalism*, 13(5), pp. 589–603.

Duncan, S. and Newton, J. (2010). How do you feel? Preparing novice reporters for the death knock. *Journalism Practice*, 4(4), pp. 439–53.

Dworznick, G. (2008). Journalism and trauma. *Journalism Studies*, 7(4), pp. 534–53.

Eagle, R. B. (2015). Loitering, lingering, hashtagging: Women reclaiming public space via #BoardtheBus, #StopStreetHarassment, and the #EverydaySexism Project. *Feminist Media Studies*, 15(2), pp. 350–3.

Edwards, D. (1999). Emotion discourse. *Culture & Psychology*, 5(3), pp. 271–91.

Eksner, J. (2015). Indexing anger and aggression: From language ideologies to linguistic affect. In: H. Flam and J. Kleres, eds., *Methods of exploring emotions*. New York: Routledge.

Ekström, M. (2000). Information, storytelling and attractions: TV journalism in three modes of communication. *Media, Culture & Society*, 22(4), pp. 465–92.

Ekström, M. and J. Firmstone, eds. (2017). *The mediated politics of Europe: A comparative study of discourse*. Basingstoke: Macmillan.

Elias, N. (2000). *The civilizing process* (E. Jephcott, Trans.) (revised edition). Malden, MA: Blackwell.

Eliasoph, N. (1998). *Avoiding politics: How Americans produce apathy in everyday life*. New York: Cambridge University Press.

Engesser, S., Ernst, N., Esser, F. and Büchel, F. (2017). Populism and social media: How politicians spread a fragmented ideology. *Information, Communication & Society* 20(8), pp. 1109–26.

English, J. F. (2002). Winning the culture game: Prizes, awards, and the rules of art. *New Literary History*, 33(1), pp. 109–35.

Enli, G. (2015). *Mediated authenticity. How the media constructs reality*. New York: Peter Lang.

Enroth, H. (2017). Fear as a political factor. *International Political Sociology*, 11(1), pp. 55–72.

Ettema, J. S. and Glasser, T. L. (1998). *Custodians of conscience*. New York: Columbia University Press.

Epstein, E.J. (1973). *News from nowhere*. New York: Vintage.

Fernback, J. (1994). The individual within the collective: Virtual ideology and the realization of collective principles. In: S. Jones, ed., *Virtual culture: Identity and communication in cybersociety*. Newbury Park, CA: Sage.

Fiegerman, S. (2017). Facebook is closing in on 2 billion users. *CNN*, February 1. *http://money.cnn.com/2017/02/01/technology/facebook-earnings/index.html*

Flam, H. (2005). Emotions' map: A research agenda. In: H. Flam and D. King, eds., *Emotions and social movements*. London: Routledge.

Flam, H. (2015). Introduction: Methods of exploring emotions. In:

H. Flam and J. Kleres, eds., *Methods of exploring emotions*. London: Routledge.

Fletcher, R. and Nielsen, R. K. (2017). Are news audiences increasingly fragmented? A cross-national comparative analysis of cross-platform news audience fragmentation and duplication. *Journal of Communication*, 67(4), pp. 476–98.

Flyvbjerg, B. (1998). *Rationality and power: Democracy in practice*. Chicago: University of Chicago Press.

Foucault, M. (1978). *The history of sexuality* (R. Hurley, Trans.). New York: Pantheon.

Foucault, M. (1980). *Power/knowledge: Selected interviews and other writings, 1972–1977* (C. Gordon et al., Trans.). New York: Pantheon.

Franklin, B. (1997). *Newzak and news media*. London: Arnold.

Fraser, N. (1992). Rethinking the public sphere: A contribution to the critique of actually existing democracy. In: C. Calhoun, ed., *Habermas and the public sphere*. Cambridge, MA: MIT Press.

Fredrickson, B. L. (2001). The role of positive emotions in positive psychology: The broaden-and-build theory of positive emotions. *American Psychologist*, 56(3), pp. 218–26.

Frier, S. (2016). Inside facebook's decision to blow up the Like button. *Bloomberg Businessweek*, January 27. *https://www.bloomberg.com/features/2016-facebook-reactions-chris-cox/*

Fröhlich, M. (2005). Emotional intelligence in peace journalism. *Global Media Journal*, 4(7).

Furedi, F. (2004). *Therapy culture: cultivating vulnerability in an uncertain age*. London and New York: Routledge.

Gaber, I. (2014). The "othering" of "Red Ed", or how the *Daily Mail* "framed" the British Labour leader. *The Political Quarterly*, 85(4), pp. 471–9.

Galtung, J. and Ruge, M. (1965). The structure of foreign news: The presentation of the Congo, Cuba and Cyprus crises in four newspapers. *Journal of International Peace Research*, 1, pp. 64–90.

Gamson, W. A. (1992). *Talking politics*. Cambridge: Cambridge University Press.

Gendron, M. (2010). Defining emotion: A brief history. *Emotion Review*, 2(4), pp. 371–2.

Gerbaudo, P. (2018). Social media and populism: An elective affinity? *Media, Culture & Society*, 40(5), pp. 745–53.

Gerlitz, C., and Helmond, A. (2013). The Like economy: Social buttons and the data-intensive Web. *New Media & Society*, 15(8), pp. 1348–65.

Gilroy-Ware, M. (2017). *Filling the void*. London: Verso.

Glasser, T. L. (1991). Communication and the cultivation of citizenship. *Communication*, 12(4), pp. 235–48.

Goleman, D. (1996). *Emotional intelligence*. London: Bloomsbury.

Goodwin, I., Griffin, C., Lyons, A., McCreanor, T. and Moewaka Barnes, H. (2016). Precarious popularity: Facebook drinking photos, the attention economy, and the regime of the branded self. *Social Media + Society*, 2(1).

Goodwin, J., Jasper, J. M. and Polletta, F., eds. (2001). *Passionate politics: Emotions and social movements*. Chicago: University of Chicago Press.

Gould, D. B. (2010). On affect and protest. In: J. Staiger, A. Cvetkovich and A. Reynolds, eds., *Political emotions*. London: Routledge.

Gould, D. B. (2012). Political despair. In: P. Hoggett and S. Thompson, eds., *Politics and emotions: The affective turn in contemporary political studies*. New York: Continuum.

Gould, D. B. (2015). When your data make you cry. In: H. Flam and J. Kleres, eds., *Methods of exploring emotions*. London: Routledge.

Gould, S. and Harrington, R. (2016). 7 charts show who propelled Trump to victory. *Business Insider*, November 11. *http://uk.businessinsider.com/exit-polls-who-voted-for-trump-clinton-2016-11/#more-young-people-voted-for-clinton-but-that-bloc-did-not-include-as-many-voters-as-those-over-40-who-as-a-majority-voted-for-trump-2*

Gray, J. (2007). The news: You gotta love it. In: J. Gray, S. Sandvoss and L. C. Harrington, eds., *Fandom: Identities and communities in a mediated world*. New York: NYU Press.

Gray, J., Sandvoss, C. and Harrington, L. C. (2007). Introduction: Why study fans? In: J. Gray, S. Sandvoss and L. C. Harrington, eds., *Fandom: Identities and communities in a mediated world*. New York: NYU Press.

Greco, M. and Stenner, P., eds. (2013). *Emotions: A social science reader*. London: Routledge.

Greer, C. and McLaughlin, E. (2010). We predict a riot? Public order policing, new media environments and the rise of the citizen journalist. *British Journal of Criminology*, 50(6), pp. 1041–59.

Gurău, C. (2013). Codes of ethics in discussion forums. In J. Bishop, ed., *Examining the concepts, issues and implications of internet trolling*. Hershey, PA: IGI Global.

Gürsel, Z. D. (2010). US newsworld: The rule of text and everyday practices of editing the world. In: S. E. Bird, ed., *The anthropology of news and journalism*. Bloomington: Indiana University Press.

Habermas, J. (1989). *The structural transformation of the public sphere*

(Thomas Burger with the assistance of Frederick Lawrence, Trans.). Cambridge, MA: MIT Press.

Hagdu, A. T., Garimella, K. and Weber, I. (2013). Political hashtag hijacking in the US. In *Proceedings of the 22nd International Conference on World Wide Web*. ACM, pp. 55–6.

Hall, S., Critcher, C., Jefferson, T., Clarke, J. and Roberts, B. (2013). *Policing the crisis: Mugging, the state and law and order*. Basingstoke: Palgrave Macmillan.

Hanisch, C. (2000). The personal is political. In: B. A. Crow, ed., *Radical feminism: A documentary reader*. New York: New York University Press.

Harbers, F. and Broersma, M. (2014). Between engagement and ironic ambiguity: Mediating subjectivity in narrative journalism. *Journalism*, 15(5), pp. 639–54.

Hardt, M. (1999). Affective labor. *boundary 2*, 26(2), pp. 89–100.

Harry Potter Alliance. (No date). What we do. Harry Potter Alliance website. *http://www.thehpalliance.org/what_we_do*

Hartsock, J. C. (2000). *A history of American literary journalism: The emergence of a modern narrative form*. Amherst: University of Massachusetts Press.

Harvey, D. (2000). *Spaces of hope*. Berkeley: University of California Press.

Held, D. (2006). *Models of democracy*. Stanford, CA: Stanford University Press.

Hermida, A. (2014). *Tell everyone: Why we share and why it matters*. Toronto: Doubleday Canada.

Hesmondhalgh, D. and Baker, S. (2008). Creative work and emotional labour in the television industry. *Theory, Culture & Society*, 25(7–8), pp. 97–118.

Hesmondhalgh, D. and Baker, S. (2011). *Creative labour: Theoretical synthesis*. London: Routledge.

Hewitt, R. (2017a). *A revolution of feeling: The decade that forged the modern mind*. London: Granta Books.

Hewitt, R. (2017b). From May's tears to angry Trump, is modern politics too emotional? *New Statesman*, October 9. *https://www. newstatesman.com/politics/uk/2017/10/mays-tears-angry-trump-modern-politics-too-emotional*

Heyman, R. and Pierson, J. (2015). Social media, delinguistification and colonization of lifeworld: Changing faces of Facebook. *Social Media + Society*, 1(2).

Higgins, M. (2008). *Media and their publics*. Maidenhead: Open University Press.

Higgins, M. and Smith, A. (2016). *Belligerent broadcasting: Synthetic argument in broadcast talk.* London: Routledge.

Hill, A. (2005). *Reality TV: Audiences and popular factual television.* London: Routledge.

Hill, A. (2017). Trump's plain speaking fuels the leadership cult of authenticity. *Financial Times,* February 6. *https://www.ft.com/content/f168807e-e8a8-11e6-893c-082c54a7f539*

Hills, M. (2002). *Fan cultures.* London: Routledge.

Hills, M. (2015). The "most unlikely" or "most deserved cult": Citizen-fans and the authenticity of Milifandom. In: D. Jackson and E. Thorsen, eds., *UK election analysis 2015: Media, voters and the campaign.* The Centre for the Study of Journalism, Culture and Community, Bournemouth University. *http://www.electionanalysis.uk/*

Hochschild, A. R. (1983). *The managed heart.* Berkeley.

Hochschild, A. R. (2003). *The commercialization of intimate life: Notes from home and work.* Berkeley: University of California Press.

Hochschild, A. R. (2016). *Strangers in their own land: Anger and mourning on the American right.* New York: The New Press.

Holmes, M. (2004). Introduction: The importance of being angry: Anger in political life. *European Journal of Social Theory,* 7(2), pp. 123–32.

Holmes, S. (1995). *Passions and constraint: On the theory of liberal democracy.* Chicago: University of Chicago Press.

Honneth, A. (2014). *Freedom's right: The social foundations of democratic life.* New York: Columbia University Press.

Hopper, K. M. and Huxford, J. E. (2015). Gathering emotion: Examining newspaper journalists' engagement in emotional labor. *Journal of Media Practice,* 16(1), pp. 25–41.

Hopper, K. M. and Huxford, J. (2017). Emotion instruction in journalism courses: An analysis of introductory news writing textbooks. *Communication Education,* 66(1), pp. 90–108.

Horeck, T. (2014). #AskThicke: "Blurred lines," rape culture, and the feminist hashtag takeover. *Feminist Media Studies,* 14(6), pp. 1105–7.

Hui, V. T. B. (2015). The protests and beyond. *Journal of Democracy,* 26(2), pp. 111–21.

Hyde, M. (2017). In Stoke, May marches on with familiar neuron-crushing dullness. *Guardian,* May 16. *https://www.theguardian.com/politics/2017/may/16/in-stoke-may-marches-on-with-familiar-neuron-crushing-dullness*

Illouz, E. (2007). *Cold intimacies: The making of emotional capitalism.* Cambridge: Polity.

Inglehart, F. and Norris, P. (2016). Trump, Brexit, and the rise of populism: Economic have-nots and cultural backlash. Harvard Kennedy School: Faculty Research Working Paper Series, August, RWP16-026. *https://papers.ssrn.com/sol3/papers.cfm?abstract_id=2818659*

Itule, B. D., and Anderson D. A. (2003). *News writing and reporting* (sixth edition). Boston: McGraw-Hill.

Jalan, I. (2015). Researching dark emotions: Eliciting stories of envy. In: H. Flam and J. Kleres, eds., *Methods of exploring emotions*. London: Routledge.

James, S. (1999). *Passion and action: The emotions in seventeenth-century philosophy*. Oxford: Oxford University Press.

James, W. (1884). What is an emotion? *Mind*, 9, pp. 188–205.

Jarzebowski, C. (2015). "My heart belongs to daddy": Emotion and narration in early modern self-narratives. In: H. Flam and J. Kleres, eds., *Methods of exploring emotions*. London: Routledge.

Jasper, J. M. (2011). Emotions and social movements: Twenty years of theory and research. *Annual Review of Sociology*, 37, pp. 285–303.

Jenkins, H. (2006). *Convergence culture*. New York: NYU Press.

Jenkins, H. (2012). *Textual poachers: Television fans and participatory culture* (second edition). New York: Routledge.

Jenkins, H. and Shresthova, S. (2012). Up, up, and away! The power and potential of fan activism. *Transformative Works and Cultures*, 10.

Jensen, J. (1992). Fandom as pathology: The consequences of characterization. In: L. A. Lewis, ed., *The adoring audience: Fan culture and popular media*. New York: Routledge.

Johanssen, J. and Garrisi, D. (2017). "I am burning, I am burning": Affect, acid attacks and British tabloid newspapers. *Journalism Studies*, online first. *https://doi.org/10.1080/1461670X.2017.1389294*

Jones, J. P. (2005). *Entertaining politics: New political television and civic culture*. Lanham, MD: Rowman & Littlefield.

Jones, J. P. (2010). *Entertaining politics: Satiric television and political engagement*. Lanham, MD: Rowman & Littlefield.

Jukes, S. (2017). Affective journalism – Uncovering the affective dimension of practice in the coverage of traumatic news. PhD, Goldsmiths, University of London.

Juris, J. S. (2005). Violent performed and imagined militant action, the Black Bloc and the mass media in Genoa. *Critique of Anthropology*, 25(4), pp. 413–32.

Kant, I. (1998). *Critique of pure reason* (P. Guyer and A.W. Wood, trans.). Cambridge: Cambridge University Press.

Kaplan, A. M. and Haenlein, M. (2010). Users of the world, unite!

The challenges and opportunities of social media. *Business Horizons,* 53(1), pp. 59–68.

Karpf, D. (2017). Digital politics after Trump. *Annals of the International Communication Association,* 41(2), pp. 198–207.

Katriel, T. (2015). Exploring emotion discourse. In: H. Flam and J. Kleres, eds., *Methods of exploring emotions.* New York: Routledge.

Kellner, D. (2010). Celebrity diplomacy, spectacle and Barack Obama. *Celebrity Studies,* 1(1), pp. 121–3.

Kemp, S. (2017). Digital in 2017: Global overview. We Are Social, January 24. *https://wearesocial.com/uk/special-reports/digital-in-2017-global-overview*

Kertzer, D. I. (1989). *Ritual, politics, and power.* New Haven, CT: Yale University Press.

Khan, K. and Blair, D. M. (2013). Writing Bill Clinton: Mediated discourses on hegemonic masculinity and the 2008 Presidential Primary. *Women's Studies in Communication,* 36(1), pp. 56–71.

Khoja-Moolji, S. (2015). Becoming an "intimate publics": Exploring the affective intensities of hashtag feminism. *Feminist Media Studies,* 15(2), pp. 347–50.

Kitch, C. (2000). "A news of feeling as well as fact": Mourning and memorial in American newsmagazines. *Journalism* 1(2), pp. 175–95.

Kitch, C. (2003). "Mourning in America": Ritual, redemption and recovery in news narrative after September 11. *Journalism Studies,* 4(2), pp. 213–24.

Klein, A. (2012). Slipping racism into the mainstream: A theory of information laundering. *Communication Theory,* 22(4), pp. 427–48.

Kleinginna, P. R. and Kleinginna, A. M. (1981). A categorized list of emotion definitions, with suggestions for a consensual definition. *Motivation and Emotion,* 5(4), pp. 345–79.

Knobloch, S., Patzig, G., Mende, A. M. and Hastall, M. (2004). Affective news: Effects of discourse structure in narratives on suspense, curiosity, and enjoyment while reading news and novels. *Communication Research,* 31(3), pp. 259–87.

Koehn, D. (1998). *Rethinking feminist ethics: Care, trust and empathy.* New York: Routledge.

Koljonen, J. (2010). Dags att prata om det. *Dagens Nyheter,* December 18.

Kotišová, J. (2017a). *Cynicism ex machina*: The emotionality of reporting the "refugee crisis" and Paris terrorist attacks in Czech Television. *European Journal of Communication,* 32(3), pp. 242–56.

Kotišová, J. (2017b). When the crisis comes home: Emotions, professionalism, and reporting on 22 March in Belgian journalists' narratives. *Journalism*, online first. *https://doi. org/10.1177/1464884917748519*

Kramer, A. D., Guillory, J. E. and Hancock, J. T. (2014). Experimental evidence of massive-scale emotional contagion through social networks. *Proceedings of the National Academy of Sciences*, 111(24), pp. 8788–90.

Krug, S. (2016). Reactions now available globally. Facebook Newsroom, February 24. *https://newsroom.fb.com/news/2016/02/reactions-now-available-globally/*

Kyriakidou, M. (2008). Rethinking media events in the context of a global public sphere: Exploring the audience of global disasters in Greece. *Communications*, 33, pp. 273–91.

Kyriakidou, M. (2009). Imagining ourselves beyond the nation? Exploring cosmopolitanism in relation to media coverage of distant suffering. *Studies in Ethnicity and Nationalism*, 9(3), pp. 481–96.

Laclau, E. (2005). *On populist reason*. London: Verso.

Lagorio-Chafkin, C. (2016). Reddit and the God Emperor of the Internet. *New York Times*, November 19. *https://www.nytimes. com/2016/11/20/opinion/sunday/reddit-and-the-god-emperor-of-the-internet.html*

Lakoff, G. (2016). Language and emotion. *Emotion Review*, 8(3), pp. 269–73.

Langer, A. I. (2010). The politicization of private persona: Exceptional leaders or the new rule? The case of the United Kingdom and the Blair effect. *The International Journal of Press/Politics*, 15, pp. 60–76.

Langer, A. I. (2011). *The personalisation of politics in the UK: Mediated leadership from Attlee to Cameron*. Manchester: Manchester University Press.

Lazzarato, M. (1996). Immaterial labour. *http://strickdistro.org/wp-content/uploads/2011/09/Week-1_Immaterial-Labour_Lazzarato.pdf*

Lea, M., O'Shea, T., Fung, P. and Spears, R. (1992). *"Flaming" in computer-mediated communication: Observations, explanations, implications*. Hemel Hempstead: Harvester Wheatsheaf.

Levy, M. R. (1979). Watching TV News as para-social interaction. *Journal of Broadcasting & Electronic Media*, 23(1), pp. 69–80.

Levy, M. R. and Windahl, S. (1984). Audience activity and gratifications: A conceptual clarification and exploration. *Communication Research*, 11(1), pp. 51–78.

Lewis, J. and Stearns, P. N. (1998). Introduction. In: P. N. Stearns and J. Lewis, *An emotional history of the United States*. New York: NYU Press.

Lewis, L. A., ed. (1992). *The adoring audience: Fan culture and popular media*. New York: Routledge.

Lewis, S. C. and Westlund, O. (2015). Actors, actants, audiences, and activities in cross-media news work: A matrix and a research agenda. *Digital Journalism*, 3(1), pp. 19–37.

Lichterman, J. (2016). Nearly half of US adults get news on Facebook, Pew says. Nieman Lab, May 26. *http://www.niemanlab.org/2016/05/ pew-report-44-percent-of-u-s-adults-get-news-on-facebook/*

Lim, E. T. (2002). Five trends in presidential rhetoric: An analysis of rhetoric from George Washington to Bill Clinton. *Presidential Studies Quarterly*, 32(2), pp. 328–48.

Livingstone, S. and Lunt, P. (1994). *Talk on television*. London: Routledge.

Loken, M. (2014). #BringBackOurGirls and the invisibility of imperialism. *Feminist Media Studies*, 14(6), pp. 1100–1.

Loyn, D. (2003). Witnessing the truth. Open Democracy, February 20. *https://www.opendemocracy.net/media-journalismwar/article_993.jsp*

Lunt, P. and Pantti, M. (2007). The emotional public sphere: Social currents of feeling in popular culture. In R. Butch, ed., *Media and public spheres*. Basingstoke: Palgrave.

Lunt, P. and Stenner, P. (2005). *The Jerry Springer Show* as an emotional public sphere. *Media, Culture & Society*, 27(1), pp. 59–81.

Lutz, C. (1988). *Unnatural emotions: Everyday sentiments on a Micronesian atoll and their challenge to Western theory*. Chicago: University of Chicago Press.

Lutz, C. and Abu-Lughod, L., eds. (1990). *Language and the politics of emotion*. Cambridge: Cambridge University Press.

Lyman, P. (1981). The politics of anger. *Socialist Review*, 11, pp. 55–74.

Lyman, P. (2004). The domestication of anger: The use and abuse of anger in politics. *European Journal of Social Theory*, 7(2), pp. 133–47.

Macdonald, M. (2000). Rethinking personalization in current affairs journalism. In: C. Sparks and J. Tulloch, eds., *Tabloid tales: Global debates over media standards*. Oxford: Rowman & Littlefield.

Manning, N., Penfold-Mounce, R., Loader, B.D., Vromen, A. and Xenos, M. (2017). Politicians, celebrities and social media: A case of informalisation? *Journal of Youth Studies*, 20(2), pp. 127–44.

Mansch, L. D. (2005). *Abraham Lincoln, president-elect: The four critical months from election to inauguration*. London: McFarland.

Maras, S. (2013). *Objectivity in journalism*. Cambridge: Polity.

Marcus, G. E. (2010). *Sentimental citizen: Emotion in democratic politics*. University Park, PA: Penn State University Press.

Marcus, G. E., Neuman, W. R. and MacKuen, M. (2000). *Affective intelligence and political judgment.* Chicago: University of Chicago Press.

Martin, J. (2017). Inscribing virtues in Australian literary journalism: An investigation into how journalists communicate emotions to readers of the magazine-style Walkley Award winning features, 1988–2014. PhD, University of Melbourne.

Martin, J. R. and Rose, D. (2003). *Working with discourse.* London and New York: Continuum.

Marwick, A. E. (2013). *Status update: Celebrity, publicity, and branding in the social media age.* New Haven, CT: Yale University Press.

Massanari, A. (2017). # Gamergate and The Fappening: How Reddit's algorithm, governance, and culture support toxic technocultures. *New Media & Society,* 19(3), pp. 329–46.

Massumi, B. (2002). *Parables for the virtual: Movement, affect, sensation.* Durham, NC: Duke University Press.

May, B. (2017). Theresa May's Stance on Fox Hunting Has Proved She is a Dangerous Woman, Hell-Bent on Establishing Herself as a Virtual Dictator. *Mirror,* June 7. *https://www.mirror.co.uk/news/ politics/brian-may-theresa-mays-stance-10581169*

McLeod, D. M. (2007). News coverage and social protest: How the media's protest paradigm exacerbates social conflict. *Journal of Dispute Resolution,* 12(1), pp. 1–10.

McNair, B. (2012). *Journalism and democracy: An evaluation of the political public sphere.* London: Routledge.

Mendes, K., Ringrose, J. and Keller, J. (2018). #MeToo and the promise and pitfalls of challenging rape culture through digital feminist activism. *European Journal of Women's Studies,* 25(2), pp. 236–46.

Meštrović, S. (1996). *Postemotional society.* London: Sage.

Meyer, R. (2013). Facebook considers adding a "Sympathize" button. *The Atlantic,* December 13. *https://www.theatlantic.com/technolo gy/archive/2013/12/facebook-considers-adding-a-sympathize-button/ 282126/*

Meyer, R. (2015). Facebook says it's introducing a "Dislike" button. *The Atlantic,* September 15. *https://www.theatlantic.com/technology/ archive/2015/09/facebook-says-its-introducing-a-dislike-button/405514/*

Miller, C. (2015). Life in the new media landscape: Ritual communication and distributed cognition on Reddit. *Gnovis,* 16(2), pp. 1–15.

Milner, R. M. and Philips, W. (2016). Dark magic: The memes that made Donald Trump's victory. In: D. Lilleker, D. Jackson, E. Thorsen and A. Veneti, eds., *US election analysis 2016: Media, voters and the campaign.* The Centre for the Study of Journalism,

Culture and Community, Bournemouth University. *http://www. electionanalysis.uk/*

Mindich, D. T. Z. (1998). *Just the facts: How "objectivity" came to define American journalism.* New York: NYU Press.

Mishra, P. (2017). *Age of anger: A history of the present.* London: Macmillan.

Moeller, S.D. (1999). *Compassion fatigue: How the media sell disease, famine, war and death.* New York: Routledge.

Montgomery, M. (2001). Defining "authentic talk." *Discourse Studies,* 3(4), pp. 397–405.

Mouffe, C. (2000). *The democratic paradox.* London: Verso.

Mouffe, C. (2005). *The return of the political.* London: Verso.

Mouffe, C. and Holdengräber, P. (1989). Radical democracy: Modern or postmodern? *Social Text,* 21, pp. 31–45.

Mudde, C. (2007). *Populist radical right parties in Europe.* Cambridge: Cambridge University Press.

Mudde, C. and Kaltwasser, C. R., eds. (2012). *Populism in Europe and the Americas: Threat or corrective for democracy?* Cambridge: Cambridge University Press.

Neiger, M. (2007). Media oracles: The cultural significance and political import of news referring to future events. *Journalism,* 8(3), pp. 309–21.

Newmyer, T. (2017). Trump Inauguration: In fiery speech, POTUS doubles down on populist promises. *Fortune,* January 20. *http:// fortune.com/2017/01/20/trump-inauguration-trump-channels-angry-populism-in-inaugural-address/*

Ngai, S. (2005). *Ugly feelings.* Cambridge, MA: Harvard University Press.

Noff, A. (2011). Happy birthday to Facebook's Like button. Socialmedia. biz, April 22. *http://insidesocialmedia.com/2011/04/22/facebooks-like-button/*

Nussbaum, M. C. (2016). *Anger and forgiveness: Resentment, generosity, justice.* Oxford: Oxford University Press.

Oberschall, A. (1973). *Social conflict and social movements.* New York: Prentice Hall.

Olesen, V. and Bone, D. (1998). Emotions in rationalizing organizations. In: G. Bindelow and S. J. Williams, eds., *Emotions in social life: Critical themes and contemporary issues.* London: Routledge.

Ong, J. C. (2009). The cosmopolitan continuum: Locating cosmopolitanism in media and cultural studies. *Media, Culture & Society,* 31(3), pp. 449–66.

Oremus, W. (2015). Is Facebook finally building a "Dislike" button? Not exactly. *Slate,* September 15. *http://www.slate.com/blogs/future_*

tense/2015/09/15/facebook_dislike_button_not_exactly_mark_zuckerb erg_confirms_new_buttons.html

Osborne, C. (2016). UK to prosecute online trolls, cyberbullies and fake account creators. ZDNET, March 3. *http://www.zdnet.com/arti cle/uk-to-prosecute-online-trolls-cyberbullies-and-fake-account-creators/*

Ost, D. (2004). Politics as the mobilization of anger emotions in movements and in power. *European Journal of Social Theory,* 7(2), pp. 229–44.

Ost, D. (2006). *The defeat of solidarity: Anger and politics in postcommunist Europe.* Ithaca, NY: Cornell University Press.

Ott, B. L. (2017). The age of Twitter: Donald J. Trump and the politics of debasement. *Critical Studies in Media Communication,* 34(1), pp. 59–68.

Pantti, M. (2010). The value of emotion: An examination of television journalists' notions on emotionality. *European Journal of Communication,* 25(2), pp. 168–81.

Pantti, M. K. and Wahl-Jorgensen, K. (2011). "Not an act of God": Anger and citizenship in press coverage of British man-made disasters. *Media, Culture & Society,* 33(1), pp. 105–22.

Pantti, M., Wahl-Jorgensen, K. and Cottle, S. (2012). *Disasters and the media.* London and New York: Peter Lang.

Papacharissi, Z. (2009). The virtual geographies of social networks: A comparative analysis of Facebook, LinkedIn and ASmallWorld. *New Media & Society,* 11(1–2), pp. 199–220.

Papacharissi, Z. A. (2010). *A private sphere: Democracy in a digital age.* Cambridge: Polity.

Papacharissi, Z. (2015). *Affective publics: Sentiment, technology, and politics.* Oxford: Oxford University Press.

Pariser, E. (2011). *The filter bubble: What the internet is hiding from you.* London: Penguin UK.

Parkinson, H. J. (2017). Was it Corbyn memes wot won it? Here are some of the best. *Guardian,* June 9. *https://www.theguardian.com/ politics/2017/jun/09/corbyn-memes-wot-won-it-some-of-the-best*

Pawlik-Kienlen, L. (No date). 10 tips for interviewing sources for articles. *https://www.theadventurouswriter.com/blogwriting/10-tips-for-interviewing-sources-for-articles/*

Peter, L. (2017). Kurz and charisma: What propels young leaders to power? BBC News, October 17. *https://www.bbc.co.uk/news/world-europe-41640326*

Peters, C. (2011). Emotion aside or emotional side? Crafting an "experience of involvement" in the news. *Journalism,* 12(3), pp. 297–316.

Peters, J. D. (1999). *Speaking into the air: A history of the idea of communication.* Chicago: University of Chicago Press.

Pettifor, A. (2017). Causes and consequences of President Donald Trump. *Real-World Economics Review*, 78, pp. 44–53.

Puente, M. (2017). What's up with Melania Trump's cyber bullying campaign? It's "a work in progress." *USA Today*, May 9. *https://www.usatoday.com/story/life/people/2017/05/09/whats-happening-melania-trumps-cyberbullying-campaign-not-much-yet/101212182/*

Raboy, M. (1997). Cultural sovereignty, public participation, and democratization of the public sphere: The Canadian debate on the new information infrastructure. In: B. Kahin and E. J. Wilson, eds., *National information infrastructure vision and policy design.* Cambridge, MA: MIT Press.

Read, A. (2016). Where social media is headed in 2017: The biggest trends to watch for. Buffer Social. *https://blog.bufferapp.com/state-of-social-media*

Reddy, W. M. (2001). *The navigation of feeling: A framework for the history of emotions.* Cambridge: Cambridge University Press.

Rehg, W. (1994). *Insight and solidarity: The discourse ethics of Jurgen Habermas.* Berkeley: University of California Press.

Reinecke, L. and Trepte, S. (2014). Authenticity and well-being on social network sites: A two-wave longitudinal study on the effects of online authenticity and the positivity bias in SNS communication. *Computers in Human Behavior*, 30, pp. 95–102.

Remnick, D. (2017). A hundred days of Trump. *New Yorker*, May 1. *https://www.newyorker.com/magazine/2017/05/01/a-hundred-days-of-trump*

Rentschler, C. (2015). # Safetytipsforladies: Feminist twitter takedowns of victim blaming. *Feminist Media Studies*, 15(2), pp. 353–6.

Rheingold, H. (1993). *The virtual community: Homesteading on the electronic frontier.* Cambridge, MA: Addison Wesley.

Richards, B. (2004). The emotional deficit in political communication. *Political Communication*, 21(3), pp. 339–52.

Richards, B. and Rees, G. (2011). The management of emotion in British journalism. *Media, Culture & Society*, 33(6), pp. 851–67.

Richardson, J. E. (2007). *Analysing newspapers: An approach from critical discourse analysis.* Basingstoke and New York: Palgrave Macmillan.

Rieff, P. (1979). *Freud: The mind of the moralist.* London: Chatto & Windus.

Robertson, L. (2002). Romancing the source. *American Journalism Review*, May. *http://ajrarchive.org/article.asp?id=2520*

Robin, C. (2004). *Fear: The history of a political idea*. Oxford: Oxford University Press.

Rosenstiel, T. and Kovach, B. (2005). Media anger management. *Washington Post*, October 2. *http://www.washingtonpost.com/wp-dyn/content/article/2005/10/01/AR2005100100928.html??noredirect=on*

Ross, A. A. G. (2013). *Mixed emotions: Beyond fear and hatred in international conflict*. Chicago: University of Chicago Press.

Rossman, S. (2017). Hillary Clinton lost the presidential Twitter war, study shows. *USA Today*, July 13. *https://www.usatoday.com/story/news/politics/onpolitics/2017/07/13/hillary-clinton-lost-presidential-twitter-war-study-shows/473576001/*

Roy, J. (2016a). "Cuck," "snowflake," "masculinist": A guide to the language of the "alt-right." *Los Angeles Times*, November 16. *http://www.latimes.com/nation/la-na-pol-alt-right-terminology-20161115-story.html*

Roy, J. (2016b). How "Pepe the Frog" went from harmless to hate symbol. *Los Angeles Times*, October 11. *http://www.latimes.com/politics/la-na-pol-pepe-the-frog-hate-symbol-20161011-snap-htmlstory.html*

Rupar, V. and Broersma, M. (2010). The power of narrative journalism: A comparative approach to award winning reporting. In: Conference of the International Association for Literary Journalism Studies, Roehampton University, May 22.

Sandvoss, C. (2005). *Fans: The mirror of consumption*. Cambridge: Polity.

Sandvoss, C. (2012). Enthusiasm, trust and its erosion in mediated politics: On fans of Obama and the Liberal Democrats. *European Journal of Communication*, 27(1), pp. 68–81.

Sandvoss, C. (2013). Toward an understanding of political enthusiasm as media fandom: Blogging, fan productivity and affect in American politics. *Participations*, 10(1), pp. 252–96.

Sandvoss, C. (2015). It's the neutrosemy, stupid! Fans, texts and partisanship in the 2015 General Election. In: D. Jackson and E. Thorsen, eds., *UK election analysis 2015: Media, voters and the campaign*. The Centre for the Study of Journalism, Culture and Community, Bournemouth University. *http://www.electionanalysis.uk/*

Sanghani, R. (2015). #Milifandom: Ed Miliband's teen groupies are not a joke. *Telegraph*, April 22. *http://www.telegraph.co.uk/women/womens-politics/11554357/Milifandom-Labour-leader-Ed-Milibands-teen-groupies-are-not-joking.html?placement=CB1*

Sawyer, M. (2017). The Week in Radio. *Observer*, June 4.

Sayej, N. (2017). Alyssa Milano on the #MeToo movement: "We're not going to stand for it any more." *Guardian*, December 1. *https://www.theguardian.com/culture/2017/dec/01/alyssa-milano-mee-too-sexual-harassment-abuse*

Scherer, K. R. (1993). Neuroscience projections to current debates in emotion psychology. *Cognition and Emotion*, 7(1), pp. 1–41.

Schrøder, K. C. (2015). News media old and new. *Journalism Studies*, 16(1), pp. 60–78.

Schudson, M. (1978). *Discovering the news*. New York: Basic Books.

Schudson, M. (1982). *The power of news*. Cambridge, MA: Harvard University Press.

Schudson, M. (2001). The objectivity norm in American journalism. *Journalism*, 2(2), pp. 149–70.

Schultz, I. (2006). Bag nyhederne: Værdier, idealer og praksis. PhD, University of Roskilde.

Seargeant, P. and Tagg, C., eds. (2014). *The language of social media: Identity and community on the internet*. New York: Springer.

Shapiro, S. (2006). Return of the sob sisters. *American Journalism Review*, June/July. *https://www.ijpc.org/uploads/files/Return%20 of%20the%20Sob%20Sisters%20-%20American%20Journalism%20 Review.pdf*

Sharman, J. (2017). Theresa May to nurse who says she hasn't had a pay rise in eight years: "There's No Magic Money Tree." *Independent*, June 2. *https://www.independent.co.uk/news/uk/politics/theresa-may-nhs-nurses-election-2017-bbc-question-time-leaders-special-a7770371. html*

Shaw, F. (2014). Emotional investments: Australian feminist blogging and affective networks. In: T. Benski and E. Fisher, eds., *Internet and emotions*. London and New York: Routledge.

Shepherd, T., Harvey, A., Jordan, T., Sray, S. and Miltner, K. (2015). Histories of hating. *Social Media + Society*, 1(2).

Sills, S., Pickens, C., Beach, K., Jones, L., Calder-Dawe, O., Benton-Greig, P. and Gavey, N. (2016). Rape culture and social media: Young critics and a feminist counterpublic. *Feminist Media Studies*, 16(6), pp. 935–51.

Singer, P., Flöck, F., Meinhart, C., Zeitfogel, E. and Strohmaier, M. (2014). Evolution of Reddit: From the front page of the internet to a self-referential community? In: *Proceedings of the 23rd International Conference on World Wide Web*. ACM.

Smythe, D. W. (1981). *Dependency road: Communications, capitalism, consciousness, and Canada*. Norwood, NJ: Ablex.

Snakenborg, J., van Acker, R., and Gable, R. A. (2011). Cyberbullying: Prevention and intervention to protect our children and youth. *Preventing School Failure: Alternative Education for Children and Youth*, 55(2), pp. 88–95.

Society of Professional Journalists. (2014). SPJ Code of Ethics. *http://www.spj.org/ethicscode.asp*

Soldani, B. (2016). 16 surprising stars-turned-politicians from around the world. Special Broadcasting Service, November 11. *http://www.sbs.com.au/topics/life/culture/article/2016/11/11/16-surprising-stars-turned-politicians-around-world*

Sparks, C. (2000). Introduction: The panic over tabloid news. In: C. Sparks and J. Tulloch, eds., *Tabloid tales: Global debates over media standards*. Oxford: Rowman & Littlefield.

Stache, L. C. (2015). Advocacy and political potential at the convergence of hashtag activism and commerce. *Feminist Media Studies*, 15(1), pp.162–4.

Staiger, J., Cvetkovich, A. and Reynolds, A., eds. (2010). *Political emotions: New agendas in communication*. London and New York: Routledge.

Stanyer, J. (2013). *Intimate politics: Publicity, privacy and the personal lives of politicians in media saturated democracies*. Oxford: John Wiley & Sons.

Stark, L. and Crawford, K. (2015). The conservatism of emoji: Work, affect, and communication. *Social Media + Society*, 1(2).

Statista. (2017a). Number of Facebook users in the United States as of January 2017, by age group (in millions). *https://www.statista.com/statistics/398136/us-facebook-user-age-groups/*

Statista. (2017b). Percentage of US population who currently use any social media from 2008 to 2017. *https://www.statista.com/statistics/273476/percentage-of-us-population-with-a-social-network-profile/*

Stemplowska, Z. and Swift, A. (2012). Ideal and nonideal theory. In: D. Estlund, ed., *The Oxford handbook of political philosophy*. Oxford: Oxford University Press.

Stenvall, M. (2008). On emotions and the journalistic ideals of factuality and objectivity –Tools for analysis. *Journal of Pragmatics*, 40(9), pp. 1569–86.

Stenvall, M. (2014). Presenting and representing emotions in news agency reports: On journalists' stance on affect vis-à-vis objectivity and factuality. *Critical Discourse Studies*, 11(4), pp. 461–81.

Stets, J. E. and Turner, J. H. (2008). The sociology of emotions. In: M. Lewis, J. M. Haviland Jones and L. F. Barrett, eds., *Handbook of emotions* (third edition). New York: Guilford.

Stinson, E. (2016). Facebook reactions, the totally redesigned Like button, is here. *Wired*, February 24. *https://www.wired.com/2016/02/facebook-reactions-totally-redesigned-like-button/*

Stoker, G. and Hay, C. S. (2016). Understanding and challenging populist negativity towards politics: The perspectives of British citizens. *Political Studies*, online first. *http://journals.sagepub.com/doi/abs/10.1177/0032321715607511#*

Street, J. (2001). *Mass media, politics and democracy*. London: Palgrave Macmillan.

Street, J. (2003). The celebrity politician: Political style and popular culture. In: J. Corner and D. Pels, eds., *Media and the restyling of politics*. London: Sage.

Subramani, S. (2013). Occupy Wall Street: A hybrid counterpublic. *Student Anthropologist*, 3(2), pp. 156–71.

Svensson, J. (2014). Power, identity and feelings in digital late modernity. In: T. Benski and E. Fisher, eds., *Internet and emotions*. London: Routledge.

Swart, J., Peters, C. and Broersma, M. (2017). Navigating cross-media news use. *Journalism Studies*, 18(11), pp. 1343–62.

Tester, K. (2001). *Compassion, morality and the media*. Buckingham: Open University Press.

Think Digital First. (2018). The demographics of social media users in 2018. *http://www.thinkdigitalfirst.com/2016/01/04/the-demographics-of-social-media-users-in-2016/*

Thompson, J. B. (1995). *The media and modernity: A social theory of the media*. Stanford, CA: Stanford University Press.

Thompson, J. B. (2000). *Political scandal: Power and visibility in the media age*. Cambridge: Polity.

Thompson, J. B. (2005). The new visibility. *Theory, Culture & Society*, 22(6), pp. 31–51.

Thrift, N. (2008). *Non-representational theory: Space, politics, affect*. New York: Routledge.

Thrift, S. C. (2014). #YesAllWomen as feminist meme event. *Feminist Media Studies*, 14(6), pp. 1090–2.

Thumim, N. (2012). *Self-representation and digital culture*. Basingstoke: Palgrave Macmillan.

Tuchman, G. (1972). Objectivity as strategic ritual: An examination of newsmen's notions of objectivity. *American Journal of Sociology*, 77, pp. 660–79.

Turner, G. (2010). *Ordinary people and the media: The demotic turn*. London: Sage.

Turner, J. (2017). Seductive Jezza leaves us with a painful choice. *Times*, June 3. *https://www.thetimes.co.uk/article/seductive-jezza-leaves-us-with-a-painful-choice-vdsgk9wrc*

Turner, J. H. and Stets, J. W. (2005). *The sociology of emotions*. Cambridge: Cambridge University Press.

Umbach, M. and Humphrey, M. (2016). Keeping it real? Corbyn, Trump, Sanders and the politics of authenticity. *The Conversation*, February 6. *https://theconversation.com/keeping-it-real-corbyn-trump-sanders-and-the-politics-of-authenticity-54506*

Utz, S. (2015). The function of self-disclosure on social network sites: Not only intimate, but also positive and entertaining self-disclosures increase the feeling of connection. *Computers in Human Behavior*, 45, pp. 1–10.

van Dijck, J. (2013). *The culture of connectivity: A critical history of social media*. Oxford: Oxford University Press.

van Hensbergen, C. (2017). The world speaks the language of men, but after #MeToo women must find their voice. *The Conversation*, October 25. *https://theconversation.com/the-world-speaks-the-language-of-men-but-after-metoo-women-must-find-their-voice-86107*

van Leeuwen, T. (2001). What is authenticity? *Discourse Studies*, 3(4), pp. 392–7.

van Zoonen, L. (1998). A professional, unreliable, heroic marionette (m/f): Structure, agency and subjectivity in contemporary journalisms. *European Journal of Cultural Studies*, 1(1), pp. 123–43.

van Zoonen, L. (2005). *Entertaining the citizen: When politics and popular culture converge*. Lanham, MD: Rowman & Littlefield.

Wahl-Jorgensen, K. (2001). Letters to the editor as a forum for public deliberation: Modes of publicity and democratic debate. *Critical Studies in Media Communication*, 18(3), pp. 303–20.

Wahl-Jorgensen, K. (2007). *Journalists and the public*. Creskill, NJ: Hampton Press.

Wahl-Jorgensen, K. (2013a). The strategic ritual of emotionality: A case study of Pulitzer Prize-winning articles. *Journalism*, 14(1), pp. 129–45.

Wahl-Jorgensen, K. (2013b). Subjectivity and storytelling in journalism: Examining expressions of affect, judgment and appreciation in Pulitzer Prize-Winning stories. *Journalism Studies*, 14(3), pp. 305–20.

Wahl-Jorgensen, K. (2014). Changing technologies, changing paradigms of journalistic practice: Emotionality, authenticity and the challenge to objectivity. In: C. Zimmerman and M. Schreiber, eds., *Technologies, media and journalism*. New Haven, CT: Campus/Yale University Press.

Wahl-Jorgensen, K. (2016). The emotional politics of the EU Referendum: Bregrexit and beyond. In D. Jackson, E. Thorsen and D. Wring., eds., *EU Referendum analysis 2016: Media, voters and the campaign*. Centre for the Study of Journalism, Culture and Community, Bournemouth University. *http://www.referendumanalysis.eu/*

Wahl-Jorgensen, K. (2017a). The battle for authenticity. In: D. Jackson and E. Thorsen, eds., *UK election analysis 2017: Media, voters and the campaign*. The Centre for the Study of Journalism, Culture and Community, Bournemouth University. *http://www.electionanalysis.uk/*

Wahl-Jorgensen, K. (2017b). Public displays of disaffection: The emotional politics of Donald Trump. In: P. Bozcowski and Z. Papacharissi, eds., *Trump and the media*. Cambridge, MA: MIT Press.

Wahl-Jorgensen, K. (2018a). The emotional architecture of social media. In: Z. Papacharissi, ed., *Networked self: Platforms, stories, connections*. New York: Routledge.

Wahl-Jorgensen, K. (2018b). Media coverage of shifting emotional regimes: Donald Trump's angry populism. *Media, Culture & Society*, 40(5), 766–78.

Wahl-Jorgensen, K. (2018c). Towards a typology of mediated anger. *International Journal of Communication*, 12, pp. 2071–87.

Wahl-Jorgensen, K. and Hanitzsch, T. (2009). Introduction: On why and how we should do journalism studies. In: K. Wahl-Jorgensen and T. Hanitzsch, eds, *Handbook of journalism studies*. London: Routledge.

Wahl-Jorgensen, K., Williams, A. and Wardle, C. (2010). Audience views on user-generated content: Exploring the value of news from the bottom up. *Northern Lights*, 8, pp. 177–94.

Walzer, M. (1986). Pleasures and costs of urbanity. *Dissent*, 33(4), pp. 470–5.

Warner, M. (2002). Publics and counterpublics. *Public Culture*, 14(1), pp. 49–90.

Weaver, M. (2015). Teenage founder of #milifandom says her parents really hate Ed Miliband. *Guardian*, April 22. *https://www.theguardian.com/politics/2015/apr/22/teenage-founder-of-milifandom-says-her-parents-really-hate-ed-miliband*

Westen, D. (2007). *The political brain: The role of emotion in deciding the fate of the nation*. New York: Public Affairs.

Wettergren, Å. (2005). Mobilization and the moral shock: Adbusters Media Foundation. In: H. Flam and D. King, eds., *Emotions and social movements*. London: Routledge.

Wettergren, Å. (2015). How do we know what they feel? In H. Flam and J. Kleres, eds., *Methods of exploring emotions*. New York: Routledge.

Wheeler, M. (2013). *Celebrity politics*. Cambridge: Polity.

Williams, S. (2015). Digital defense: Black feminists resist violence with hashtag activism. *Feminist Media Studies*, 15(2), pp. 341–4.

Williams, S. J. (2001). *Emotions and social theory*. London: Sage.

Williams, S. J. (2009). Modernity and the emotions: Corporeal reflections in the (ir)rational. In: J. Harding and E. D. Pribram, eds., *Emotions: A cultural studies reader*. London: Routledge.

Wood, M., Corbett, J. and Flinders, M. (2016). Just like us: Everyday celebrity politicians and the pursuit of popularity in an age of anti-politics. *British Journal of Politics and International Relations*, 18(3), pp. 581–98.

Wouters, C. (2007). *Informalization: Manners and emotions since 1890*. London: Sage.

Wray, K. (2017). Reddit's r/The_Donald is eating itself over Net neutrality. *Inverse Culture*, July 12. *https://www.inverse.com/article/34071-net-neutrality-the-donald-debate*

Wright, K. (2008). Theorizing therapeutic culture: Past influences, future directions. *Journal of Sociology*, 44(4), pp. 321–36.

York, C. (2015). Ed Miliband's #Milifandom is yet another indicator of his unstoppable rise to sexpot. *Huffington Post*, April 22. *http://www.huffingtonpost.co.uk/2015/04/22/ed-milibands-milifandom_n_7115110.html?1429695262*

Zacharek, S., Dockterman, E. and Edwards, H. S. (2017). *Time* person of the year 2017: The silence breakers. *Time*, December 17. *http://time.com/time-person-of-the-year-2017-silence-breakers/*

Zillmann, D. (1991). Empathy: Affect from bearing witness to the emotions of others. In: J. Bryant and D. Zillmann, eds, *Responding to the screen: Reception and reaction processes*. Mahwah, NJ: Lawrence Erlbaum Associates.

Zillmann, D. (2013). Empathy: Affective reactivity to others' emotional experiences. In: J. Bryant and P. Vorderer, eds., *Psychology of entertainment*. London and New York: Routledge.

Index

Note: Page numbers with *italic f* and *t* denote figures and tables, respectively.

Act Up 95
affective expression 51, 153, 176n3
  anti-social, online 155
  negative 156
  positive 160
affective turn 15, 26–7, 31, 36
Affordable Care Act (US 2010)
  125
African-Americans 105, 120, 121
Agudat Achim 127
Ahmed, Sara 12, 28, 97, 129, 173
airline stewardesses 156
alt-right movement 138, 139
Ancient Greece *see* Greece
Ancient Rome 22
Andrejevic, Mark 157–8
anecdotal leads 46, 47, 52–3
  frequency of 50
  key storytelling tropes
    characterized by 48
  prevalence of 49
  role of 49
anger 1, 11, 13, 14, 118, 142, 169,
    177n2 (Ch. 5)
  acceptable 127
  age of: global 115; rise of 3
  aggressive 98, 101–2
  analysis of 92, 170
  anti-globalization 125
  collective 91–2, 95
  compassion vs 104
  constructed as normatively
    undesirable 105

current mobilization of 113
dangerous 126–7
dangers of 91
directed 119, 125
disruptive 98, 101–2
economic 111, 112
essentializing of 124
exclusionary 105
framing and interpretation
    of 119
illegitimate 94, 98, 102–6
illiberal 126–7
importance of 108
individual 91–2, 96
irrational 98, 102–6
journey to happiness and hope
    from 121
justified 100
legitimate 93, 98–100, 101,
    119
love articulated with hate and
    146
newsworthy 127
normatively appropriate 91
opportunistic 126–7
organizing 112
performative 108, 126
political 109, 111, 112, 114, 128,
    129
populist 116, 127
protesters united in 122
rational 91, 93, 98–100
reactionary 111

anger (*cont.*)
  references to 120, 121, 123, 124
  role of 12, 93, 95, 107, 109,
    127, 170;
  productive 112
  subjects of 121*t*
  targets of 120, 121, 125, 126
  unspecified 119*t*, 123, 124
  see also construction of anger;
    expression of
  anger; mediated anger; public
    anger; Transition-Anger
anti-globalization 125
anti-Semitism 127
anxiety 11, 12
appraisal 47, 54, 176n6
Arendt, Hannah 77
Aristotle 57, 90–1
Assange, Julian 86
Associated Press 122
Atlanta Journal-Constitution 120
Atlantic, The 113, 161
audience engagement 28, 48,
    157
  emotional 9, 31, 32, 35, 37, 49,
    54, 66
  mainstream media 67
audiences 1, 5, 10, 20, 51, 68,
    72, 93
  anticipating emotional
    reactions of 58
  apathetic 28
  broader 137
  circulation of stories to 83
  connection with 55, 71
  eliciting emotional reactions
    in 37, 41, 52, 53, 64–5
  emotional impact of
    journalists' work upon 56
  empathy of 82
  energizing 136
  facilitating understanding of
    32, 43–4
  imagined 33, 76
  media 156
  multiple 87

news 35, 36, 97, 100, 149, 161
  particular forms of
    emotionality valued by 16
  pleasing 31
  political and social knowledge
    of 32, 43
  responses of 15, 33, 41, 46, 53,
    167
  selected 8
  selling information about 158
  user-generated content views
    of 74, 76, 88
Australia 12, 95, 131
Austria 2, 128
authenticity 4, 16, 30, 151, 162
  characteristics vital to
    emerging notions of 137
  cultivation of 88, 90, 166,
    169
  discursively produced 69–70
  emotional 76, 93
  emotional as ordinary in
    political life 70–2
  guarantor/guarantee of 34, 65,
    66, 68
  mastery of 71
  mediated 66, 67, 68
  perceived 74
  performance of 68, 69, 70,
    76, 142
  personalized storytelling
    68–70, 73, 88
  Trump described as
    generating cult of 71
  truth equated with 76
  winning the battle for 71

Bachchan, Jaya 131
Baker, Sarah 56
Bakersfield-Californian 120
Baldoni, John 71
Bangladesh 97
Barnes, Lyn 32–3, 55, 57, 59, 60,
    63, 65
Barrett, Lisa Feldman 8
Baym, Nancy 156, 177n3

BBC (British Broadcasting
  Corporation) 74–5
Question Time 72
Beasley, Berrin 32
Beasley, Vanessa 118
Beck, Ulrich 79
Beckett, Charlie 33, 43
Bedford Today 100
Beecham, Ray 105–6
Benhabib, Seyla 25, 78
Bennett, Lucy 130
Benson, Rodney 44, 98
Berkman, Michael 126
Berlant, Lauren 28, 67
Berners-Lee, Tim 158–9
Berry, Jeffrey 3, 13, 111
Bieber, Justin 131
Big Brother 69
Bird, Liz 42–3, 46, 48–9
Bishop, Jonathan 154
Blaagaard, Bolette 34
Blair, Diane M. 144
Bleiker, Roland 79
Boehner, Kirsten 7
Bollywood 131
Boltanski, Luc 41, 79
Bourdieu, Pierre 44
boyd, danah 151
Brader, Ted 28
Brain, David 148
Breakthrough 86
Brexit 2
Bristol Post 98–9
Broersma, Marcel 43, 45, 46, 133
Brough, Melissa M. 130
Bruce, Geoff 122
Burke, Tarana 85
Burkitt, Ian 6, 8
Bush, George W. 51, 119*t*, 121

California 29
  see also Hollywood; San
    Francisco
Cameron, David 133
Cammaerts, Bart 71
Cardiff 97

Carlson, Matt 10
Carter, Brian 160
Carter, Jimmy 123
Cepernich, Cristopher 21
change *see* cultural change;
  economic change;
  physiological change;
  political change; social
  change; technological
  change; value change
Chicago Daily Herald 125
Chivers, C. J. 49
Chouliaraki, Lilie 14, 34, 79–80,
  83
Chowdhry, Amit 162
Cilizza, Chris 113, 127
citizen journalism 34
Clark, Rosemary 84–5
Clarke, Richard A. 51
Clay-Warner, Jody 10
Clinton, Hillary 113, 138, 140,
  141, 143, 145
CMC (computer-mediated
  communication) 155
CNN (Cable News Network)
  124
cognitive psychology 6
Coleman, Stephen 27–8, 29, 67,
  70, 137
compassion 3–4, 60, 106
  ability to show 105
  clear opposition to 104
  conditions for 14, 81
  creating the grounds for
    76
  expression of 161
  fostering 14, 81–2, 86, 173
  generating 9, 77, 78
  personalized storytelling and
    77–88
  significance of 61
  storytelling elicits 64, 65
  see also cultivation of
    compassion
Confederate flag (US) 104–5
conspiracy 11, 114

construction of anger 101, 119,
123
 discursive 94
 mediated 97, 106, 129
Corbyn, Jeremy 71–2, 136
 Corbynistas 137
Cornell Daily Sun 126
Corner, John 69, 131
Costera Meijer, Irene 35
Coward, Ros 33, 67
Cramer, Katherine J. 13, 142
Crawford, Kate 159
Creators Syndicate 125
Crossley, Nick 25
Crown Prosecution Service (UK)
154
Croydon 105–6
cultivation of compassion 67,
77, 169
 democratizing 81
 discursive construction of
 authenticity closely tied to
 88
 emotional storytelling and
 166
 facilitating new and bottom-up
 ways of 87
 fostering forms of engagement
 based on 90
 means of 65, 66
 mediated 82
 personalized storytelling has
 powerful role to play in
 16
 questions around conditions
 for 34
 spaces for identification
 through 80
cultural change 115
cyberbullying 154–5, 177n2 (Ch.
7)
cyberoptimists 152, 153

Dahlberg, Lincoln 25, 26, 28
Daily Cardinal 126
Damiani, Jesse 87

Dardenne, Robert 42–3, 46,
48–9
Davidson, Joyce 8
Dean, Howard 113
DeGregory, Lane 55
Delhi gang rape (2012) 86, 131
Delli Carpini, Michael 115
DeLuca, Kevin 94, 107, 108, 148
demonstrations 100, 105–6, 107,
121*t*
 coverage of 97, 101
 disruptive violent behavior
 seen to discount
 legitimacy of 102
 frequency of stories about 96
demotic turn 67
Dennis, Everette 30
Deuze, Mark 33, 43
Dionne, E. J. 123
disgust 11, 12, 28
domestic violence 84–5, 95
Dori-Hacohen, Gonen 13
Duffy, Elizabeth 5
Duterte, Rodrigo 2

economic change 115
Eksner, Julia 93
electronic agora 152
Elias, Norbert 4, 24, 57
Eliasoph, Nina 13
Ellison, Nicole 151
emotion(s) 37–65
 circulation of 166, 171–2
 collective 32, 43, 95
 conscious 6
 dangerous 12, 118, 128
 defining 4–10
 elicitation of 37, 52
 emancipation of 4
 historical neglect in political
 life 21–6
 individual 32, 43, 45, 91, 94–5
 invocation of: explicit 54–5;
 widespread 48
 journalism and 30–5, 40–4
 labeling of 95

mediated politics and 27–30,
166–9
mobilization of 26, 127
normative 4, 115
propositions about 166–74
public 95
regulation in public discourse
58
research agendas in media and
politics must consider the
role of 172–4
scholarship on the role of
31
taking seriously 20–36
towards a nuanced analysis of
10–14
uncontrollable 113, 118
understanding, in mediated
public life 1–19
see also negative emotion(s);
political emotion(s); positive
emotion(s); also under
various emotions, e.g. anger;
compassion; disgust; fear;
happiness; hatred; love
emotional architecture 18, 19,
146, 171
public debate and 159–65
social media 18, 147–65
emotional attachments 152
positive 14
emotional connection
creating 112
strong unexplainable 135
emotional culture
changing 2–4
emergence of 33
emotional expression 1, 3, 10,
30, 31, 37, 45, 51–2, 68, 147,
176n3
appropriateness of 57
authenticity performed
through 70
careful 69
carefully managed/policed 39,
64, 149

complexities in charting 53
divisive 12
elicitation of 152
governing 24
heavily policed and disciplined
16
hostile 153
importance of 32
issues around 155
negative 12, 52
parameters for 64
positive 143, 145
public 4, 25
as speech act 8
structurally encouraged 18,
157
universalized 160
see also expression of anger
emotional intelligence 56–7, 59
popular valorization of 3
requirements for 60
strategic ritual of emotionality
requires 64
emotional labor
behind-the-scenes 65
commercialization on
Facebook 157–9
commodification of 18, 19,
147, 155–9
differences in types of 63
journalists and 16, 31, 32, 37,
39, 40, 55–65
outsourcing 16, 39, 52, 64
relational labor as distinctive
from 177n3
scholarship on the role of 31
unacknowledged 57
emotional language 45–6, 52,
77–8, 93, 167
studying changes in use of
116
emotional regimes 57
challenging 9
changing 27, 110, 114–17, 170
detailed historical exploration
of 116

emotional regimes (*cont.*)
  eras characterized by 4
  establishing 9, 93
  perpetuating 9, 93
  prevailing 17, 109, 110, 168
  prevalence of 9
  shifting 17, 89, 110–28
  significant contemporary
    transformations in 109
emotional storytelling 14, 29, 33,
  36, 45, 46, 52
  authenticity and compassion
    cultivated through 166,
    169
  centrality to rituals of public
    mourning 42
  circulation in public in era of
    social media 87
  key social and political issues
    made visible in 65
  main objective of 43–4
  Pulitzer Prize-winning stories
    rely heavily on 64
  storytelling value of 32
emotionality 11
  abstract ideas around 175n1
    (Intro.)
  authenticity through 70
  centrality to journalistic
    storytelling 40
  complex interaction between
    objectivity and 58
  contemporary culture
    increasingly characterized
    by 2
  embodied 24
  how it is constructed and
    embedded in
  journalistic texts 34
  personal storytelling and 16,
    88–9
  rationality and 166,
    167–8
  regimented use of 40
  social interaction always
    suffused with 4

  strategic ritual in journalism
    15, 16, 37–65, 168, 175n2
  uncontrollable 113
empathy 57, 59, 75, 78, 91
  creation of 41
  emotional 72
  potential to cultivate 34
Enli, Gunn 68, 69, 71, 74
Enlightenment thought 23
Epstein, Edward 30–1
Essex Chronicle 103
Ettema, James 42, 45, 63
EU (European Union) 97, 99,
  103
  British referendum on
    membership 12
  Greek referendum over bailout
    package 101
Eureka Times-Standard 122, 125
European Parliament 2, 70
expression 150
  facial 6
  mediated 8
  negative 164
  political 133
  positive 18, 50, 147, 161, 163,
    164
  pro-social 147, 155–9, 163
  public 36, 115–16
  shared injustice 96
  structurally bolstered 139
  sympathetic 162, 163
  see also affective expression;
    emotional
    expression
expression of anger 34, 95, 98,
  121, 123
  complexities of 128
  deliberate 17, 117
  disruptive 94
  politicized 100
  post-election 116

Facebook 82
  commercialization of
    emotional labor 157–9

emotional architecture 146,
149–50, 159–65, 171–2
reactions emoji 1, 18, 146, 147,
159–65, 171
relative flexibility of 158
Trump fans on 138
fandom *see* political fandom
fascism 13, 127, 147
fear 11, 20, 28, 43, 50, 77, 123
compassion has given way to
104
political 12
feminism 5, 34, 78–9, 88, 95,
144
hashtag activism 77, 82, 84–5,
86
Fernback, Jan 155, 156
filter bubble thesis 14
Firmstone, Julie 70, 137
Flam, Helena 8, 13
flaming 153, 154, 155
Fletcher, Richard 14
Flyvbjerg, Bent 173
Focus (German news website)
101
Forbes 71, 162
Foucault, Michel 10, 173
Franklin, Bob 41
Fraser, Nancy 25, 87, 172
Fredrickson, Barbara L. 6
Furedi, Frank 3

G8 summit 2005 102
Gamson, William 42
Garrett, Peter 131
Gaza activists 121
Gerbaudo, Paolo 2
Gerlitz, Carolin 159, 160
Glasser, Ted 42, 45, 63, 77
globalization 111
Goodwin, Ian 27, 28, 150
Goodwin, Jeff 95
Gould, Deborah 13, 28, 95
Gray, Jonathan 130, 132
Great Recession (2000s) 122
Greco, Monica 6

Greece 2
Ancient 22
anti-austerity protests 98
referendum over EU bailout
101
grief 11, 60
appropriate 58
grievances 91, 99, 101, 104
collective 89, 106, 109
dramatizing 124
legitimate 101, 126
political 122
shared 92, 109, 111, 122, 170
Guardian 72, 134
Gurău, Călin 154
Gürsel, Zeynep 32, 46

Habermas, Jürgen 24–5
Hagdu, Asmelash Teka 87
Hall, Harriet 122
Hanisch, Carol 78–9
Hanitzsch, Thomas 30
happiness 11, 45, 47, 51, 77, 83,
120, 136
journey from anger to hope
and 121
representations of 159, 162
Harbers, Frank 45
Hardt, Michael 157
Harry Potter Alliance 130
Hartsock, John C. 40, 48
hate speech 155
online, high-profile examples
of 154
uninhibited circulation of 11
hatred 11, 28, 105, 122, 125, 173
acceptable 127
love articulated with anger
and 146
Hay, Colin S. 13
Held, David 22
Helmond, Anne 159, 160
Hesmondhalgh, David 56
Hewitt, Rachel 2, 27
Heyman, Rob 157
Higgins, Michael 41–2, 112

Hill, Annette 69, 71, 76
Hills, Matt 130, 134, 137
Hirschbeck, John 51
Hispanic voters 140
Hochschild, Arlie 3, 9, 13, 32,
    57–8, 59, 63, 65, 71, 90, 105,
    113, 114, 141, 142, 156, 168,
    177n3
Holdengräber, Paul 25
Hollywood 85, 124, 131, 132
Hollywood Reporter 124
Holmes, Mary 8, 90, 92, 96
Hong Kong 108
hope 11, 47, 51, 120, 121
Horeck, Tanya 84
Howard, John 12
Huffington Post 136
Humans of New York Refugee
    Stories 16, 66, 77,81–4, 86,
    88, 169
Humphrey, Matthew 71
Hutchison, Emma 79
Hyde, Marina 72

immaterial labor 157
India 131
informalization 4, 30, 36, 70
informational capital 159
Inglehart, Fred 2, 111
Instagram 82
instrumentalized hypersociality
    158
investigative journalism 42, 63
Iowa 113
irritation 11, 92
Israeli online comments 13
Italy 2

Jackson, Glenda 131
James, Susan 23, 27
James, William 5
Jasper, James M. 95
Jenkins, Henry 130, 132, 135
Jones, Jeffrey P. 28, 131
journalism 9–10, 27, 93
    award-winning 36, 67, 88

emotion and 20, 30–5, 36,
    40–4
historians of 116
opinionated 98
personalized storytelling and
    66
sensationalized 41
strategic ritual of emotionality
    in 37–65, 175n2
see also citizen journalism;
    investigative journalism;
    photojournalism; tabloid
    journalism
journalism studies 15, 19, 20,
    36, 167
journalistic objectivity 30–6, 58
    direct challenge to 76
    emphasis on 20
journalistic storytelling 15, 36,
    38, 64
    award citations often focus on
        excellence of 43
    award-winning 1
    compelling 42
    embedding emotion within
        176–7n2 (Ch. 5)
    emotional resonance of 55
    emotionality in 40, 58
    emotionalized form of 46
    objectivity in 58
    outsourcing of emotional labor
        52
joy 58, 163
Jukes, Stephen 33, 37, 43, 52, 56,
    57, 60, 63, 65

Kaltwasser, Cristóbal Rovira 110
Kant, Immanuel 23
Kenyan citizens 121
Khan, Imran 131
Khan, Kherstin 144
Khoja-Moolji, Shenila 84
kinship 132
Kitch, Carolyn 42
Klein, Adam. 12
Kleinginna, Anne M. 7

Kleinginna, Paul R. 7
Knobloch, Sylvia 35
Koehn, Daryl 78
Koljonen, Johanna 86
Kotišová, Johana 33
Kovach, Bill 64
Kovaleski, Serge 113
Kramer, Adam D. 164
Ku Klux Klan 104–5
Kurz, Sebastian 2
Kyriakidou, Maria 79

Labour Party (UK) *see* Corbyn,
    Jeremy; Miliband, David;
    Miliband, Ed
Laclau, Ernesto 110
Lady Gaga 130
Lagorio-Chafkin, Christine 139
language 29, 85, 87, 97, 114,
    138
    angry 117
    borrowed 135
    collaboratively created
        142–3
    distinctive 139, 144
    odd non-verbal 113
    openly racist 104
    positive 51, 52
    rational 148
    shared 145, 171
    spontaneous, unpolished 71
    see also emotional language
Lazzarato, Maurizio 157
Le Pen, Marine 128
Levy, Mark R. 35
Lewis, Jan 27
Lewis, Lisa A. 130
Lewis, Seth C. 174
Likes (Facebook) 160–1, 162,
    163*f*
Lim, Elvin T. 71
Livingstone, Sonia 29
Loken, Meredith 84
Los Angeles Times 123
Louis CK 85
love 11, 14, 28, 77, 108, 163

motivation to engage in
    politics 166, 170–1
politics of 17–18, 129–46
Loyn, David 42
Lunt, Peter 28, 29
Lyman, Peter 12, 90, 96

Mail Online 102-3, 104
mainstream media 81
    coverage of anger in protest
        96
    journalists seeking to reach
        and engage
    audiences 67
    Trump and 116–17, 139, 142
Maras, Steven 30
Marcus, George 21, 23, 26
Martin, J. R. 11, 51, 53
Martin, Jennifer 45, 64
Marwick, Alice E. 151
Massachusetts 127
Massumi, Brian 7
May, Brian 72
May, Theresa 71, 72
McNair, Brian 174
media 3, 7, 8, 15, 18, 21, 98, 135
    biased and adversarial 143
    conventional 148, 151, 152
    dynamic ecology 70
    emerging forms 88
    emotional labor in 56, 63
    hybrid 116, 127, 129
    living life through 151
    long-lived participatory
        formats within 148
    long-standing vilification in
        71
    mass 145
    new technologies 153
    nine propositions about 19,
        166–4
    norms of presentation 29
    predictable, professionalized
        134
    reports on global crises and
        disasters 79

media (*cont.*)
　research agendas in 166,
　　172–4
　spin controlling 134
　tabloid 41
　see also mainstream media;
　　news media; social media
media content 9
　authentic 69
　trust in 68, 72, 76
　user-generated 16, 66, 74–6,
　　88, 138, 169
media coverage 89, 93, 94, 127
　anger in 96, 101, 110
　negative 133
　Trump in 116–17, 124, 125,
　　126
media organizations 68, 102–3,
　113
　mainstream 81
　see also social media
　　organizations
media practices 14, 27
　political life and 1
media regime 115
mediated anger 170
　discursive constructions of
　　17
　insights around the nature of
　　110
　typology of 17, 89, 90–109
mediated politics 19, 36, 40,
　67
　anger in 13, 129
　emotions in 11, 14, 27–30, 35,
　　77, 90, 127, 166–9
　key building block of 1
　role of mediated anger in
　　shaping 90
Mendes, Kaitlynn 86
Merrill, John 30
Mexico 50, 140
Meyer, Robinson 161–2
Midnight Oil 131
Milano, Alyssa 85
Miliband, David 133

Miliband, Ed 18, 129, 132, 170
　Milifandom 133–8, 142, 145,
　　168, 171
Miller, Chris 139
Milligan, Christine 8
Milner, Ryan M. 138
Mindich, David T. Z. 40, 47
Mirror 72
Mishra, Pankaj 2–3, 115
Montgomery, Martin 68
Morocco 97
Mouffe, Chantal 25, 26, 173
Mudde, Cas 110, 123

negative emotion(s) 3, 11, 12, 36,
　52, 109, 129
　anger as 90, 128, 170
　discursive climate dominated
　　by 13
　expression and elicitation of
　　156
　potential consequences of 61
　reactions emoji enable 163
Neveu, Erik 98
New Black Panther Party 104
New York Times 51, 55, 82, 175n2
New York Times Magazine 49
New Yorker 114
Newmyer, Tory 117
news media 10, 36
　emotion in 4, 9, 24–6, 27, 33,
　　35, 37
　scholarship on 20
Nexis UK 96, 118, 176n2 (Ch. 5)
NGOs (non-governmental
　organizations)
　collaborations between
　　news organizations and 83
　global human rights 86
NHS (UK National Health
　Service) 72, 103–4
Nielsen, Rasmus Kleis 14
Noff, Ayelet 160
Norris, Pippa 2, 111
Nussbaum, Martha 12, 91–2, 96,
　106

Obama, Barack 116, 117, 118–22,
    127, 131, 143, 177n2 (Ch. 5)
objectivity 33–4, 36, 42, 43, 45,
    48, 58, 76, 83, 175n1 (Ch. 2)
  allegiance to 38
  attachment to 63
  commitment to 33
  conventional practices of
    169
  emotion and 32, 56
  emphasis on 35–6
  heyday of 40
  long reign of 37
  long-standing practices of 64
  maintenance of 57
  overriding emphasis on 64
  professional 57
  strategic ritual of 16, 38–40,
    47, 58
  see also journalistic objectivity
Observer 72
Occupy Wall Street movement
    94, 148
Ong, Jonathan Corpus 79
open-mindedness 155, 156, 158
ordinariness 142
  extraordinary 141
  performance of 69
O'Reilly, Bill 85
Oremus, Will 162
Ost, David 26, 111, 112
Ott, Brian L. 3, 127

pain 5, 77, 91, 134
  emotional 13
Pantti, Mervi 28, 31–4, 40, 43,
    44, 79, 80, 98, 100, 116, 123
Papacharissi, Zizi 7, 14, 22, 28,
    76, 86–7, 134, 150, 158
Paris terrorist attacks (2015) 33
Pariser, Eli 14, 160–1
Patel, Priti 103
Pels, Dick 131
Perry, Katy 131
personalized storytelling 14, 16,
    29, 41, 66–89

anecdotal leads and 46, 47,
    48, 50
  authenticity in 68–70
  compassion and 77–88
  compelling 168–9
  defined 47
  editors' preference for 73
  emotional 168
  emphasis in 65
  valorization of 73
Peter, Laurence 2
Peters, Chris 32, 40
Peters, John Durham 13
Pettifor, Ann 111
Philippines 2, 128
Philips, Whitney 138
photojournalism 32, 62
physiological change 6
Pierson, Jo 157
pleasure 5, 34
Podemos 2
police violence 108
political change 88, 115, 116, 145
  affective communities
    oriented towards 170–1
  aim for broader forms of 87
  broader audiences for 137
  practices evolving in response
    to 31
  projects for 173
political community
  creation of 95, 137–45
political emotion(s) 17, 34, 89,
    129
  essential 166, 169–70
political fandom 14, 17–18, 170–1
  social change and 129–46
  see also Miliband, Ed; Trump,
    Donald J.
politics 15, 17, 61
  ability and right to participate
    in 22
  anger in 112, 114, 128
  being emotional about 21
  bringing the personal into the
    realm of 78

politics (*cont.*)
  constructive 12
  cultural 97
  emotion in scholarship on
    24–6
  energizing audiences 136
  fandom and 130–3
  gaming and 152
  image 107
  informalization of 30, 36,
    70
  intellectual deliberation over
    21
  love motivates us to engage in
    170–1
  one of the main moving forces
    in 26
  perceived shift in the
    emotional climate of 104
  personalized storytelling,
    compassion and 79
  popular culture and 20, 28,
    29, 36, 131, 167
  populist 41
  rational and constructive
    participants in 23
  research agendas in 172–4
  resentment 114
  studying how people talk
    about 42
  success of celebrities in 29
  see also mediated politics
popular culture 11, 135
  fans of texts and figures 130
  politics and 20, 28, 29, 36,
    131, 167
populism 3, 41, 104, 154
  angry 17, 89, 109–28, 145, 170,
    177n2 (Ch. 5)
  exclusionary 124
  illiberal 112
  right-wing 2, 110
positive emotion(s) 36, 51, 52,
    129, 143
  complex 170
  different uses for 145

  increasing pressure to express
    156
  pro-social, privileging of 165
protest coverage 93, 96–106,
    107, 121, 170
  anger in 1, 17; mediated
    96–106
  routine 5, 89, 90, 108
protests 91, 128
  anger in 94, 109, 122, 126
  anti-war (1960s) 108
  constructions of 107, 108
  disruptive or violent 109
  extraordinary 106
  importance of 21
  student 101
public anger 2, 90–2, 101, 111,
    118
  extent of 94
  generalized 126
public opinion 25, 157
  anger becomes a barometer
    of 100
public spaces 18, 147–8, 149,
    156, 157
  open-minded 155, 158
  single-minded 155, 158
Pulitzer Prize-winners 5, 37, 44,
    46, 48–55, 63, 175n2, 176n4
  analysis of 16, 39–40, 45
  emotional storytelling 64
  strategic ritual of emotionality
    in 168

Raboy, Marc 148
racial intolerance/resentment
    105, 114
racism 84, 104, 122, 140
  historical 119*t*, 120
  open 105
rationality 41, 103, 149
  celebrating 21–6
  claims to 173
  commitment to 30
  emotion(ality) and 11, 18, 27,
    28, 165–8, 172

language of 148
political culture that
    emphasizes freedom and 12
refracted through dynamic
    power relations 10
understanding of 78
Raw Story 104–5
Reagan, Ronald 29, 131
Reality TV 29, 69, 76, 131
Reddit 5, 170
    Trump on 18; fans of 129, 132,
    138–46, 171
Reddy, William 4, 8–9, 17, 27,
    57, 58, 109, 110, 115, 156
Rees, Gavin 33, 44, 56, 57, 60
refugees
    crisis (2015) 33
    treatment at immigration
        removal center 100
    see also Humans of New York;
        UNHCR
Rehg, William 78
Reinecke, Leonard 161
Remnick, David 114
Rentschler, Carrie 84
resentment 110
    politics of 114
    racial 114
Rheingold, Howard 152–3
Richards, Barry 29, 33, 44, 56,
    57, 60
Richardson, John E. 46, 54
Rieff, Philip 21
Rihanna 131
Robin, Corey 12
Rocky Mountain Collegian 122
Roosevelt, Franklin D. 71
Rose, David 11, 51, 53
Rosenstiel, Tom 64
Ross, Andrew A. G. 6, 9, 21
Ross, Karen 67
Rotherham 97
Rubin, Alissa J. 55
Rubin, Jennifer 125
Rupar, Verica 43, 45, 46
Russia 99

sadness 52, 162, 163
San Francisco 102–3
Sanders, Bernie 142
Sandvoss, Cornel 130, 131, 132,
    134, 135
Sanghani, Radhika 136, 137
Sarafconn, Carol 127
Sawyer, Miranda 72
Schrøder, Kim Christian 35
Schudson, Michael 30, 40, 116
Schultz, Ida 45
Schwarzenegger, Arnold 29
Seargeant, Philip 151
sensationalism 31, 41
    fear of 20
September 11 attacks 80
sexism 84, 85
sexual assault 85
    borderline 86
sexual harassment
    call for attention to 85
    taking seriously claims of 86
sexual violence 86
Shavit, Nimrod 13
Shresthova, Sangita 130
Siapera, Eugenia 26
Sills, Sophie 86
Singer, Philipp 138
Singh, Jyoti 86
single-mindedness 155, 156, 158
Slate 162
Smith, Angela 42
Smith, Leroy 105
Smythe, Dallas 156–7
Snakenborg, John 154
Sobieraj, Sarah 3, 13, 111
social change 43, 88, 92, 96, 106
    aim for broader forms of 87
    communities have potential to
        effect 66–7
    comprehensible projects for
        98
    conditions for political action
        and 35
    inability of political
        institutions to effect 3

social change (*cont.*)
  political fandom and 17–18,
    129–46
  possibility for 86
  practices evolving in response
    to 31
  projects for 173
  tangible 81
social interaction 4, 6, 171
  emotionally significant 9
  exploited for commercial
    means 158
  mediated 158
social media 14, 33, 66, 67, 81,
    83, 169, 173–4
  commodification of emotional
    labor in 19
  emotional architecture of 18,
    147–65, 171
  energization of young voters
    through 136
  hate groups enabled by
    11
  percentage in US and UK who
    use 149
social media organizations 157,
    164, 171
  see also Facebook; Instagram;
    Reddit; Twitter
socialization 156
  journalistic 39, 56, 60
  virtual 158
Soldani, Bianca 131
South Africa 101
South Bend Tribune 120
South Carolina 105
Spacey, Kevin 85
Spain 2
St Petersburg Times 55
Stache, Lara C. 84
Staiger, Janet 27
Stanton, Brandon 82
Stanyer, James 28, 29, 70
Stark, Luke 159
Stearns, Peter N. 27
Stemplowska, Zofia 172

Stenner, Paul 6, 28
Stenvall, Maija 34
Stets, Jan E. 8
Stoker, Gerry 13
storytelling 54
  carefully crafted and plotted
    49
  compelling 43
  hybrid 66, 81, 169
  key tropes borrowed from
    fiction 48
  knowledge of how to
    incorporate emotion into
    37–8
  mediated 79
  online 66, 169
  outstanding 37
  see also emotional storytelling;
    journalistic
  storytelling; personalized
    storytelling
strategic ritual
  emotionality 44–55
  objectivity 16, 38–40, 47,
    58
Subramani, Shreya 86
Sunday Times 99, 104
Svensson, Jakob 8
Swart, Joëlle 35
Swift, Adam 172
Swift, Taylor 131
Switzerland 2
sympathy 41, 98
  easy expression of 163
  garnered around the world
    108
  technical way to express regret
    or 162
Syriza 2

tabloid journalism 31, 41
tacit knowledge 39
Tagg, Caroline 151
Tea Party movement 114
technological change 33, 43, 67,
    115

practices evolving in response
    to 31
tangible 81
Tehreek-e-Insaf party 131
Telegram and Gazette 127
Telegraph 101
Thompson, John B. 29, 42
thought 147
    activated 8–9
    brief history of 15, 20–36
    private 76
Thrift, Nigel 29, 84, 85
Thumim, Nancy 151
Times 71
Tomlinson, Abby 134, 136
tragedy 60, 82
Transition-Anger 91, 96, 106
Trepte, Sabine 161
trolling 154
Trudeau, Justin 131
Trump, Donald J. 1, 2, 5, 29, 131,
    154
    angry populism 17, 71, 110–28,
        170, 177n2 (Ch. 5)
    fans on social media 18, 89,
        129, 132, 133, 138–46, 171
Trump, Melania 154–5
Trump Tower 140
TTIP (Transatlantic Trade and
    Investment
    Partnerships) 103–4
Tuchman, Gaye 16, 38, 39, 47
Turner, Jonathan H. 8
Turner, Janice 71
Twitter 18, 30, 84–7, 105, 129,
    131–8, 145, 170, 171
    feminist hashtags 5
    intersection of personal and
        political on 76
    Trump on 116–17, 139

UGC (user-generated content)
    16, 66, 74–6, 88, 138, 169
UK General Election (2017) 71
Ukraine 99, 100
Umbach, Maiken 71

UNHCR (UN High
    Commissioner for
    Refugees) 82, 83

value change 111
van Leeuwen, Theo 68–9
van Zoonen, Liesbet 28, 29, 34,
    131, 132
violence 13, 49, 50, 103, 115,
    127
    aggression and 90, 100, 101
    disproportionate 108
    disruption and 101, 102, 107,
        109
    gendered 85
    possibility of 99
    potential for 90, 94, 104
    threatened 94, 101
    see also domestic violence;
        police violence; sexual
        violence
virtual communities 86, 152,
    154
virtual world 156
    emotional life of 152–5

Wahl-Jorgensen, Karin 11, 12, 30,
    34, 43, 47, 50, 67, 73, 74, 81,
    94, 116, 123, 148, 149
Walzer, Michael 155
Warner, Michael 87
Warren, Rick 120
Washington 119
Washington Post 125
Weinstein, Harvey 85
well-being 58
    collective 12
Westen, Drew 27
Western Daily Press 100
Westlund, Oscar 184
Wettergren, Åsa 8, 9, 93
WikiLeaks 86
Wilders, Geert 128
Williams, Sherri 84
Williams, Simon J. 3, 6, 21, 27
Windahl, Sven 35

Wolff, Michael 124
Women's Marches 119
World Wide Web *see* Berners-
 Lee, Tim
Wouters, Cas 4, 30, 70
Wray, Katie 139
Wright, Katie 3

Yarl's Wood 100
York, Chris 136
young voters 133–7
YouTubers 30

Zillmann, Dolf 14
Zuma, Jacob 101